IN IRONS: U.S. MILITARY MIGHT IN THE NEW CENTURY

IN IRONS: U.S. MILITARY MIGHT IN THE NEW CENTURY

*The American Edition, Published in Cooperation with
the Center for Naval Analyses
and the
Royal United Services Institute*

HARLAN K. ULLMAN

1995
NATIONAL DEFENSE UNIVERSITY
WASHINGTON DC

NATIONAL DEFENSE UNIVERSITY PUBLICATIONS

To increase general knowledge and inform discussion, the Institute for National Strategic Studies, through its publication arm the NDU Press, publishes McNair Papers; books based on University- or Institute-sponsored symposia; authored books relating to U.S. national security, especially to issues of joint, combined, or coalition warfare, peacekeeping operations, and national strategy; and a variety of briefer works designed to circulate contemporary comment and offer alternatives to current policy. The Press occasionally publishes out-of-print defense classics, historical works, and other especially timely or distinguished writing on national security.

First published in 1995 by Gerald Duckworth & Co. Ltd., London, England. British edition ISBN 0-7156-2652-3.

The NDU Press publication is sold by the U.S Government Printing Office. For ordering information, call (202) 512-1800, or write to the Superintendent of Documents, U.S. Government Printing Office, Washington, D.C. 20402. Cite title and stock number 008-020-01353-6.

This NDU Press publication is sold by the U.S. Government Printing Office. For ordering information, call (202) 512-1800, or write to the Superintendent of Documents, U.S. Government Printing Office, Washington, DC, 20402. Cite title and stock number 008-020-01353-6.

American edition: First printing, March 1995. ISBN 0-16-045593-6

"IN IRONS"

The term "in irons" has several usages, each of which entails a measure of constraint. The most common meaning of "in irons" is to be put in chains, as to shackle a prisoner or captive. But the appropriate metaphor for this book is nautical and the distinctive cases are instructive. On one hand, "in irons" is to lose the wind temporarily, either through a mistaken sailing maneuver or through a stilling of the air. On the other hand, the more sinister meaning of "in irons" is that of becoming completely becalmed when the wind or current simply disappears. In the days of sail, the consequences of this entrapment could be desperate and even fatal if, on a lengthy ocean passage, there was no wind for days at a time. The hapless crew of a ship in this form of irons suffered the agonies of slow death as food and water ran out and as disease and the elements, usually heat, exacted a deadly toll. The only escape from "in irons" was a freshening and lasting breeze that would carry the ship and crew to safety.

In Irons: U.S. Military Might in the New Century

Contents

CONTENTS (CONTINUED)

TABLES

TABLES (CONTINUED)

FIGURES

FOREWORD

THERE IS NO QUESTION THAT THE U.S. MILITARY IS IN THE MIDST OF A reduction in size and manpower strength, the dimensions and rate of which have been the subjects of discussion since the end of the Cold War. But is this reduction merely a postwar adjustment to newly emerging regional threats, or is it the start of a precipitous decline in overall strength that will leave the United States a second rate power sometime early in the 21st century?

The haunting possibility that U.S. military power might be lapsing into strategic decline is the driving concern of this study by the distinguished military analyst, Harlan K. Ullman. What disturbs Ullman most is the possibility that this decline may be the result of inattention and neglect, rather than a deliberate—if unfortunate, in his judgment—strategic contraction of U.S. power. Thus, his first task is to convince the reader that the current reduction is, in fact, critically and historically different from other postwar decreases. This task is complicated because, on balance, most agree that the U.S. Armed Forces are today unchallenged by any credible opponent anywhere in the world. But there is cause for concern, as Ullman ably demonstrates, before going on to suggest specific remedies.

Wherever one stands, this study deserves to be read as a serious contribution to the great strategic debate about the future of U.S. military power. The NDU Press is pleased to be able to offer its readers the American edition of this study, which is being copublished in Great Britain by the Royal United Services Institute for Defence Studies. We especially appreciate the opportunity offered to us by the Center for Naval Analyses in the United States, to present this timely and thoughtful analysis of one of the central defense questions of our time.

ERVIN J. ROKKE
Lieutenant General, U.S. Air Force
President, National Defense University

IN IRONS: U.S. MILITARY MIGHT IN THE NEW CENTURY

PROLOGUE

This book is about the future condition of America's military might. The message is sobering, unsettling, and, for the moment, unheeded. Despite the best intentions of government, U.S. fighting strength is being steadily and perceptibly eroded. Unless the nation takes powerful remedial action, or is very lucky, before the end of this century, this erosion in military power will lead to profound decline, decay, or worse. "Worse" means that the debilitating form of "in irons" will become inevitable.

As will be shown, the reasons for this accelerating and downward defense spiral are now predominantly structural, domestic, and embedded in the way the United States Government does and will do business in a world that possesses but a single superpower. The larger questions of whether a dramatic cut in U.S. military capabilities and in the ability to project force on a timely and effective operational basis will matter and will harm U.S. national security are, currently, less precisely answerable. However, any message of warning is sure to be muffled and muzzled by measures of disinterest and complacency naturally arising from the public's attention on almost exclusively non-defense issues and from the immediate and overwhelming superiority of today's U.S. military forces that seemingly contradicts any forecasts of despair.

The most likely response by the administration and Congress to this warning will be to dismiss any alarm with the assertion that the current defense program seems largely in balance—which it is. Future problems and funding shortfalls always can arise. But, despite occasional reports to the contrary by watchdog organizations and the press, elected and senior appointed officials will promise with vigor and emotion that the Federal Government is not going to allow America's military might to atrophy as it did during the 1970s. Hence, overcoming this understandable reluctance to view the condition of America's future military might as a serious and looming problem is a daunting task.

The thrust of this book is prescriptive. Yet, sufficient care must be taken to show the evidence, signs, and reasons for alarm. As a nation, we may choose to accept even a precipitous contraction in U.S. military power. However, we would be irresponsible if that choice were made by default or by chance and even more irresponsible if alternatives that could prevent this decline or enhance the manner in which we provide for the common defense were left unexamined.

The metaphor for this book was described nearly two centuries ago by Samuel Taylor Coleridge. Based on the suggestion of my wife Julian, appropriate phrases from *The Rime of the Ancient Mariner* appear as section headings. I hope they serve as cautions and not accurate forecasts. Whatever parallel may be drawn between the albatross that adorned the ancient mariner and the portrayal of the more debilitating and consuming aspects of the enormous "infrastructure" supporting the defense establishment that will follow is not accidental.

In this endeavor, the lesson of Sir Norman Angell occasionally provided grounds for second thoughts. Writing in 1911, Sir Norman argued powerfully, persuasively, and entirely wrongly that economic interdependence in Europe made future war among industrial states simply too expensive to contemplate. Three years later, Angell's *The Great Illusion* was exploded at Sarajevo, and the Great War wrecked much more than the Nobel Prize winner's thesis and reputation. My own view is that the ingredients for Angell's optimism may well exist today, at least regarding the western and industrialized world. The analogue may be closer to 1815 and a century of relative if not perfect stability and not 1914 followed by three decades of revolution and conflict. The prospect of strong antireform movements present in the Russian elections of December 1993, as well as examples of civil strife as close to home as Mexico, does not yet constitute the grounds for reversing this view.

No matter which historical example applies, it is still imperative that we deal with the common defense in pragmatic, hardheaded, effective ways. The first step, however difficult, is recognizing where we are headed. Next, a course of action must be taken and acknowledged even if that decision means permitting or tolerating U.S. military power to erode substantially.

The evidence, alarm, and solutions that follow are mine alone. However, many colleagues and supporters were invaluable in helping me to undertake this effort. Principally, an enormous debt of gratitude and thanks go to Robert Murray, President of The CNA

Corporation, who sponsored this work, and to my colleagues, especially Bill Bell and Jamil Nakhleh, vice presidents at CNA, and Robin Pirie, now at DOD. I am especially grateful to many others. I recognize, particularly: former Secretaries of Defense Frank C. Carlucci, Robert S. McNamara, and James R. Schlesinger; former Chairman of the Joint Chiefs of Staff General Colin L. Powell, USA (Ret.), Admiral Huntington Hardisty, USN (Ret.), former Commander in Chief, U.S. Forces Pacific, and last, but far from least, David Bolton, until of late, Director of the Royal United Services Institute, one of the book's co-publishers. I also owe huge thanks to former shipmate and friend Commander Don Ditko for helping me set the numbers record straight. And to J. C. Owens of CNA who typed the original manuscript; Linda Dennis, who is an enormously able editor; and Sylvia Wiener, who produced the final design and layout, there was never better support. Any flaws or errors are my responsibility entirely. And, as the reader turns to *In Irons*, I leave this thought from Coleridge published as part of the complete poem in 1796:

> *Down dropt the breeze, the sails dropt down,*
> *'Twas sad as sad could be;*
> *And we did speak only to break*
> *The silence of the sea.*

Harlan Ullman
Washington, DC
Summer 1994

INTRODUCTION[1]

In his State of the Union address on January 25, 1994, President Bill Clinton pledged to the American public that the U.S. military "will remain the best-equipped, best-trained, and best-prepared fighting force on the face of the earth." These remarks, or ones like them, have been made by a succession of presidents. However, if this particular pledge is to be honored as intended, strong actions well beyond simple rhetoric will be required.

During the Cold War, the condition and health of U.S. military posture were defined by the simple formula that connected and matched "strategy, force structure, and budget." Strategy was derived from the military requirements to deter and contain the Soviet Union and, until 1972, China. Force structure was designed to meet the strategy. And the budget was to provide the necessary resources.

Mismatches often arose. Perhaps the most publicized mismatch led to the "hollow force" of the 1970s. "Hollow" describes a force that was largely unready and unprepared to fight and win at short or no notice. To deal with these mismatches, we changed strategy, force structure, and budget. But there was never any automatic or axiomatic corrective method in place. What made life easier was the unmistakable connection between this formula and the seemingly permanent threat of the Soviet Union. Threat was inseparable from the equation, and its connection assured bipartisan consensus and support for national defense.

Today, however, the post-Cold War world has denied us the luxury of an implacable adversary to underwrite defense planning. As a result, the traditional formula of strategy, force structure, and budget has been replaced by a far more complex interaction that combines two new ingredients. The first new ingredient is "threat"

---

[1] To aid the reader, footnotes are kept to a minimum. Most figures, data, and reference material were drawn from the Annual Reports of the Secretary of Defense to Congress required by the 1947 National Security Act; the Federal Budget documents by year; and open-source government publications. Other sources are noted.

or, more precisely, its absence. The second is "infrastructure," originally arising from the needs of World War II and the Cold War and including the military bases to house, train, and support the forces; the defense industrial base; logistical and support facilities; and new, quasi- or non-defense-related programs whose cost is borne by the Department of Defense.

The decoupling of threat and strategy have resulted in a pronounced and understandable uncertainty about future enemies. This uncertainty removes the long-standing basis for maintaining a permanent and broad public consensus for defense. Public support and interest must inevitably become diluted as long as the lack of a real threat or danger persists.

The infrastructure issue, which is also defined to include the process by which we select and acquire our forces and weapons, has been magnified and distorted by threat and its absence. Clearly, infrastructure must be reduced. But, despite sound attempts and rationale for these reductions, the "downsizing" of any large entity is inherently difficult.

The book uses the "threat, strategy, force structure, budget, and infrastructure" formula for organizing the presentation of evidence, analysis, and prescriptions. In a more abstract sense, this formula is representative of three broader categories that are useful in establishing the context and logic for the analysis. The categories are "strategic uncertainty," "domestic introspection and preoccupation," and the "extraordinary expense of governance." These categories are defined ahead and each serves as a specific chapter. But their consequences are important to note in advance.

"Strategic uncertainty" will contribute to the lack of a fundamental and credible argument sufficient to form or hold a defense consensus. "Domestic preoccupation" will lead to the substitution of domestic priorities for those of defense and national security. The "extraordinary expense of governance" means that the impact of those dollars spent on defense will suffer from growing inefficiencies in obtaining fair value and from demands by non- or quasi-defense programs funded under the DOD budget.

The fiscal consequences of these three broad categories can be summarized in terms of substantial future underfunding for defense;[2] a growing and gross disparity between spending for military "teeth" and "tail" in which "tooth" is being devoured by "tail";[3] and imbedded "cost creep," which means no constant level of military power can be maintained unless annual defense spending is increased well above the rate of inflation.[4]

Taken together, these fiscal consequences will be profound. Between now and the end of the century, the spending shortfall for defense is likely to be $200 or $300 billion from a projected five-year plan of $1.3 trillion. Given the other inefficiencies, this means that for every dollar DOD is planning to spend, effectively it will receive only 70 to 75 cents. The obvious conclusion must be a fundamental reduction in U.S. military might.

This impending and potentially huge mismatch leaves three basic policy choices for the nation. First, the nation can accept the consequences of a less capable future military that could become "hollow" or worse. The arguments supporting this choice emphasize the lack of immediate threat to the nation and the necessity of

---

[2] Refer ahead to page 78 for the table that lists the extent of likely underfunding. Included are shortfalls due to future pay raises, inflation, potential cuts, program overruns, costs of health care and environmental cleanup, defense conversion, assistance to the former Soviet Union, and misestimates in savings from base closings.

[3] Generally, a "ready" force should receive about half of the budget or more; 1987 was the last time "teeth" and "tail" had equal budget shares. "Tail" now receives more than 3/5 and the trend is growing worse. See the graphs on pages 156 and 157.

[4] As will be shown, the costs of weapon modernization, the all-volunteer force, and operations have increased each year by at least 2 percent and usually 3 to 5 percent above the rate of inflation. See Chapter Four.

sustaining the economy by redirecting spending priorities. Defense would be refocused toward more substantial capabilities for reconstitution should a new Soviet-like threat arise. Fewer federal resources would be spent on defense, allowing them to be used elsewhere. Defense would also support the domestic economy by preferential funding of civilian-related employment, some of it at the highest levels of technology.

Second, the current force, specified by the Clinton administration's *Bottom-Up Review* (BUR) of military needs conducted in 1993, can be maintained. This force will require substantial increases in defense resources either through more spending or through imposing major reforms and efficiencies that will free up resources already headed for defense. The arguments underlying this choice rest on the notion that maintenance of current U.S. military strength is vital to stabilizing and reassuring an otherwise dangerous and changing world.

Third, the United States could embark on a major revision of its security needs and redefine its objectives, strategy, forces, and budget in keeping with what appear to be the realities and uncertainties of the post-Cold War world.

As this new and uncertain terrain is traversed, there are two particular pitfalls. If defense is allowed to atrophy without full and open recognition of this condition and its possible consequences, the legitimacy and authority of the political process may ultimately emerge more damaged than U.S. military might. And, if reform is not imposed to correct many of the more extreme diseconomies and inefficiencies, without major and frequent increases in spending, it will be impossible to keep defense at any constant level of capability.

This book is structured and organized to present both the evidence for alarm and the alternative choices for responding to these realities and dangers. Part I assesses each of the four defense build-downs since the end of World War II. The first three build-downs provide interesting and a few contrarian insights that are applicable to the current round of reductions. The consequences and challenges posed by strategic uncertainty, preoccupation with domestic issues, and the extraordinary costs of governance are examined as they affect and influence our security needs and put in place the dynamics that would drive U.S. military power toward the condition of "in irons."

Part II establishes a range of alternative choices and policy prescriptions that set the realistic boundaries for defining the size, composition, and rationale for future military might. The range of choices and solutions focuses on the fundamental issues that shape the new century and influence our preparation for it, including the key components that cumulatively make up the common defense. These components expand on the balance of "threat, strategy, force structure, budget, and infrastructure" and include specific policy questions that will shape future military power—for example, the commitments to be undertaken by military forces; how ready those forces must be; and where to strike the balance between and among readiness, modernization, and acquisition of new and potentially "leap ahead" technologically driven weapon systems.

Part III contains a cost-benefit analysis of the three basic policy choices facing us: accept a weaker military; spend more or free up more resources; or revise our strategy. From these evaluations, specific solutions are offered. If there is a single "bottom line," it is that many of the inefficiencies and extraordinary costs of continuing to do the business of defense as we have in the past must be redressed and eliminated or reduced.

Without decisive and fundamental action, the long-term consequences of the current trends for DOD could result in an active-duty force of about 1 million (or about a third less than today's force of 1.5 million), largely unready to undertake many military tasks and no longer cushioned by the superior technology and training put into place in the 1980s and early 1990s. Worse, the expense and inefficiencies of the process will multiply those deficiencies in capability, making recovery more difficult and certainly far more expensive.

This appears to be our fate. Whether this condition proves truly injurious to the nation is, for the moment, beyond our knowledge. But, if we are bold and decisive, we can avoid a future condition of military decay and ensure the retention of a military force that is both the proper size and the finest in the world. And, in this process, if we take further action, large savings could possibly accrue. The vital question is whether government will react appropriately to these circumstances and opportunities.

Part I: "The Bird To Slay That Made the Breeze To Blow"

Chapter One: The Record of Prior American Defense Reductions

Since 1945, there have been four distinct periods of significant reduction in the military might of the United States. Each series of reductions followed in the wake of the build-ups for various "wars" that have been waged by the United States over the past six decades. The Truman administration demobilized the country after the unconditional victory of World War II and eliminated immeasurable amounts of military power made redundant by the defeat of Germany and Japan. That demobilization lasted five years until the onset of the Korean War became the last straw in a series of provocative actions by the USSR that made American rearmament and a countervailing response inevitable.

The Eisenhower administration embarked on a cautious and partial demobilization beginning in 1953 (and after an armistice halted the fighting in Korea) that emphasized U.S. superiority in nuclear and thermonuclear weapons and delivery systems while it simultaneously decreased the money spent on defense in order to support the higher priority of strengthening the domestic economy. The third and, as it turned out, the least well-conceived reduction technically began in 1969 with the reversal of the Vietnam build-up and steps ultimately to end the conflict in Southeast Asia. This drawdown persisted over three presidencies, and, by the late 1970s, U.S. military power had inadvertently eroded despite the intent of these administrations to avoid the so-called "hollowing" of the forces.

The fourth and current series of reductions began with the ending of the Cold War in 1989 and 1990 and the design of a "base force" that proposed, over time, to reduce active-duty strength by 25 percent and annual defense spending by 10 percent. This series of reductions is continuing to evolve as we move into the new century. Although conventional wisdom has been highly critical of each of the nation's defense build-downs thus far, a careful review of the record suggests that much of this criticism is misplaced. This unconventional view, when combined with the context, content, and consequences of each of the earlier reductions, offers some interesting lessons for the current drawdown.

THE TRUMAN REDUCTIONS—THE FIRST DEMOBILIZATION

Japan's unconditional surrender to the Allies ending World War II took place on board the battleship USS *Missouri* anchored in Tokyo Bay. As General of the Army Douglas McArthur closed the proceedings, squadrons of Navy fighter airplanes flew overhead. The symbolism was obvious. On that day in September 1945, the United States was not only a superpower. The United States was *the* power, perhaps even more dominant than Greece, Rome, and England had been during their golden years. With 12 million men and women in uniform, with nuclear weapons technology, with a vast arsenal of tanks, combat aircraft, and ships, and with an economy and industrial base of unprecedented size and breadth, the United States stood alone in virtually every category of power and prestige.[5] For better or for worse, as it had after World War I, the United States acted to demobilize this enormous military capacity and transform wartime America back to a normal, peacetime basis with a standing military force of about 1.5 million. Although that force numbered about 10 percent of the World War II military, in historical terms, it was the United States' largest standing peacetime Army and Navy. At the time, few Americans disagreed with the decision to demobilize, and the priority was to return the United States to peacetime as rapidly as possible.

The context of this demobilization was clear. The enemy was gone and the United States was now occupying Japan and Germany, as

---

[5] The U.S. Navy in September 1945 consisted of nearly 2,000 ships, including 96 aircraft carriers of all sizes. The U.S. Army consisted of 91 divisions. In 1994, the U.S. Navy is moving towards a fleet of fewer than 300 ships and 10 aircraft carriers, and the Army to 10 active divisions. While numbers are often misleading, this comparison suggests how much the United States had mobilized for World War II.

well as parts of Austria and Trieste. Restoring a peacetime society was the order of the day. In the Truman view, part of that restoration necessitated a balanced budget, if not one in surplus, to pay off the $250 billion national debt incurred to finance the war. This conservative fiscal policy, it was argued, would also serve to check or reduce the inflationary pressure arising from the release of pent-up consumer demand and the transition of this gargantuan wartime production base to civilian and peacetime consumption.

Publicly, while shedding vast amounts of capability, the administration voiced the determination, if not a specific plan, to maintain sufficient military strength to protect the nation. Remember, though, that the first years of Truman's administration were chaotic. Truman was roundly attacked as a little man unsuited for the presidency. His tenacity, courage, and common sense carried the day. However, only in retrospect is he seen as a great leader. In the early months of the post-war world, a coherent view of that world and a supporting strategy were far from in place.

As events that coalesced the hardening of the Cold War progressed—the Greek-Turkish communist insurgencies in 1947; the communist coups in Eastern Europe in 1948; the first Berlin Crisis in 1948; the communist victory in China in 1949; and, perhaps most troubling, the Soviet Union's acquisition of the "bomb"—the Truman administration sensed or believed that strategy, diplomacy, and economic strength were more useful instruments in assuring the nation's common defense than a large or expanded military and accompanying large defense expenditures. And Truman was growing into the job and acquiring the knowledge of international affairs denied him under President Franklin D. Roosevelt.

James Forrestal, the first secretary of defense, recognized and underscored these beliefs in his first annual report to Congress dated June 30, 1948: "As a primary precaution against war, we must strive to prevent its inception anywhere. We must do everything we can to bring order out of chaos wherever it exists and to eradicate the evils and injustices which cause war." The instruments for organizing this stability were largely non-military.

A year later, Forrestal's successor, Louis Johnson, reaffirmed in his annual report to Congress that: "Our defense policy will consist of mustering the maximum of strength, within the limits of our economy and our democracy, to back up that foreign policy and make America secure by discouraging any potential aggressors."

At the time, the defense budget was about $12 billion per year, and about 1.4 million active-duty personnel were in service. However, Washington was awash in political bloodletting, and a form of bureaucratic absolute war was being waged over defense. The level of dissention and turmoil within the Pentagon and echoed in Congress over the National Security Act of 1947, which "unified" the national military establishment and created a Department of Defense in the 1949 amendment, was extraordinarily high, and indeed contributed to the suicide of Secretary Forrestal in 1949. As a result, the furor over reorganization and draconian defense budgets, and white-hot debate over roles and missions and service responsibilities for those tasks, produced the most extreme form of internecine warfare among the U.S. military services in our history. By contrast, the interservice rivalry of later years and so often discussed in the media was of a kinder variety when compared to the fratricide of the late 1940s. Given the turbulence of both the domestic and international environments, few presidents and administrations have faced periods of parallel tumult.

In retrospect and as seen at the time, the content of the Truman demobilization was uncomplicated. The most important national security priority was restoring the economy. The "remainder method" of calculating defense budgets was in vogue in which the budget estimates for all non-defense spending were subtracted from the projected ceiling and the remainder put to defense needs. Defense rested in a standing force that would be reinforced by mobilization in time of war. Hence, an emergency production base and a huge system and network for stockpiling "critical" materials and goods were established. Truman pursued a program of "universal military training" that would complement mobilization, but it was rejected by Congress. Finally, research and development were accorded high priority in the national security hierarchy, with appropriate organizations and funding.

The administration continued to believe that Soviet ambitions stopped well short of war. Despite the international crises that were leading to extreme chill in the Cold War and the first Berlin Crisis in 1948 that came precariously close to a hot war, the administration principally relied on strategy, diplomacy, and aid as the key instruments for protecting U.S. security. The Truman Doctrine, the massive European Recovery Plan known as the Marshall Plan, and substantial emphasis on military and foreign assistance formed the operational instruments for conducting U.S. policy. The creation of NATO in 1949 was a further indication of the extent to which the Truman administration relied on strategic and diplomatic efforts supported by a modest national wallet to underwrite a defense aimed at containing or eliminating the causes of conflict rather than fighting one.

The consequences of the Truman demobilization are less clear. It is unknowable whether U.S. military restraint and its strong anti-communist stand encouraged or discouraged Soviet actions in Europe and elsewhere. By early 1950, the government was examining rearmament through the vehicle of the now famous NSC-68 study.[6] But Truman remained as resistant to increasing defense and defense spending as he had been in 1949 when General Eisenhower was recalled to serve as *de facto* Chairman of the Joint Chiefs and given the task of determining an appropriate military budget. Ike did just that, and Truman rejected it as too costly.

The Korean War ended American military restraint towards rearmament. As North Korean forces drove into South Korea on June 24, 1950, Washington time, the United States was faced with two strategic questions. The first was how or whether to respond. After all, there was no treaty with Korea, and the few U.S. forces in Korea, about 750, were part of a military assistance group. These factors did not automatically mandate a declaration of war. The second question was what was to be done about both the fear and the expectation that the Soviet Union would intervene militarily, if not in Korea, then elsewhere. Answers to these questions might or might not deal with the fact that Korea was not then seen as a vital American interest.

---

[6] In late 1949, a group of senior government officials looked at the need for U.S. rearmament. Led by Paul H. Nitze, the group produced the landmark report known by its document number, NSC-68.

Once the decision had been made for a military response and that it would be under a UN mandate, the U.S. military was ordered to fight in a region for which there had been no preparation or planning. There was a general lack of readiness for war in the U.S. forces, as well as shortages in ammunition that would cost U.S. lives. The initial bloodying of the U.S. Army's Task Force Smith by the North Koreans is usually cited as the price of this unpreparedness. But, for all its ill preparation, the United States was able to respond quite effectively. Forced into the very southeast corner of South Korea called the Pusan perimeter where U.S. and UN forces hung on for dear life, the United States mobilized in less than three months after the initial attack. By September 1950, the U.S. was about to seize the offensive. Confidence was not lacking as the U.S. senior leadership was the team that won World War II. George Marshall was the newly installed secretary of defense; McArthur, of course, commanded the forces in Korea and the Pacific; Ike was Supreme Allied Commander in Europe; and Omar Bradley was Chairman of the JCS.

The Inchon Landing that September was one of the most brilliant maneuvers in military annals, and the North Korean army was routed.[7] The U.S. military, in a period of weeks, was converted from an underfunded, "un-combat-ready" peacetime force into an effective fighting force. Indeed, had the United States not demobilized after World War II and retained a standing force of many millions and if North Korea still attacked south, it is debatable whether the outcome of the war would have been much different. The strategic blunders that followed, drawing China into the war that fall, and led to a bloody stalemate do not contradict the actual military performance of U.S. forces and the rapid conversion to wartime footing. An anecdotal piece of evidence supporting this resilience is relevant.

---

[7] Although many analysts consider the Korean War and even its early successes with less than admiration for U.S. prowess, the reader might dwell for a moment on comparing the build-up and attack in the Persian Gulf War in 1990–91 and the first four months of the Korean War in 1950.

Soviet T-34 tanks deployed by North Korea were virtually invulnerable to World War II 2.36-inch (i.e., the diameter of the rocket projectile fired by the weapon) "bazookas," which simply lacked the punch to penetrate the armor plating. In less than two months, the U.S. was able to produce and ship to Korea the more effective and larger 3.5-inch bazooka with sufficient stocks of ammunition. The newer weapon had been in testing, and, as the U.S. would experience 40 years later in another war, the ability to move rapidly from testing to combat use is significant.

The Korean War propelled the U.S. into a major rearmament and a determined effort to confront and defeat Soviet aggression on a worldwide basis. Thus, the militarization of the Cold War began in earnest. The Truman policies of putting the economy first, emphasizing mobilization and research and development, and relying on alternatives to using U.S. military might such as military assistance and foreign aid and thus keeping defense spending to the minimum—although quite effective if measured against the military performance of the first five months of the Korean War— would be reordered. Reliance on a standing force in excess of 3 million troops, large deployments overseas not for reasons of post-war occupation or assistance but for actual defense of friends and allies, and an active military competition with the USSR became the new priorities for policy. The U.S. also made the decision to develop thermonuclear weapons. Because of their vast destructive capacity that could destroy a society, thermonuclear weapons would revolutionize strategy by making the deterring of war rather than its waging the most vital national strategic priority.

As defense industries were rejuvenated and a domestic defense infrastructure made more robust, the post-World War II structural changes in the characteristics of the economy were introducing the first signs of what would become significant "cost creep" in defense. In other words, the economies of scale that may have been present during World War II in acquiring and producing vast numbers of weapons of war were being reversed. These cost comparisons illustrate the first signs of this post-war phenomenon of "cost-creep" and are taken from the annual defense reports of the period.

At the end of World War II and in then-year dollars, a P-51 fighter cost $54,000; B-17 and B-29 bombers $218,000 and $680,000, respectively. A World War II Pershing tank cost $81,000 and a Fletcher-class destroyer $7 million. In 1949, the cost of an F-86 fighter was $500,000; a B-36 bomber $3.5 million; a Patton tank $200,000; and the new class of "destroyer leaders" $20 million each. While the shift from reciprocating to jet engines, from guns to missiles, from TNT to thermonuclear explosives, and other technological advances that produced greatly increased or order-of-magnitude advances in operational performance were obvious, the relative costs of these improvements began exponential growth far above the rate of inflation. We will return to this subject later.

Part of Truman's emphasis on research and development was the decision to embark on a program to develop thermonuclear weapons. Too often, the historical myth or misperception of the alleged "revolutionary" impact of nuclear weapons was created by confusing the destructive power of nuclear and thermonuclear weapons. Prior to thermonuclear weapons with explosive capacity extending into the megaton range, fission weapons had yields of between 10 and about 100 kilotons, or the equivalent of 10,000 to 100,000 tons of TNT. A nuclear weapon, despite its destructive capacity, was to a thermonuclear weapon in nearly the same ratio as a double-ought buckshot is to an 8-inch artillery round.

Two single bombs destroyed Hiroshima and Nagasaki, but thousands of conventional bombs had imposed more damage and killed more people on raids over Tokyo, Haruna, Dresden, Berlin, and other World War II targets. Prior to thermonuclear weapons, the military view was that atomic weapons were important but not strategically decisive. In 1950 and after Russia obtained the "bomb," the Joint Chiefs noted that Soviet delivery of 100 nuclear weapons on U.S. targets would do only "serious damage." And, despite the so-called nuclear monopoly, the U.S. had only a handful of these weapons: 9 in 1946, 13 in 1947, and 50 in 1948. It was not until the advent of thermonuclear weapons and the first detonation in 1952 of an "H-bomb" that fusion weapons would eventually be seen as playing a decisive strategic role.

After the post-war demobilization and the hardening of the Cold War, the foundations for future U.S. national security policy were put firmly in place. The philosophy of "containment" of the threat was the principal basis for that policy. A series of alliances and security arrangements were being assembled to that end, with primary focus on NATO Europe. Economic strength was essential, and only in crisis would defense spending be allowed to consume large portions of the nation's resources. As nuclear and thermonuclear strength grew, "deterrence" would emerge as the bedrock for national security. Emphasis on exploiting both the littoral advantages of geography in surrounding and containing the USSR through systems of alliances and the advantages of technological superiority became permanent fixtures on the national security landscape and policy of the United States.

Finally, despite the temptation to use the national security argument either to limit political debate or to impose autocratic decisions on government or the public, Truman was exceedingly careful to consult at length with Congress on these matters. The reality that Congress was dominated and disciplined by relatively few powerful leaders and strict seniority and party systems no doubt simplified Truman's success and effectiveness in these security matters. But, the experiences of World War II and the emergence of another "totalitarian" threat meant that foreign policy was viewed as genuinely bipartisan, and the executive branch took great pains to ensure the continuity of that relationship. Although secrecy was important, public trust and confidence in government were sufficiently credible to permit major and formidable policies to be put in place and, more importantly, sustained.

THE EISENHOWER REDUCTIONS

U.S. forces mobilized to fight in Korea. By the time of the presidential elections in 1952, the United States was spending more than the equivalent of 250 billion of today's dollars on defense, and the forces totalled over 3 million men and women in uniform. The fact that, for political and strategic reasons, the Korean War was a stalemate did not resonate well among the U.S. public, who were expecting another unconditional and total victory, as in 1945. Thus, in the presidential elections, General of the Army Dwight David Eisenhower not only promised that he was the right man for the country at this "time for change," he also assured voters he would end the war, which he did in 1953.

The context of Eisenhower's view of defense was conditioned by his experiences in World War II, his understanding of the Soviet Union, and his instinctive grasp of the importance of preserving and nurturing national economic strength. In a sense, politics and personalities aside, the similarities and consistencies with Truman's view are striking. Although the Soviet Union was America's military, political, and ideological adversary, Ike felt certain that Soviet ambitions did not envisage world war. He also believed that the American thermonuclear advantage could and should be translated into policy actions and specific strategies to exploit those advantages. Hence, the shift to the strategic "new look," as it was called, followed, with emphasis on a doctrine of "massive retaliation" and U.S. technological superiority.

The new look assumed that Soviet conventional military power, which Eisenhower probably felt was exaggerated anyway, could be ultimately contained and checked by the threat of a U.S. massive thermonuclear weapons response. The implication followed that fewer U.S. conventional forces would be required, replaced as they were by the destructive power of the atom, which would lessen long-term costs of defense. In this case, nuclear weapons were not only more effective than manpower, they were less expensive. The military was cut back, a popular step with the ending of the Korean War, and a second but premeditated post-war build-down began.

The new look placed continuing emphasis on research and development and a further broadening of the effort to exploit technology and U.S. technical advantages, particularly as nuclear targeting and delivery systems required a new generation of improved capabilities. Although the non-nuclear or conventional capability of the U.S. military was reduced, including the actual readiness to fight, the integration of tactical and strategic nuclear weapons was seen by the administration as more than compensating for any erosion in conventional strength.

This emphasis on R&D was made permanent by the 1958 amendment to the National Security Act that, among other actions, established both the directorate for research, development, and engineering within DOD and the Defense Advanced Research Projects Agency (DARPA), since renamed ARPA. The combination of less spending on defense and more emphasis on R&D was probably good for the economy—although the U.S. economy was robust enough then, even in recession, that the absolute contribution of shifting resources from defense to the private sector was impossible to calculate.

The content and structure of this second post-war build-down were well planned and well executed. Defense budgets and force levels were cut and force structure was recast to reflect this strategic new look. Figure 1 shows the breakdown of the new look in terms of the budget.

Figure 1. DOD expenditures for military functions (1951-1959)

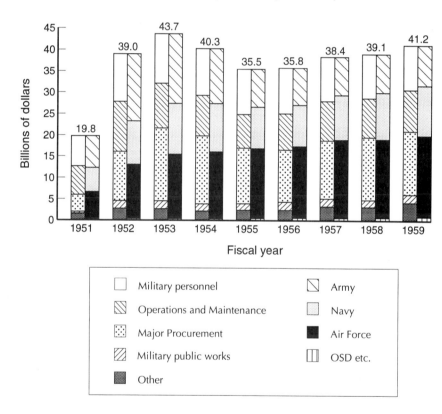

As was the case under Truman, Eisenhower's demobilization made certain assumptions that were not without long-term flaws. These shortcomings would have serious future political consequences. The strategy of nuclear superiority could be defeated or neutralized if and when the USSR caught up and deployed comparable strategic forces. If the U.S. were engaged in conflict against other, non-nuclear adversaries outside the Soviet protective sphere, conventional and not nuclear force would be the only usable military instrument.[8] To be sure, this was a longer-term consideration but not one to be ignored. Finally, emphasis on R&D could lead to a permanent institutionalization of a military industrial complex with a long-term and powerful claim on resources and, as this industrial base grew stronger, a potential bureaucratic check on innovation that was not in keeping with the innovative assumptions of the new look.

Thus, in the fifteen years after World War II ended, U.S. national security policy had dramatically shifted from wartime demobilization and traditional reliance on a small standing force. A muscular R&D program, a strong mobilization and stockpile base, a strong reserve, the need for mobilization in crisis, and an active foreign assistance and aid program, including alliances, were products of the Cold War. Thermonuclear deterrence, militarily strong alliances, and containment, all underwritten by a large standing force and a strong and mobilizable industrial base with robust R&D programs to exploit U.S. technological superiority, had become the new foundations for security.

Like the Truman administration, the Eisenhower team sought and maintained a bipartisan approach to foreign and defense policy. There were few substantive differences in the nature of Executive and Congressional relations in these matters or in the control of power and authority within Congress. As a result and despite the crises of the era—Suez, Hungary, Sputnik, Lebanon, and the U-2 shootdown—the constitutional questions and tensions over the foreign policy and commander-in-chief responsibilities were relatively minor. It is also important to note that Eisenhower used personal diplomacy with Chairman Khrushchev to improve U.S.-Soviet

---

8 In 1954, the U.S. chose not to consider the use of nuclear weapons in relieving the Viet-Minh siege of French forces trapped in Dienbienphu. This refusal, correct as it was, revealed both the strategic and military inapplicability of the "new look" to actual non-Soviet, non-nuclear conditions of war.

relations. The "Spirit of Geneva," the "Open Skies" proposal for arms inspection, and steps towards nuclear testing moratoria were a very real part of the foreign policy agenda. And trust and confidence between government and the governed, the horror of McCarthyism withstanding, were still in partial bloom.

THE POST-VIETNAM NIXON–FORD–CARTER REDUCTIONS

Less than two decades after World War II ended, the United States was engaged in another land war in Asia, this time in Indo-China. From the war in Korea until the conflict in Vietnam began in earnest, U.S. defense policy had rapidly matriculated from Eisenhower's "new look" to Kennedy's "flexible response." The "new look" of the 1950s was based on nuclear and thermonuclear superiority and a policy of "massive retaliation" that placed a premium on nuclear and not conventional forces. "Flexible response," on the other hand, while maintaining a strong industrial and mobilization flavor, aspired to fight not only on conventional and nuclear levels of conflict but also in unconventional and guerrilla forms of warfare. This versatility across the entire spectrum of conflict was presumed to be the best means to prevent conflict. In this sense, as the personal views of Truman and Eisenhower had shaped U.S. defense policy, John F. Kennedy also had strong views on the need for a strong defense as the best means to prevent Soviet aggression.[9]

Ike had trimmed military spending following the armistice in Korea on the grounds of seizing strategic and fiscal advantages by emphasizing strategic nuclear forces and by deemphasizing conventional force. The Kennedy administration came to office highly critical of what it saw as Eisenhower's failure to keep pace with alleged advances in Soviet military power and convinced of the need to spend a great deal more on defense. Not only was the so-called

---

[9] In this regard, Kennedy was no doubt influenced by his experiences in Europe in 1939 as the world moved to war. Kennedy feared that a democracy's weakness was waiting too long to rearm in time of danger. And, as he wrote in 1940 in *Why England Slept*, he was not about to repeat that error.

"missile gap" a strategic chasm that had to be closed, but the Eisenhower administration's preoccupation with nuclear forces, in Kennedy's view, had atrophied U.S. conventional might to dangerously low levels. Notwithstanding what would turn out to be a fundamentally mistaken assessment of Soviet military capability and intent by the new team, U.S. defense expenditures soared during first the Kennedy and then the Johnson years. Certainly, Vietnam proved a significant factor for these increases, but the Soviet Union remained the prime reason for increasing U.S. defense expenditures.

During the transition from the "new look" to "flexible response," the Kennedy administration adopted and upgraded planning scenarios for rationalizing and defining force structure. The so-called "2-1/2 war" scenario that began in the late 1950s was reinforced by extensive analysis in which the U.S. planned on simultaneously being able to fight the USSR, China, and a "1/2 war" elsewhere. As will be noted in Chapter Six, the assumptions and criteria on which planning was based were vital. And this need for rigor in planning forces in turn led to a preoccupation with "analysis." It was also clear that, at all times, a substantial and probably unclosable gap existed between what forces would be needed in those scenarios for 2-1/2 wars and what forces and capabilities were actually bought by the budgets.

One of the so-called revolutions of this period was Secretary of Defense Robert McNamara's use of and reliance on quantitative analysis. McNamara then believed every problem had a solution that, in turn, was resolvable through some form of analytical appraisal. This fascination with and dependence on analysis would have two long-term consequences. The first was the assumption that all (or even many) military problems were resolvable by analysis. Simply because a numerical response could be calculated to what it might take to defeat, say, a Soviet attack into Europe did not mean that answer was valid or even relevant.[10] Yet, analysis became an enduring legacy of the decision-making process.

---

10 For example, in 1982, the Naval War College in Newport was asked to "wargame" on its computers the 1942 Battle of Midway in which a vastly numerically inferior U.S. force decisively beat a much larger Japanese naval force. The one result that this gaming did not produce was a U.S. victory—the actual outcome.

Second, the military services quickly realized that the only way to become relevant in the decision process was to acquire analytical capabilities at least equal to those of the Office of the Secretary of Defense (OSD). This the services did and were eventually able to "out-analyze" a series of different future OSDs.

But even when a real, quantifiable threat existed, the limits of analysis were severe if not always deemed to be so. Faith in the enduring application of analysis is not necessarily useful in a world of nonspecific threats for which analysis may have less or little use. And relating military solutions to politically driven problems simply may not work.

The debate over whether Vietnam would have become a debacle had Kennedy lived is moot. Lyndon Johnson assumed Kennedy's promise to "pay any price and bear any burden," and within months of Kennedy's assassination, the United States was building up its forces and escalating the war in Vietnam. In August 1964, a series of North Vietnamese attacks against U.S. Navy warships, since disputed and shown to be exaggerated by the U.S., precipitated the Tonkin Gulf Resolution—a nearly unanimous act of Congress that Johnson would use as authorization, if not *de facto* declaration, to carry on the war.

The history of the Vietnam War is well known and beyond the scope of this text. However, several of the legacies of that war were vitally important in shaping the contemporary political environment and mood of the nation. Most importantly and tragically, a crisis of confidence and trust between the public and its government and between the White House and Congress tore apart much of American society. The extraordinary and frequent protests and riots, accompanied by many Congressional hearings and, ultimately, the War Powers Act that limited executive power and required Congressional approval for deployment of U.S. forces into combat (or pseudo-combat) conditions, were expressions of this crisis. Despite its opposition, Congress never shut off funding for the war until after the U.S. withdrew, which was one sure way to end the conflict.

The consquences were clear and tragic. Not only could an administration no longer be trusted; public expectation and cynicism routinely assumed that government would prevaricate and could not be trusted to tell the truth. The war in Vietnam that would kill nearly 60,000 Americans and unknown numbers of Vietnamese, combined with its mismanagement, pressurized and exacerbated the fundamental constitutional tensions over war powers and foreign policy.

The war also cast the military into the role of villain. To the politicians, the military was seen as incompetent because it could not win a war against a small, ill-armed, largely primitive foe. To much of the public, with television images of U.S. forces burning Vietnamese villages and wantonly killing enemy and civilians alike thrust on the evening news, the military was held in contempt and vilified as "warmongers."

To the military, who saw the war as unwinnable as long as political constraints prevented invading the north or massively destroying the many dams, bridges, and other targets that would cripple North Vietnam, the oath to obey civilian leadership became the larger escape mechanism for repressing frustration and anger and living with the consequences of defeat. In fact, no flag or general officer resigned in protest of that war largely on the grounds that such an act would have had no effect. But the situation was untenable for the military. Implicitly and over time, veterans of that war individually came to the recognition that in future conflicts there would have to be specific, achievable, and supportable military objectives. Otherwise, "new Vietnams" were too likely to occur. Two decades later, these bloody and painful lessons coalesced into the so-called Weinberger Doctrine that set six principles for the decisive deployment of U.S. forces in harm's way—each one a legacy and reminder of Vietnam.

The vast antagonism between Congress and the presidency over Vietnam, which was even more vitriolic than the interservice wars of 1947–1950 in the Pentagon, effectively ended the era of bipartisanship and unleashed any lingering constraints on the constitutional tensions between the branches. The military, as well as future political leaders, vowed never again to be trapped between the Scylla of unachievable military objectives and the Charybdis of applying insufficient force.

In November 1968, President-elect Richard Nixon was charged by the U.S. public to end the most unpopular war in American history, a mandate that would take nearly seven years to complete.

This charge implicitly meant that a third post-war build-down in U.S. military capability was inevitable. As in the case of Ike's reductions, there was the enticement that by cutting defense expenditures American economic health could be improved.

Simultaneously, the nation ended the draft and put in place an all-volunteer military force. But, unlike the defense demobilization of 1945–46 (and more like Eisenhower's build-down—during which Nixon served as vice president), this reduction entailed continuing to meet the military threat of a superpower while waging a bloody and protracted war in Vietnam. Following the direction set in the Eisenhower administration, but with a Nixonian twist, the U.S. partly relied on its technological advantages—particularly in strategic nuclear systems, which were readily seen by the Soviet Union as representing the most valuable military currency of the realm—to compensate for lower overall defense expenditures.

During and partially because of America's painful and humiliating withdrawal from Vietnam, the Nixon administration implemented the highly innovative and simple strategy of moving China from the category of U.S. enemy to one of *de facto* strategic friend. This transition was part of a fundamental reassessment of national security policy undertaken for President Nixon by his National Security Advisor Henry Kissinger in 1969. This was the last time any administration embarked on both a sweeping review of and sweeping changes in national security. This review led the U.S. to move from planning for 2-1/2 wars to a 1-1/2 war plan, with the USSR as the single adversary under the umbrella of the Nixon Doctrine in which regional states would assume larger responsibilities for their security.

The intent of playing the so-called and misnomered China "card" was to induce the USSR to improve strategic and political relations with the West and moderate its hostile and belligerent policies. Arms control agreements with the Soviet Union would follow and strengthen the sense of detente and the success of the Nixon foreign policy. The net result of these broader strategic actions permitted the United States to continue reducing defense expenditures and to build down the size of its non-nuclear forces. Table 1 shows the budgetary comparisons of these three post-conflict defense reductions.

Table 1. GNP, federal budget, and DOD budget for selected years (in billions of current-year dollars)

FY		GNP	Net total	DOD	Other	Offsets[a]	GNP	Federal budget
			Federal budget outlays				DOD outlays as percent of:	
1950	Lowest year since World War II[b]	$263.3	$43.1	$11.9	$31.2	NA	4.5	27.7
1953	Korea peak[b]	358.9	76.8	47.7	29.1	NA	13.3	62.1
1961	—	506.5	97.8	44.6	55.7	−2.5	8.8	44.5
1964	Last prewar year	612.2	118.6	50.8	70.7	−2.9	8.3	41.8
1968	Southeast Asia peak[b]	822.6	178.9	78.0	105.5	−4.6	9.5	42.5
1969	Last actual year	900.6	184.6	78.7	111.0	−5.1	8.7	41.5
1970	Johnson budget	960.0	195.3	81.6[c]	119.4	−5.7	8.5	40.6
1970	Current estimate	960.0	197.9	77.0	127.0	−6.1	8.0	37.7
1971[d]	Budget estimate	1,020.0	200.8	71.8	135.6	−6.6	7.0	34.6
1971	In 1964 dollars	—	—	54.6	—	—	—	—
Changes 1964 to 1971		+407.8	+82.2	+21.0[e]	+64.9	−3.7		
	1969 to 1971	+119.4	+16.2	−6.9	+24.6	−1.5		

a   These amounts are undistributed intragovernmental transactions deducted from government-wide totals. They include government contribution for employee retirement and interest received by trust funds.

b   Measured in terms of defense outlays as a percentage of GNP and federal budget.

c   Includes the $2.6 billion cost of the July 1, 1969, pay raise. The pay-raise costs were not shown in the agency totals, but were included in a government-wide contingency estimate in the FY 1970 Johnson budget.

d   Lowest percent of GNP since 1951; lowest percent of federal budget since 1950.

e   5.2 percent of the GNP growth during this period, and 24.4 percent of the increase in the federal budget.

The Nixon administration had managed to reduce the top line for defense spending in real terms by about 30 percent in four years. A strong but less costly military was still viewed as essential to guarding national security. However, because of cost creep and accumulating growth in the overhead and infrastructure costs of defense, a powerful erosion in U.S. military might was taking place. These costs and inefficiencies reduced what a dollar could purchase as well as distorted how spending directly contributed to effective military output.

The war in Vietnam, the role of the presidency in waging that war, and the subterfuge, real or imagined, symbolized the so-called "imperial presidency" in which the White House was seen as responsible to no one. In that perspective, the Watergate fiasco became a political nuclear blast detonated by an act of supreme executive misconduct. Congressional and public reaction to this scandal was more than profound. Aside from nearly impeaching Richard Nixon and driving him out of office, the actual and perceived power, prestige, and influence of the presidency plummeted to unprecedented depths. The War Powers Act, passed in 1973, required specific Congressional approval for deploying U.S. forces for more than three months to serve in regions where conflict was likely or occurring. About the same time and partly motivated by the Vietnam backlash, the seniority system in Congress was overturned, further diffusing both the political power and self-disciplining mechanisms of government.

One consequence of this crisis in trust, confidence, and failure by the executive branch was an activist Congress that led to a proliferation of its staffs and committees and increasing involvement in the oversight and regulation of the executive branch. The crisis over the handling of Vietnam was exacerbated by the excesses of Watergate, and public wrath turned against the president and his White House. In many ways, Congress became an instrument of this wrath, and tensions over constitutional prerogatives continued to worsen as Congress attempted to redress a balance of power swung too far in the direction of 1600 Pennsylvania Avenue.

The Carter administration took office in 1977, promising, among other things, a president who "would always tell the truth to the American people" and a commitment to continue progress in improving relations with the USSR. Detente was extended. Arms reduction negotiations continued. By then, the United States was well out of Vietnam, and a principal focus on "human rights" was a hallmark of the new administration. Like the Nixon team in 1969, the Carter administration attempted a "zero-base" review of national security. Unlike the Nixon team, however, the Carter conclusion was to continue along the same track, including further, modest reductions to defense.

The Brezhnev Doctrine to maintain Soviet dominance in Eastern Europe, the Soviet invasion of Afghanistan, and the seizure of the U.S. Embassy and staff in Tehran by so-called Irani "students" were seen as direct challenges to U.S. leadership and to the Carter presidency. Despite the success of the Camp David Accords that produced peace between Egypt and Israel, the Carter administration was seen by its critics as "soft" or weak in foreign policy. The failed raid to free the U.S. hostages in Tehran in 1980 was perhaps the last straw that would break the administration's chances for reelection by perpetuating the perception of a weak White House.

Meanwhile, the quantitative trend in diminished readiness of the armed forces continued well into the late 1970s even though, after 1978, defense spending was increased every year through the mid 1980s. The most publicized and unintended consequence of this implicit or *de facto* military build-down was the "hollow force," that is, a military that was judged by its uniformed leadership to be largely unready to carry out both its peacetime and wartime missions. A series of real and alleged U.S. military failures in the 1970s and early 1980s reinforced this perception of unreadiness and has been well documented in the Congressional record and by many narratives and studies of the reasons for this standard of performance.

The causes of this "hollowness" were driven by shortfalls in spending or, put another way, by a broader inability to meet the financial demands needed to sustain the forces on hand at appropriate levels of combat readiness. Not enough quality recruits were entering service; not enough quality personnel were being retained in service; not enough money was going to training; and not enough money was being applied to maintain combat systems at acceptable levels of operational readiness. Thus, although it is clear that the long-term effects of this third build-down were never premeditated and may have had little strategic consequence, the costs of reversing this condition would prove enormous. The consequences were the condition of "in irons" through gradual decay of the forces rather than a catastrophic single military failure.

Comparing these three instances of earlier defense reductions across categories of budget, force size, and industrial base capacity measured by employment, we see the results shown in tables 2 through 4. Table 2 compares defense spending and military manpower for selected years; table 3 displays uniform and civilian DOD manning for selected years; and table 4 provides a selective breakdown of federal spending for outlays from 1945 through 1994.

Understanding the breakdown of defense expenditures provided further insight into the effects of the changing social and economic structure of the nation on military capability (table 5).

Furthermore, it is useful to compare the changing costs of individual weapon systems during this period (table 6). Although the capabilities and technologies in newer systems reflected major and often extraordinary improvements in performance, the relative and absolute cost increases have grown far greater than inflation.

Table 2. Comparison of defense spending and manpower[a]

	Truman FY 1945–47	Eisenhower FY 1955	Johnson FY 1965	Nixon-Ford FY 1975	Reagan FY 1988
Defense outlays	$120 billion	$208 billion	$199 billion	$190 billion	$290 billion
Active-duty strength	1.4 million	3.0 million	2.7 million	2.1 million	2.2 million
Selected reserves	N/A	1.0 million estimated	1.2 million	0.9 million	1.2 million

a In FY 1988 dollars.

Table 3. Department of Defense manpower (endstrength in thousands)

Active-duty military[a]

FY	Army	Navy[b]	Marine Corps	Air Force[c]	Full-time Guard and Reserve	Total military
1940	218	161	28	51	—	458
1941	1,310	284	54	152	—	1,801
1945	5,984	3,320	470	2,282	—	12,056
1948	554	418	85	388	—	1,444
1950	593	381	74	411	—	1,459
1953	1,534	794	249	978	—	3,555
1960	873	617	171	815	—	2,475
1966	1,200	745	261	887	—d	3,094
1967	1,442	751	285	897	—d	3,377
1968	1,570	765	307	905	—d	3,548
1969	1,512	776	310	862	—d	3,460
1970	1,322	692	260	791	1	3,066
1971	1,123	623	212	755	1	2,715
1972	811	588	198	726	1	2,323
1973	801	564	196	691	1	2,253
1974	783	546	189	644	1	2,162
1980	777	527	188	558	13	2,063
1985	781	571	198	602	55	2,206
1986	781	581	199	608	64	2,233
1987	781	587	200	607	69	2,243
1988	772	593	197	576	71	2,209
1989	770	593	197	571	72	2,202
1990	751	583	197	539	74	2,143
1991	725	571	195	511	75	2,077
1992	611	542	185	470	72	1,880
1993	572	510	178	445	71	1,750
1994	540	471	174	426	68	1,611

a Active-duty military includes the activation of 25,652 National Guard and Reservists in FY 1990 pursuant to sections 673b, Title 10 U.S.C.; 17,059 National Guard and Reservists in FY 1991; and 954 National Guard and Reservists in FY 1992 pursuant to sections 672 and 673, Title 10 U.S.C. to support Operation Desert Shield/Desert Storm.

b Navy reserve personnel on active duty for Training and Administration of Reserves (TARS) are included in the active Navy before FY 1980 and in the full-time Guard and Reserve thereafter.

c Air Force civil service employment is included in the Army before 1948 and identified separately thereafter.

d Indicates less than 500 full-time National Guardsmen and Reservists. Data before 1966 not available.

(Continued on next page)

Table 3. *(Continued)*

DOD civilian work force[a]

FY	Army	Navy, including Marines	Air Force	Defense agencies and other	Total civilians	Total DOD man-power
1940	137	119	—	—	256	714
1941	329	227	—	—	556	2,357
1945	1,881	747	—	—	2,628	14,684
1948	303	347	152	1	804	2,248
1950	261	293	154	2	710	2,170
1953	884	470	382	2	1,738	5,293
1960	473	365	355	2	1,195	3,671
1966	450	367	336	69	1,222	4,316
1967	516	416	349	76	1,357	4,733
1968	510	429	339	75	1,352	4,900
1969	531	438	349	72	1,390	4,849
1970	480	388	328	68	1,264	4,330
1971	452	362	313	63	1,189	3,904
1972	446	353	300	60	1,159	3,482
1973	406	334	288	72	1,099	3,352
1974	409	335	289	75	1,108	3,270
1980	361	309	244	77	990	3,053
1985	420	353	264	92	1,129	3,335
1986	413	342	263	94	1,112	3,345
1987	418	353	264	98	1,133	3,376
1988	393	348	253	96	1,090	3,299
1989	403	354	261	99	1,117	3,319
1990	380	341	249	103	1,073	3,216
1991	365	329	233	117	1,045	3,122
1992	334	309	214	149	1,006	2,886
1993	294	285	202	156	937	2,763
1994	293	269	201	160	923	2,608

[a] Beginning in 1953, the civilian work force figures include both U.S. and foreign national direct hires and the foreign national indirect-hire employees that support U.S. forces overseas.

Table 4. Federal outlays FY 1945–1994 (FY 1987 dollars in billions)

FY	National defense	Veterans, Space, Internat'l	Net interest	Social & economic	Agency total	Undist. offset. receipts	Grand total
		Federal unified budget					
1945	714.6	18.0	23.6	61.4	817.6	−16.3	801.3
1948	64.9	32.4	22.4	74.3	194.0	−12.2	181.8
1950	94.6	72.8	24.2	71.0	262.6	−12.5	250.1
1953	315.2	31.6	23.6	78.7	449.1	−23.2	425.9
1960	217.9	34.3	26.6	133.8	412.6	−23.1	389.5
1966	229.6	60.8	32.3	200.8	523.5	−26.2	497.3
1967	274.6	59.9	34.2	226.4	595.1	−28.7	566.4
1968	299.5	54.3	35.5	254.1	643.4	−29.8	613.6
1969	283.4	50.3	38.7	250.2	622.6	−27.5	595.1
1970	264.4	48.5	41.6	271.0	625.5	−27.7	597.8
1971	238.4	47.2	40.8	303.5	629.9	−28.9	601.0
1972	220.3	49.1	40.5	333.9	643.8	−25.5	618.3
1973	197.2	48.1	43.1	364.4	652.8	−32.5	620.3
1974	185.3	51.1	49.6	377.1	663.1	−37.7	625.4
1980	187.1	54.1	74.4	545.0	860.6	−28.5	832.1
1985	261.2	52.4	137.3	584.7	1,035.6	−34.3	1,001.3
1986	276.4	48.8	140.1	586.0	1,051.3	−34.0	1,017.3
1987	282.0	45.4	138.7	574.3	1,040.4	−36.5	1,003.9
1988	283.3	46.4	146.5	586.7	1,062.9	−35.8	1,027.1
1989	285.9	45.8	156.4	604.1	1,092.2	−34.3	1,057.9
1990	272.3	47.9	163.1	659.3	1,142.6	−32.4	1,110.2
1991	238.4	50.7	165.2	752.7	1,207.0	−33.2	1,173.8
1992	253.0	51.6	164.6	752.0	1,221.2	−32.1	1,189.1
1993	240.6	53.4	162.4	808.3	1,264.7	−29.7	1,235.0
1994	223.6	54.7	166.7	828.1	1,273.1	−29.1	1,244.0

Table 5. Defense expenditures by percentage of annual budgets

	Personnel (salaries, benefits)	Operations, maintenance, and training	Procurement (including military construction)	Research and development
Truman (1946–1950)	47	31	19	3
Eisenhower (1953–1960)	34	26	32	8
Nixon/Ford/Carter (1969–1979)	34	30	27	9

Table 6. Cost of individual weapon systems (all figures in FY 1988 dollars)

	Tanks	Fighter aircraft	Nuclear attack submarines	Surface warships
1945	M-48 $400,000	F-51 $540,000	—	DD-692/710 $20 million
1965	M-60 $800,000	F-4 $7 million	SSN-594 $250 million	DDG-2 $150 million
1990	M-1A1 $2.3 million	F-15C/D $40 million	SSN-688 $700 million	CG-47 $1.1 billion

In comparison, there are important observations and conclusions from these three periods of demobilization and military reductions. Among the significant observations, it is clear that the Truman demobilization, the Eisenhower partial demobilization, and the Nixon reductions were well planned and were based on similar premises: namely, downsizing of threat assessment; reliance on technology, alliances, foreign aid and assistance, and diplomacy as national security tools rather than on overwhelming force; recognition of the vital role of a healthy and expanding economy; and the sense that bipartisanship within the branches of the government would overcome any inefficiencies or roadblocks of constitutional tensions over national defense responsibilities. The last stages of the third defense drawdown in the 1970s produced a "hollow force" that was never the objective or intent of any administration and highlights both the pernicious nature of the factors that induce this condition as well as the long-term vulnerability of any level of military capability to this type of atrophy.

Presidents Truman, Eisenhower, and Nixon had strong views about national security and strong convictions over drawing down defense. No doubt, as in other areas, strong presidential leadership remains the vital factor. Indeed, on the build-up side, Presidents Kennedy and Reagan had very strong views on enhancing defense. Although the Kennedy and Reagan views may have been strategically flawed or mistaken, during their terms of office, those same views were largely responsible for inducing two build-ups that, on purely tactical and operational criteria, strengthened U.S. military might.

More important are the conclusions to be drawn from this comparison of the three post-World War II defense reductions. First, in each case, there was always a superpower threat to be countered and the perception that the military advantages of the West over the East, especially in advanced and nuclear systems, were at least being closed by the Soviet Union. The Soviet military threat was also vital in shaping the size and contours of the U.S. defense budget, whether spending was waxing or waning, and provided a quantitative as well as qualitative basis for defending and justifying U.S. force structure.

Second, in each case, the perceived (and probably actual) readiness of the forces to carry out their military missions suffered and declined. There have been, however, no objective or quantitative measures to determine the exact level of military readiness in place at a given time, and the subjective nature of this art makes it unlikely that this lack of objectivity will change.[11] Yet, in qualitative terms, during times of budgetary constraints, the universal view has been one of injury to the forces. Figures 2 and 3 show this trend between drawdowns and readiness.

---

[11] For example, in his FY 1979 report, Secretary of Defense Harold Brown noted that we have no exact means to determine readiness: "We have not yet developed the methodological tools to show the precise sensitivity of readiness to changes in our commitment of resources. But loss of readiness is a cumulative process that takes time as well as money to reverse." p. 10.

Figure 2. Nominal Army readiness

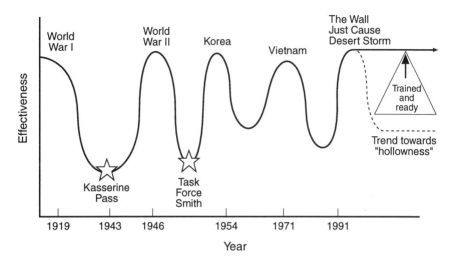

Figure 3. Composite of Navy and Air Force readiness

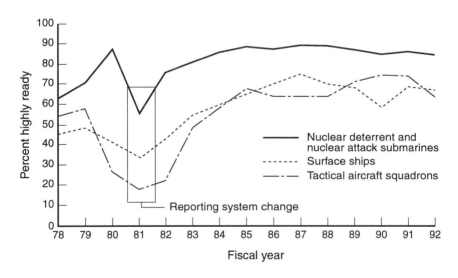

Third, in every budget expenditure category, whether for people or weapons, unit costs have increased by multiples over inflation. In the case of personnel, the end of the draft in 1973 and the higher pay levels needed for maintaining a volunteer force explain cost growth in this account. Similar built-in cost drivers apply to the other categories of defense goods and services as well. To keep pace with these inherent cost drivers that rise well above the rate of inflation, either annual defense spending had to be increased sufficiently or capability was reduced accordingly even if spending was adjusted only for inflation. The point is that no long-term steady-state level of military capability is sustainable unless annual spending is increased or the inefficiencies and cost drivers are decreased.

Fourth, through the late 1970s, the system of military bases and installations put in place to fight and win World War II was still largely functioning three-and-a-half decades later. By 1945, the U.S. had over 12 million troops in uniform out of a population of about 150 million. In 1979, there were 2.2 million in uniform out of a population of 225 million, and roughly 90 percent of the World War II installations remained in service.

Fifth, during the Eisenhower and post-Vietnam reductions, the domestic budget realities were far different. Transfer payments, federal liabilities, and non-discretionary accounts were much smaller, and domestic programs had none of the built-in pressures for annual growth as in the 1980s and beyond. Federal debt was still a consequence of the world war and was becoming a smaller and smaller percentage of GDP. Annual federal deficits were relatively small, and the issue was never "guns or butter" but balancing priorities within a federal budget that had fiscal flexibility. None of these conditions obtains in the shadow of the new century.

Sixth, and rather sensibly, the U.S. tried to exploit its technological superiority as an offset to Soviet numerical and geographical advantages. In the first instance, nuclear and thermonuclear improvements in weapons were married up with the "triad" of land- and sea-based missile and bomber forces. As conventional force became more relevant, advanced technology across virtually all systems was put to use to give the U.S. "qualitative" superiority over Soviet numerical advantage. Thus, for example, a U.S. nuclear submarine force of fewer than 100 attack boats was acceptable even though the Soviet Union maintained two or three times that number on the grounds that U.S. superior technology, namely quietness of the ships and better torpedoes, counterbalanced numerical inferiority.

Seventh, although the demobilization in 1945–46 sustained a force that, in three months, reversed the gains of the surprise North Korean attack in 1950 (but may not have been able to repel a Soviet invasion of Europe), diplomatic, economic, and strategic initiatives were successfully protecting the security of the West *vis a vis* the USSR. This use of instruments to complement U.S. military forces, in conjunction with a sensible build-down, could form a relevant model for the future.

Finally, and outside the above analysis, regulations concerning the acquisition and oversight of goods and services for defense, while increasing in costs and other impositions placed on the system, were in check in the sense these were manageable and affordable. This suggests nothing about the extent of procurement fraud or criminality and loss to the government by illegal actions. But in 1947, for example, there were about 2,000 pages of government procurement and regulatory procedures. And every dollar spent on buying goods and services cost about 2 to 5 cents to administer. In 1979, the rules and regulations grew to about 20,000 pages, and the costs of regulation increased to about 10 cents on the dollar.[12] The effect of these cost drivers and other factors that escalated defense expenses is manifested in figure 4, which displays U.S. defense spending from 1948 to 1984 in then-year dollars.

Figure 4. Fluctuations in U.S. defense spending, 1948-1984

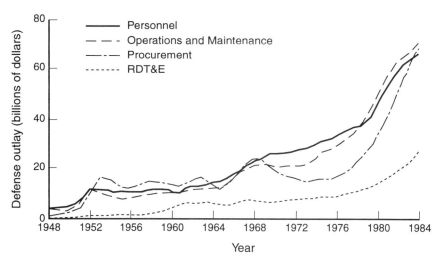

Source: The U.S. Government, *The Budget of the United States*, Appendix, 1948-1985

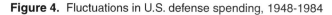

[12] The use of simple numbers is metaphoric and not analytical. In fact, the regulatory drain was probably more expensive and burdensome than this comparison suggests.

Note that beginning in about 1978, U.S. defense spending begins an asymptotic increase well above the inflation rate even though the actual increases in force size and capability were relatively modest. Some of this growth was due to the costs of the volunteer force. Much was not. It is this phenomenon that underscores the effect of the growing expense and inefficiency of governance.

The conclusions drawn from these earlier instances of defense downsizings highlight the extent of the current structural problems that must be resolved if U.S. future military might is to be maintained at levels and standards of readiness and capability likely to be needed in protecting the nation's interests.

THE FOURTH AND CURRENT BUILD-DOWN

In late 1989, largely if not entirely in response to the political and physical destruction of the Berlin Wall and the prospect of the Germanys being unified (and the new state remaining in NATO), the then new chairman of the Joint Chiefs of Staff General Colin Powell began a major review of military posture and strategy. Through sheer strength of personality, the chairman was able to persuade not only his colleagues in the Pentagon but also, most importantly, President George Bush that the Cold War was over and the U.S. must respond appropriately. The development of what became known as the "Base Force 1989–1992" was well documented in a study conducted by the Joint History Office of the Office of the Chairman of the Joint Chiefs of Staff (OCJCS).[13]

The "base force" envisaged reducing American active-duty military strength from 2.2 million to 1.6 million, or by about 25 percent, and the budget by 10 percent over a five-year period. Force structure was to be gradually reduced as shown in table 7.

The Bush "base force" was projected to be supported by budgets that grew slightly from $288.4 billion in FY 1993 to $300.6 billion in FY 1997. To allow a comparison with the last year of the Carter administration, table 8 shows the size and structure of U.S. forces for the past decade and a half.

---

[13] See Lorna S. Jaffee, *The Development of the Base Force 1989–1992*, published by the OCJCS. Perhaps the most revealing statement in that study was, "The Chairman would have preferred greater reductions...but he did not wish to increase resistance to his proposals."

Table 7. Reduction of U.S. force structure

Forces	FY 1990	FY 1993	Base force
Army			
Active divisions	18	14	12
National Guard division equivalents	10	6 (+2 Cadre)	6 (+2 Cadre)
Navy			
Aircraft carriers	15 + 1	13 + 1	12 + 1
Active/Reserve air wings	13 / 2	11 / 2	11 / 2
Ships	546	447	429
Air Force			
Active fighter wings	24	16	15.3
Reserve fighter wings	12	12	11.2
Marine Corps			
Active endstrength	197,000	185,000	170,000[a]
Reserve endstrength	44,000	42,000	35,000
Strategic nuclear forces			
Ballistic missile subs	34	22	18
Strategic bombers (PAA)	301	201	180
ICBMs	1,000	787	550

[a] USMC endstrength is scheduled to reach 159,000 in FY 1997 under the base force.

Table 8. Force structure past and future

FY	Endstrength (act/res, in 000s)	Army divisions (act/res)[a]	Marine Corps divisions (act/res)	Navy ships/ aircraft carriers	USAF tac ftr wings (act/res)	Annual budgets in then-year dollars (BA)[b]
1980	2,050/851	16/8	3/1	479/13	26/11	142.3
1985	2,152/1,088	17/10	3/1	541/14	25/12	286.8
1987	2,174/1,151	18/10	3/1	568/15	24.5/12	279.4
1990	2,069/1,128	18/10	3/1	545/15	24/12	292.9
1991	2,002/1,138	16/10	3/1	526/15	22/13	290.9
1992	1,808/1,114	14/10	3/1	466/14	16/14	286.3
1993	1,746/1,080	14/8	3/1	447/13	16/12	288.4

[a] Active/reserve.
[b] BA = budget authority.

The Bush "base force" was put into effect. Despite significant events such as the Gulf War waged throughout 1990 and ending in an overwhelming 100-hour victory in 1991 and, more importantly, the failed Soviet coup followed by the demise of both the USSR and the Warsaw Pact in August 1991, the base force remained largely unchanged. In the fall of 1991, following the failed coup, the Bush administration attempted to develop a new and bold arms-reduction initiative and seek major cuts across nuclear and conventional forces of both superpowers. However, Bush and Defense Secretary Dick Cheney were uncomfortable with the timing, and, as a result, the only forces that were cut back were theater nuclear.

To the degree that the base force had any industrial policy implications, the thrust was to let the market determine winners and losers. Government played little or no role in shaping the direction of the industrial base other than through its procurement expenditures. Thus, the first stages in this fourth downsizing would lead to a gradual reduction in manpower by about 400,000 active personnel and 300,000 reserves and to annual defense spending at just under $300 billion.

The Clinton administration assumed office in January 1993 but took a long time to settle in. Regarding defense, the first crisis was over the president's campaign pledge to end discrimination against homosexuals serving in uniform. Whatever individual views on that issue may have been, the Pentagon was seized in a huge controversy over social and legal matters and not the business of producing a first-rate plan for defending the nation.

At the time, the White House gave the new secretary of defense Les Aspin virtually no guidance on its view of defense policy or specific strategic objectives. Because very few of the top civilian positions were then filled in the Pentagon, the few senior OSD appointees had to rely on the Joint Chiefs and the Chairman for help. In practice, the reexamination of the nation's defenses, which became known as the Bottom-Up Review, would turn out more as a series of internal negotiations within the Pentagon than as a top-down presidentially directed mandate.[14]

For a number of understandable reasons, without political direction from the White House, the uniformed military was not

---

14 Discussions with many senior civilian and uniformed officials in DOD involved with the Bottom-Up Review revealed to the author the extent of this process of internal negotiations.

prepared to embark on a unilateral dismantlement of the Bush base force and cut the level of military power it believed was required to protect the nation's interests. The continued absence of any political guidance from the White House hardened this view. The unsettling nature of the world at large was taken as strong evidence for preserving U.S. military strength. Years of working with Congress had yielded the experience that making major concessions without any *quid pro quo* from Capitol Hill was not smart. The result would be a *de facto* military strategy and force posture accepted by the White House and Congress, largely by default, and without serious debate and examination of alternative policies in an appropriate interagency government forum.

Put in its public form, the Bottom-Up Review[15] focused on answering two questions. First, how should the armed forces be structured for the future? Second, how much defense is enough in the post-Cold War era?

The answers to those questions were used to define the strategy, force structure, modernization programs, industrial base, and infrastructure needed to meet new dangers and seize new opportunities. The new dangers were ordered in four broad categories:

- Dangers posed by nuclear weapons and other weapons of mass destruction to include proliferation

- Regional dangers leading to instability and conflict

- Dangers to democracy and reform principally in the FSU and Eastern Europe

- Economic dangers.

Furthermore, the review specified three guiding principles for sustaining the forces: U.S. forces must be ready to fight, they must maintain the quality of their people, and the U.S. must maintain technological superiority.

The planning for the future forces was based on the demands of meeting two illustrative contingency scenarios, one in the Gulf and the other in Korea, on a near-simultaneous basis. In addition to the forces required to win two major regional conflicts or contingencies (MRCs), other missions for peace enforcement and intervention and

---

[15] Refer to *The Bottom-Up Review: Forces for a New Era*, September 1, 1993, Office of the Secretary of Defense.

overseas presence were assessed to derive estimated numbers of forces needed for those roles as well. The conclusions led to requirements for an active-duty force of about 1.4 million and a force structure as shown in table 9. Defense budgets were as shown in table 10.

Table 9. U.S. force structure—1999

Army	• 10 divisions (active) • 5+ divisions (reserve)
Navy	• 11 aircraft carriers (active) • 1 aircraft carrier (reserve/training) • 45–55 attack submarines • 346 ships
Air Force	• 13 fighter wings (active) • 7 fighter wings (reserve) • Up to 184 bombers
Marine Corps	• 3 Marine Expeditionary Forces • 174,000 personnel (active endstrength) • 42,000 personnel (reserve endstrength)
Strategic Nuclear Forces (by 2003)	• 18 ballistic missile submarines • Up to 94 B-52H bombers • 20 B-2 bombers • 500 Minuteman III ICBMs (single warhead)

Table 10. Clinton plan: Defense discretionary funding (current-year dollars in billions)

	FY					
	1993	1994	1995	1996	1997	1998
January 1992 Bush baseline						
BA (Budget Authority)	288.4	289.3	292.8	295.2	300.6	—
Outlays	291.0	285.0	289.4	294.2	298.6	—
Proposed Clinton level						
BA	274.3	263.7	262.8	253.8	248.4	254.2
Diff. from Bush		−11.8	−15.2	−24.5	−36.2	−39.2
Cum. diff. from Bush		−11.8	−27.0	−51.5	−87.1	−126.9
Outlays	294.3	277.7	272.6	264.9	249.1	252.7
Diff. from Bush		−6.7	−11.7	−19.7	−37.4	−36.3
Cum. diff. from Bush		−6.7	−18.4	−38.1	−75.5	−111.8

The Bottom-Up Review also identified new initiatives to deal with the four dangers and promised to address the issues of readiness, acquisition reform, and infrastructure. Finally, although no formal statement on an industrial policy was released, the decision was made to preserve the nuclear submarine (SSN) and nuclear carrier (CVN) industrial base at least for a few years through award of a contract for a new SSN to the Electric Boat Shipyard and a contract for another CVN to Newport News.

In addition to the explicit rationale for the BUR found in both public and internal DOD documents, other broad geostrategic reasons supported the Pentagon's conclusions. Whether or not the world is a more dangerous place, the reality and presence of American military strength have been traditionally viewed as stabilizing and reassuring, particularly by U.S. friends and allies. As uncertainty abounds, collapsing or weakening this long-standing international pillar of strength and security can be argued as a most unwise step.

Furthermore, because of the complex and ponderous nature of the U.S. political process, finetuning a structure as large and diverse as DOD is difficult. Attempts at imposing major change, especially in downsizing DOD, can face formidable obstacles. Thus, a structural argument can be made for a consistent glide slope for reductions that is steep, but not too steep. These broader and implicit arguments can be debated and challenged. However, they also form perhaps the stronger and more useful way to make this military case to Congress, by appealing to judgment and emotion as well as to a quantitative and reasoned formula.

Despite the attempts to devise a framework for determining force structure and the intent of undertaking comprehensive solutions that would encompass issues across all defense sectors from acquisition reform to reducing social inequalities, the BUR had several serious flaws. These flaws stemmed largely from the absence of policy guidance from the White House and the inherent limitations of DOD trying to supply surrogate answers to questions the president should have been asking or answering himself.

Conceptually, although the four principal dangers may indeed define much of the new national interest, it is difficult to show why dangers to the economy, to reform in Russia, and even the threat of proliferation[16] should be the major missions for the DOD. Certainly the MRCs and fighting wars are the principal DOD function. Countering or preventing proliferation is a subset of those tasks. However, the BUR established new roles and objectives that exceeded both the authority and capacity of DOD to address in effective and comprehensive ways.

Second, the BUR was underfunded. Before his resignation in January 1994, and pressed by the military, who saw the underfunding in the many tens of billions of dollars, Secretary Aspin finally admitted publicly to a shortfall of $50 billion. Evidence that follows shows this shortfall will grow to hundreds of billions of dollars. In the summer of 1994, Deputy Secretary of Defense John Deutch released a memo cautioning the services that the future funding gaps could require delaying or canceling major programs across DOD. Although no action has been taken yet, many analysts regard this memo as the first acknowledgement of a much larger funding problem than has been previously admitted.[17] But, no matter the actual size of the shortfall, the BUR is simply not fiscally maintainable as is.[18]

Third, U.S. military capabilities were perhaps understated, threats overstated, and the role of allies and mobilization certainly underplayed. In other words, the requirements of the MRCs may

---

[16] For example, regarding proliferation of nuclear weapons, the case will be made that a more important objective for the U.S. is to prevent the use of nuclear weapons should nonproliferation efforts fail. And, antiproliferation ultimately must reside in planning for the MRC.

[17] Reported in the *Washington Post*, August 22, 1994, p. A1.

[18] For a critique of the BUR as well as evidence of underfunding, see Andrew F. Krepinevich "The Bottom-Up Review: An Assessment," Defense Budget Project, February 1994, 63 pp.; and Anthony Cordesman, "A Critique of the BUR," a presentation to the Center for Naval Analyses, May 1993. A report by the General Accounting Office released in August 1994 put the underfunding at $150 billion. The DOD has not publicly objected in strong terms to that estimate as of this writing but in private disagrees with the amount.

have exaggerated the necessary capabilities, and fewer forces, provided they were well-trained, perhaps could suffice.[19] In any event, the general scenario was predicated on U.S. unilateral action even though, politically, allies would have to be brought aboard.

As a result, unless action is taken to redress these flaws, the BUR force is headed to a condition of "in irons." As will be shown, the only questions are when this will happen and how badly capability will erode. Sadly, the question of whether this downward spiral will occur no longer applies. In addressing these flaws in the BUR, it also might be in the broader public interest to engage in a major debate over national security that so far has been deferred or dismissed as an unnecessary or fruitless exercise given what are seen as more vital national issues.

---

[19] See Krepinevich and C. Bowie et al. *The New Calculus* (Santa Monica, CA: The Rand Corporation, 1993).

Chapter Two: Strategic Uncertainty

The Constitution of the United States of America commands the government "to provide for the common defense." Congress, in Article I, Section 8, is assigned the power "to raise and support armies" and "to provide and maintain a navy."[20] The President, in Article II, Section 1 is vested "The Executive Power" and in Article II, Section 2, is assigned the title and responsibility of "commander in chief" of the armed forces.

The presumption, then as now, was the need to specify the separate and unique function of government to protect the nation and its security from military threats. The persisting tensions and irreversible but premeditated contradictions over Article I and II powers between the legislature and the executive and the abutment of political (and economic and social) challenges onto the national military domain have not softened over the past 200 years. Indeed, the structural inefficiencies mandated by the system of checks and balances are only likely to worsen in an era without a single powerful enemy and with far greater demands on an ever-constrained and contested national expense account.

The Founding Fathers were entirely purposeful in sacrificing the efficiency of government in order to maximize the liberty and freedom of the individual from excessive imposition and intervention of government. Because military security 200 years ago was viewed in terms of direct military aggression and attack against the nation and the individual states themselves, the inherent constitutional contradictions that ensured permanent tension among the branches of government could be relaxed in time of crisis. Subordinated by a clear and apparent danger, presumably in the form of invasion and direct attack, a unified government would be led by the commander in chief for the duration of the crisis. It also proved true that because of the fabulous resources possessed by this country, the ability to spend our way clear of past dangers was

---

20 The Constitution also specifies that, for armies, "no appropriation of money to that use shall be for a longer term than two years." No such stricture applies to the Navy.

both practical and possible. Strategic misjudgment or inaction could be remedied by the expenditure of additional and available resources.

The classic comingling, in later years, of a unifying and heinous threat and expending virtually unlimited resources was inadvertently and inexorably assured when the first of Yamamoto's torpedo bombers lifted off the Japanese aircraft carrier *Akagi* on December 7, 1941, en route to attacking Pearl Harbor. That "day of infamy" instantly transformed American apathy towards fascism and the war in Europe into anger, outrage, and determination, making the ultimate outcome of World War II inevitable.

Subsequently, the Soviet Union (and, before 1972, China) provided the unifying threat that enabled so-called bipartisan coalitions of Republicans and Democrats to forge a stable foreign and national security policy and, at least in this one area, mitigate the tensions between both ends of Pennsylvania Avenue. Although it is too early to tell how bipartisanship will work in the post-Cold War world, the similarities between the Bush and Clinton foreign policies suggest that the executive branch is likely to maintain a certain continuity across different administrations on many vital international issues. Whether Congress responds in a bipartisan way to this "threatless" or less threatening world will very much determine how well or how badly the nation will deal with the post-Cold War environment.[21]

It is exceedingly unlikely, however, that the coalescing of threat and massing of resources will or could recur either as dramatically as in December 1941 or, for that matter, during much of the Cold War. This lack of a coalescing or unifying threat poses a fundamental problem for the United States. On one hand, Americans have learned from hard experience that isolation and withdrawal from foreign affairs are both temporary and shortsighted international postures. Although the euphemism of "keeping one's powder dry" is not inapplicable, Americans appreciate the need to have a strong, ready military force of the right size.

---

[21] The term post-Cold War world (and new world order) is in need of replacement, because the honeymoon of the collapse of communism and the USSR is over. My response is to use the phrase "era of strategic uncertainty."

On the other hand, there is little agreement on what the "right size" is for military forces, especially after making careful consideration of the real dangers and financial costs of defense. Further, while agreeing in principle to the need for a strong defense, when choosing between that objective and the loss of a job because of base closings or cuts in procurement programs that shut down factories, most Americans understandably will opt to protect themselves and not the larger public good.

In sum, most Americans don't object to having a strong military or to paying for it when necessary. But, without a palpable and plausible threat, maintaining a sizable and consistent level of defense spending will remain among the most elusive of national objectives. Furthermore, in this competition for increasingly scarce federal dollars, domestic programs will command far more public support than defense.

The strategic quandary of how to shift from a threat-specific basis for defining national security to other criteria is not easily or quickly resolvable. If daunting military threats to U.S. security are unlikely to arise for some time to come, what are the conditions and uncertainties that may lie ahead that require the actual or putative use of U.S. force to protect or advance the interests of America and the world at large? In answering these questions, we must define the characteristics of a world regime no longer dominated by an intense, bipolar, geostrategic struggle.

A commonly held view in the United States is that although the Soviet Union and Warsaw Pact are forever gone, the world still remains a dangerous place. But, basing a strategy on obtaining public or political consensus as to what does or does not constitute a "dangerous place" in times of strategic uncertainty and ambiguity is exceedingly risky for reasons that are both logical and pragmatic. This dilemma is exacerbated by the observation made by former National Security Advisor Dr. Zbigniew Brzezinski that although "there may be dangers ahead, there are no obvious disasters."

Regarding the former Soviet Union—in the first place, while it is impossible to predict how it and its republics will evolve, a rejuvenated antiwestern or anti-imperialist state emerging in Russia or in other former republics is not going to occur quickly. There are too many pressing domestic issues, most of which revolve around the economy. The report of the decision by Russia to mothball three of its five aircraft carriers on the grounds of austerity reinforces this point.[22] The absolute danger posed by the USSR has vanished; the residual nuclear weapons possessed by four former republics are vexing but not yet threatening; and the former conventional might of Soviet forces has decayed enormously. Indeed, military spending is among the lowest of Russian political priorities except to the degree that the defense budget is providing income and sustenance for a substantial part of the population still in uniform.

The conclusion is clear. The United States and its western partners must remain vigilant regarding the former Soviet Union; massive or total disarmament would be ludicrous. Whatever dangers or uncertainties may lurk within the ten time zones of the FSU, they are of political, economic, and social dimensions. The response of Boris Yeltsin in crushing the revolt of the Russian Parliament in October 1993 and keeping his country on a democratic course reinforces optimism over the long term. The rise of Vladimir Zhirinovsky—and, worse, perhaps one day a more competent version of this extremist—remains a concern.

If those problems in the FSU are left to fester, the consequences could have a serious military dimension. Unless the West is dimwitted, the risks from the former Soviet Union do not automatically contribute to making the world a more dangerous place as far as the United States is concerned, Soviet arms sales to world markets withstanding. Sale or theft of Soviet nuclear weapons is a separate issue considered later.

Second, given the absolute passage of the Soviet threat and no matter the likelihood of a possible Russian military rejuvenation, it is exceedingly difficult to envisage a serious geostrategic threat emerging by the end of and even well into the new century remotely as capable or potentially dangerous as the USSR was. A rearmed Germany or Japan, while theoretically possible, seems entirely unlikely and certainly not in the foreseeable future. For those who correctly note that it took Hitler a half decade to remilitarize Nazi

---

[22] The *Washington Post,* February 15th, 1994, p. A20. It turns out these ships were in such bad shape they were scrapped instead.

Germany, the analogy to the present is misplaced. The political, economic, and military conditions of the 1990s are profoundly and irreversibly different from those of the 1930s, not the least of which is an internationally engaged United States replete with an arsenal of thousands of nuclear weapons and the most capable military forces in the world.

Third, new threats such as an aggressive China, India, Brazil, or other emerging power are equally difficult to imagine as plausible grounds for establishing a coherent, overarching U.S. security strategy. Both the Bush and Clinton administrations have recognized these realities and, as a result, have argued for military forces designed to deal with contingencies more likely than not to occur where conflict or tension is already present in the region. Korea and the Persian Gulf are the two obvious cases in this regard, although it is extremely difficult to argue that North Korea or Iraq could pose a threat to Western and allied interests remotely close to that of the former Soviet Union.

In the case of Korea, the south has double the population of the north, an immeasurably larger GDP, and a highly trained army of 650,000 in well-defended positions supported by U.S. forces and U.S. advanced systems. It is hard to see how the United States could let the strategic balance swing in favor of the north unless it chose to do so. Despite occasional reports that Saddam Hussein is rebuilding Iraq's army, does it seem possible that another Desert Storm operation could produce a substantially different outcome?

Just because no society-menacing threats are likely to arise in the world of the new century, that condition does not mean U.S. military power is nonessential or unimportant. Nor does it mean the United States can or should take a more relaxed view of its security, because, although the absolute danger is less, the complexity and uncertainty in this new era are greater, and U.S. leadership seems no less a contributor to global stability than in the past. This condition of strategic uncertainty does demand, however, that an especially careful and rigorous assessment be made of the level of military capability deemed necessary and, in particular, that the judgments and assumptions underlying these conclusions are clearly and coherently put. Because there is no unambiguous or obvious threat, the only basis for these findings must rest on judgment and experience. If the world is indeed a "more dangerous place," the questions are where is the world more dangerous, for whom is it more dangerous, what does this mean for the U.S., and what can be done about reducing or isolating the real dangers and threats to the U.S. and its interests?

Some in the United States argue that although military conflict and local privation or instability make the world more deadly for Bosnians, Somalis, Kurds, and Sudanese, among others, the direct foreign dangers to Americans at home are minuscule. The real dangers to Americans, in this view, reside within these shores: crime, violence, drugs, and matters that pertain to law enforcement. Resolving such problems is not a traditional task for national defense. In June 1993, when federal and state law-enforcement agencies arrested a group of terrorists suspected of plotting to destroy vulnerable sites in New York and assassinate federal and state elected officials, sixteen people were gunned down or murdered in Washington, DC, over the same two-day period. A dangerous place must be defined in relative terms.

To the degree that national security is viewed increasingly in terms of economic security and well-being, a measure of international stability among trading partners is an obvious necessity. That stability has several components: economic in the sense that financial, trade, currency, and associated markets function well; political in the sense that civil unrest or civil war does not spill across borders or cut off access to key resources and markets; strategic in the sense that threats or crises do not disrupt this order; and conceptual in that the notion of collective or cooperative security has continuing if not increasing relevance.

There are obvious potential threats and challenges to this system of western stability that come from within and outside the network of advanced states. Regional problems like Bosnia challenge stability on three grounds. The first is that ethnic hostility and civil war could spread, perhaps uncontrollably, to parts of the FSU or become the catalyst for expanding regional violence such as through direct intervention into Bosnia by Greece, Turkey, or another external state. The second is exposing the inability of the West's major security instrument—NATO—to cope with the first post-Cold War security problem that, parenthetically, is occurring in Europe. The third is to lay bare the extent of policy tools available to restoring order, giving rise to the fear that preventing or containing regional conflict as in the former Yugoslavia is beyond the ability of any outside state that may see it in its interests to take some form of action.

Regional bullies or bad actors beyond a militant Iran, Iraq, or Libya could prove disruptive to this order. But these situations, exemplified by Haiti and U.S. attempts to remove its military dictatorship, are likely to pose problems that are inherently domestic in nature and not strategic. Haiti offers no conceivable threat to international order. Yet two American administrations tried unsuccessfully to resolve the Haitian situation, although, as this book goes to press, U.S. intervention seems inevitable.

Two of the most discussed and publicly worried about threats to U.S. security have been the proliferation of weapons of mass destruction and terrorism (and, indeed, the possible connection between the two). The revelation that South Africa secretly possessed the "bomb" reinforced legitimate worries about an Iran, Iraq, or North Korea obtaining even one nuclear weapon. But there is also the tendency to exaggerate the extent of this threat. In this case, "nuclear paranoia" is not new. Four decades ago, the prospect of a Soviet Union or China armed with nuclear weapons provoked debate over preemptive elimination of that threat and, later, led to a policy of "massive retaliation" that would have destroyed Soviet society in the event of a world war. But, because nuclear war was avoided then, when fear was both justified and exaggerated, does not mean the same calculus will always apply in the future.

On the one hand, simply because the East-West conflict never led to world war—partly because vital interests never were at issue and partly because the balance of terror wrought by nuclear weapons made war an avoidable option—does not guarantee that powers armed with a relatively few bombs would immutably conform to this standard. On the other hand, even if an Iraq or a North Korea were to acquire nuclear weapons, the overwhelming superiority of U.S. military power should not be assumed away. And, were Iraq or North Korea bent on doing real harm to the United States, courses of action that do not involve nuclear weapons are available, including the use of biological agents to contaminate or kill large segments of the U.S. population. Perhaps miraculously, biological agents have not been widely used by any state or subnational group—thus far.

The point is that potential vulnerability to weapons of mass destruction can never be entirely eliminated. Since major powers are not likely to attack each other with nuclear weapons, the actual use of mass destruction weapons seems remote, particularly if intelligence and law-enforcement agencies remain fixed on this potential problem. Should these mass destruction agents be used or threatened, the role of military power would be to deter, preempt, or retaliate. But, on the basis of countering proliferation alone, when the would-be proliferators are not first-rate powers, justifying a very large and expensive standing military force would be extremely difficult.

Terrorism presents a parallel danger. Ironically, the best leverage that terrorists possess within the United States is through the protection of the Bill of Rights of the U.S. Constitution. Acts of terrorism against Americans—the destruction of Pan American Flight 103 and the bombing of the World Trade Center in New York withstanding—while tragedies to those affected, have been relatively unusual. Yet the publicity has been vast and the media coverage extensive—perhaps well in excess of the actual acts because of the rarity of such occurrences. And, terrorists benefit not only from the First Amendment; the rights of due process also apply, even in absentia. The remedy, when specific evidence is available and the perpetrators are safe from U.S. prosecution, is force. The military instrument is usually applied bluntly and forcibly. Very rarely, as in the capture of the *Achille Lauro* hijackers, it is applied in a highly discrete and precise way.

A final aspect of this threat assessment can be addressed in terms of a double paradox. One part of this paradox applies to the international environment where U.S. force might be used. The other part of the paradox applies to the nation itself that must support or tolerate future uses of U.S. force. The irony is that this double paradox arises from the relative and absolute increase in U.S. military strength occasioned by the end of the USSR.

Internationally, and despite fears of spreading ballistic missile technology and associated agents of mass destruction, the level of potential military threat facing the United States has declined dramatically. Thus, instead of large, Soviet-style military forces massed against NATO across the plains of central Europe, likely adversaries will be equipped with fewer and less sophisticated weapons. Tactics such as urban or "hit and run" warfare will fit these situations and not necessarily be suited for the strengths of American military might. Applying the most formidable U.S. military capabilities—namely, intense, highly accurate, mobile, massed firepower from the battlefield dimensions of sea, air, and land—will be far harder against an adversary lacking these means to conduct war.

At the same time, these more modestly equipped adversaries will have access to extraordinarily advanced intelligence-gathering systems ranging from CNN and other real-time media networks to the most sophisticated space photographic products now on the open market. Sold by Russian and French outlets, these products make use of national surveillance satellites. This access to advanced systems can generate political advantages by providing both information for and coverage of the actual targeting of U.S. forces. The first paradox is this inversion of military capabilities and possible operational consequences in which "superior" force may not work or may not be relevant.

The second paradox arises partly from U.S. military competence and partly from the U.S. declaratory policy that force would not be used except "overwhelmingly or decisively"; that there would be explicit and obtainable military objectives; that these objectives would be supported by the public; and finally that military force would work rapidly, with minimal casualties to ourselves and with minimal "collateral damage." Hence, while U.S. military force has increased in both relative and absolute terms, the very conditions that are likely to determine whether force will be used in anger impose substantial constraints. These constraints may not be in keeping with the realities of the post-Cold War world, namely that "decisiveness" may be not relevant or obtainable, and sustaining even a handful of injuries or deaths to ourselves or to inhabitants of the region where force is used may preclude taking otherwise appropriate action. Learning to deal with this double paradox may not be an easy matter.

The sum and substance of this review of threats lead to the conclusion that while there are legitimate grounds for maintaining strong and ready forces to assure military and physical security, the extent of real and potential dangers to the nation can be exaggerated, especially in light of the collapse of the huge military challenge of the USSR. Without a concrete threat, the strategic uncertainties of the new century are likely to prove divisive, resulting in varying opinions on what may or not be needed regarding U.S. military might. Furthermore, the huge political pressures generated by the gap between national resources and obligations and liabilities manifested in a permanently (or long-term) unbalanced federal budget will intensify the tension inherent in the checks and balances of Articles I and II of the Constitution. The result must exacerbate the differences in the policies and preferences of the commander in chief and the protectors of the public purse no matter which party dominates the collective houses of government.

The president also has constitutional responsibility for conducting the nation's foreign policy. The Senate has the specific responsibility for approving treaties and ambassadors, and the whole Congress the responsibility for all government spending and for declaring war. Congress also regulates commerce. Under all circumstances, Congress represents its constituents and the electorate with its overwhelmingly domestically oriented agenda.

Collision between national and local interests and between constitutional responsibilities is inherent to the process of government. But without some basis for ensuring consensus on means and ends, protracted warfare over domestic and national security in the budget process is too likely to produce even greater government "gridlock" and greater inefficiency in using our resources. Decisions—on how to cut defense-related infrastructure, for example—will be delayed or diluted and, without a clarifying or unifying theme, as will be shown, the current military build-down risks suffering from the similar ills of past reductions.

An indication of the power and longevity of gridlock is that partisan politics over administration policy towards Somalia and Haiti have been displaced by more traditional conflict over constitutional prerogatives between Congress and the president. Congress, led by a majority of the president's own party, saw their prerogatives being ignored. First it was the obscenity of a dead U.S. serviceman paraded through Mogadishu and then a U.S. warship driven out of Port-au-Prince by Haitian thugs that engaged Congress. The debate on Haitian intervention was an obvious clash over constitutional authority.

This pessimism over governmental impotence and its particular effect on security and defense, however, is neither inevitable nor immutable. There are powerful grounds for making the case for strong and ready forces and overcoming many of these governmental standoffs. The defense debate will continue over the size, shape, and composition of the forces, and the focus will be the level of spending and spending priorities within that context. Put another way, the question of the 1960s made famous by former Defense Secretary Robert S. McNamara of "how much is enough" will be recast. Few Americans would vote for a weak military, and bromides like "second to none" will be smoke screens for making do with less. But, there may be a minimum level of military force below which the nation will not be prepared to go, although defining this level will prove elusive.

There are specific and highly legitimate roles and uses for military force. Understanding these roles and uses can sustain a consensus of public and governmental support, certainly as far as what those uses are, even if agreement cannot be reached on how many forces we need or how much of the nation's resources should be put into defense. The first and most important use for U.S. military force is as guarantor and principal agent for maintaining order: to underwrite U.S. commitments to its allies; to maintain international stability; and to provide a responsive and appropriate capability for contingencies and crises that may occur.

A corollary assertion is that, as the sole remaining superpower, the United States is obligated to maintain military forces reflecting that status. However, although this assertion may have psychological and rhetorical value, the actual strategic or political benefit of superpower status is no longer quite so obvious or inherent. To our friends, whom we are unlikely to attack and who are unlikely to threaten us militarily, "superpower" signifies little because there is no longer any leverage with which to apply this status now that the Soviet menace is gone. To our most likely foes, who are relatively weak, superpower status has little direct relevance outside a military confrontation and provides the inducement of offering a small state the opportunity to be seen standing against the U.S. bully. This caveat of single superpower status aside, the United States will still be able to exercise global leadership and influence, if not set broad direction for the international community, and indeed continue in this responsibility. Military forces are among the most visible and perhaps most symbolic policy instrument to manifest this commitment and intent.

It would prove quite shortsighted and probably dangerous for the United States to withdraw substantially or entirely, for example, from Europe, Korea, or Japan. Presence is essential for the political message it sends and for underwriting the leadership role the United States must accept if it is to promote international stability and safeguard its own well-being. Yet, showing definitive proof or evidence of the value of presence is extremely difficult even though judgment, instinct, and experience can be used to validate its utility. The proper questions for this examination must be what is an appropriate or acceptable level of commitment, how much force and presence are necessary to affirm this degree of commitment, and what combat capability needs to be deployed or stationed in these regions.

The second use for U.S. military force is to be ready and able to deal with conflicts likely to be regional in nature. Criteria need to be set and agreed to over the types and intensity of those conflicts in terms of levels of U.S. commitment that may be required and the degree to which we could or would respond to these conflicts simultaneously or consecutively.

The third use for U.S. military force is to serve with international coalitions, perhaps in conjunction with the United Nations. Peacekeeping, peacemaking, and peace-imposing roles would constitute the most likely tasks. However, as the U.S. would present a prime political target, as will be argued, we might best provide strategic "sinews" and support to other states who assume the roles of peacekeepers on the ground. In other words, rather than becoming the world's "911 force" in emergency, the U.S. would be a permanent "411 force," assuring the availability of support and success in the form of strategic sinews.

These sinews include transportation, lift, and logistics; the vast C^3I network; and military muscle should it be needed. Indeed, given the visibility of U.S. presence in peacekeeping and the cultural, emotional, and domestic constraints imposed by American society, namely a reluctance to tolerate any losses, the U.S. would be well-advised to examine exactly what roles and at what levels it should play. And contingencies or conflicts noted above could be dealt with through some form of international coalition.

It should be clear that this hierarchy of roles and uses is a significant departure from the Cold War taxonomy that stressed the need for deterring conflict or containing it. The argument will be presented that the deterrent-based calculus of the Cold War, originally rooted in strategic and theater nuclear weapons and the ability to threaten massive and instant destruction, is not broadly relevant to this world of strategic uncertainty. It is likely that, despite the existence of substantial numbers of weapons of mass destruction in general and thousands of nuclear weapons in particular, the conduct of international politics and the role of force in that context have returned to the centuries old and traditional non-nuclear basis for protecting and advancing national interests. If the nuclear threat of massive societal destruction no longer conditions international politics, the strategic vocabulary and grammar that served the past four decades will have to be revised.

* * *

In sum, the world of the new century may in fact not be as dangerous a place as some suggest regarding absolute or relative risks to the United States. Although serious harm and damage could be done to the nation by terrorists or hostile states relying on surprise to employ mass destruction agents or to target important U.S. facilities with conventional explosives, these instances are likely to be rare. And, barring the highly improbable rejuvenation of a militarized and aggressive Russia, a world war among advanced states is beyond comprehension, perhaps for decades. This analysis suggests that while U.S. force must be sustained at appropriate levels and kept at appropriate standards of readiness to be effective, there is no objective reason why that level could not be well below the current BUR force. In any event, whatever level is determined appropriate, without adequate funding that force will not be able to carry out its assigned duties.

That aside, it would be folly to believe that the U.S. will not have to use force to protect itself, perhaps frequently and in substantial amounts. It is interesting that since the Berlin Wall came down and the Cold War ended, the United States has employed force rather substantially: in Panama, in Desert Storm, in Somalia, in Macedonia, and in the former Yugoslavia, and in a variety of humanitarian and retaliatory roles in the Persian Gulf. Since German reunification in 1989, for example, the U.S. Army has awarded over 600 Purple Hearts to its personnel killed or wounded in action. We should not assume that the international order will become simpler or more peaceful. That notion must underlie the national consensus on the need for force and on the way force may have to be used.

CHAPTER THREE: DOMESTIC PREOCCUPATION

In the shadow of the new century, if polls are to be believed, the mood of the nation is one of uncertainty and concern about the future. There is deep and continuing, if not building, disillusionment with the Federal Government. Despite the actual state of the economy, national confidence is low regarding the likelihood that a major and sustained economic recovery will maintain or increase the standard of living and quality-of-life indices enough to meet public expectations. Indeed, there is increased recognition that the national standard of living is unlikely to rise and may well shrink. When issues such as health care, education, and public safety are considered, frustration and pessimism about the future are widespread.

Moods obviously change and can change rapidly. However, at a time when the international structure has been in profound flux, the reaction of many Americans will be to insist that sorting out domestic priorities must assume precedence over many or most international issues. Thus, a fundamental task of U.S. political leadership, if the U.S. is to remain effectively engaged abroad, must be to educate and convince itself and the public of the need to maintain an effective and balanced posture towards international security. That task will become more difficult.

Over the past four decades, the United States voluntarily and premeditatively entangled itself within the constraints of socio-economic expectations and promises that had been awarded legal, regulatory, and budget status. This led to national obligations and liabilities with line items in the federal budget. These "non-discretionary" or mandatory payments are vast and continue to grow within a strained budget. This demand for resources must have negative consequences for future defense spending unless the national debt and annual deficit are allowed to grow even more. Similarly, overall spending on defense—including the employment created, the technology and industry stimulated, and other positive contributions—must be balanced against the opportunity costs of using a portion of defense resources elsewhere and the negative economic effects arising from keeping a relatively large standing military force and supporting infrastructure in place at a time of national fiscal austerity.

There is, of course, no magical formula to calculate a precise or optimum level for defense spending. Indeed, using the entire annual defense appropriation to balance the federal budget will not necessarily close the deficit in any given year and will not pay off the debt. Only a rigorous imposition of ceilings and cuts on all discretionary and non-discretionary programs (and perhaps a further tax increase) can balance the budget. But, without an overwhelming external threat to justify defense spending, assessing how the economy would be helped or hindered by various levels of defense spending is an exercise in politics and judgment and unlikely to be determined by precise quantitative analysis.

One of the largest and most difficult problems facing the nation involves making more efficient and effective use of its vast resources in both the public and private sectors. The issue is not so much one of outright stupidity or ineptness as it is the nonproductive ways in which too many of the nation's dollars are wasted or spent without compensating return. A huge "overhead structure" that grows much faster than the rate of inflation has been embedded across American society. This structure is expensive, and the "value added" is questionable and even negative.

In part, some of this "overhead" goes to pay the huge debt-service bill for both private and public sector borrowers. The total interest payments for both government and private debt continue to grow and siphon off a goodly share of the GDP. Part goes to the escalating expenses for huge local, state, and federal bureaucracies; for large and growing bureaucracies in the private sector required by government regulation, decree, or other factor; for administering health care; for litigation disproportionately higher than in any other advanced state; and for other administrative functions that, in many ways, provide little added value to the nation and its productivity while costing dearly.

In 1993 and 1994, about 2/5 of the GDP was spent on a combination of health care (1/7); debt servicing for all private and public liabilities (1/6 or more); and the costs of conforming with super-regulation (1/10).

These percentages have more than doubled in 30 years. What they suggest is declining value added for the nation and less discretionary income for investment and savings.

The other side of the inefficiency coin has to do with the inability of government to live within its financial means. This inability goes beyond "gridlock" in which the Federal Government appears trapped by the checks and balances and by the ultimately partisan nature of the political system. Government inherently aspires to solve or alleviate the fundamental problems and dangers confronting the electorate. Despite the best motives and intentions, governmental solutions too often exacerbate rather than resolve problems at hand.

Two examples demonstrate how government can turn good intentions into huge and unexpected costs that ultimately must be borne by the taxpayer. In late 1979, recognizing that the nation's savings and loan industry was being steadily bankrupted by high interest rates and inflation, Congress took bipartisan action to remove the strict regulation on areas where these banks could conduct business. These so-called "thrifts" had been originally chartered to provide low-cost mortgages and therefore allow more Americans to purchase their own homes. Set up during the Great Depression, the thrifts were granted certain tax advantages that reduced operating expenses and translated into lower mortgage rates for borrowers. These banks were prevented by law from expanding into other business and banking areas to guarantee that their competitive advantage lay only in supplying lower-cost home loans. However, in the late 1970s, double-digit inflation pushed interest rates to unprecedented levels of 20 percent and more. The S&Ls simply could not survive by loaning at low rates while inflation and the interest rates at which they had to pay investors climbed steeply.

At about the same time, the Federal Deposit Insurance Corporation (FDIC) was legally authorized by Congress to raise its coverage to $100,000 per individual account—meaning the government insured each account for any loss up to that figure. Or, as it would turn out, this expanded coverage would become an unintended insurance policy for the S&Ls to invest deposits at *no apparent risk* to themselves or to their depositors. The government had guaranteed any and all losses.

In 1981 and 1982, Congress passed a major overhaul of the tax system that included large tax cuts and tax incentives for business. Huge amounts of money became available for investment by the private sector and helped to fuel the so-called "junk bond" or leveraged buy-out (LBO) and real estate markets. S&Ls, now that deregulation of these banks became law, sought to maximize returns and, in many instances, jumped into these new markets. More often than not, S&L management had neither the knowledge nor the experience in these areas of new business permitted by the law.

In time, real estate tax credits were withdrawn, tax rates were increased, credit and the money supply shrank, and the economy faltered. By the mid 1980s, many of the S&Ls found themselves overextended as these once seemingly attractive and no-risk investments began to fail. And fail they did, in vast numbers. At the end of the day, the savings and loan industry cost the U.S. taxpayer about half a trillion dollars in the form of FDIC insurance to bank depositors whose funds had been lost or squandered away by the thrift managers.

Thus, despite the best intent, the collective action of the U.S. government to address a significant problem posed by the S&Ls turned out to be a fiscal catastrophe, and another half trillion or so dollars was piled on top of the national debt. It is arguable how much of that expense served any productive use or benefited the nation as a whole. Still, the nation will pay for this excess.

The second example of government's capacity to do unintended harm to the nation was in the Great Budget Compromise of 1990. A Republican president and a Democratic Congress were at an impasse over how to deal with an exploding fiscal deficit. In 1985, Congress passed the once-famous Gramm-Rudman-Hollings Deficit Reduction Act that mandated ceilings on federal spending and promised a balanced budget by 1990. But, none of the original Gramm-Rudman deficit targets was ever met. Instead, Congress, in collaboration with the White House, chose to move the budget ceilings ever upwards, so as not to trigger large, automatic cuts in federal programs and, no doubt, massive public reaction against this form of enforcing federal fiscal discipline. The annual deficit and total debt rose and rose.

In the summer of 1990, with a Congressional election pending that fall, the presidential race two years off, and the Gramm-Rudman law poised to shut down government through sequesters, time had run out and political agreement had to be reached on dealing with the budget deficit that seemed uncontrollable. The result was a combination of limiting growth in federal spending and a significant increase in revenues through new taxes. On the grounds that this compromise would produce a balanced budget by 1996, President Bush broke his pledge on "no new taxes." To the degree that Mr. Bush's abrogation of his most sacred campaign promise cost him the election, there can be debate. There can be no debate, however, on what happened to federal deficits, as table 11 shows.

Table 11. Gramm-Rudman-Hollings Deficit Reduction Act—projected and actual annual deficits (billions of dollars)

FY	Original 1985 targets	1987 amendment	1990 amendment	Actual
1986	171.9	—	—	221.0
1987	144.0	—	—	149.8
1988	108.0	144.0	—	155.2
1989	72.0	136.0	—	152.5
1990	36.0	100.0	—	221.4
1991	0	64.0	327.0	269.5
1992	—	28.0	317.0	290.4
1993	—	0	216.0	254.7
1994	—	—	108.0	234.7 (est.)
1995	—	—	83.0	165.1 (est.)

The point of these examples is that government has the capacity to impose unintended damage on the nation, even when the intent is pure. No senior government official would responsibly argue for downsizing defense in a chaotic or injurious manner. However, there is no sign that government is better or even as well-equipped as in the past to reduce defense and military power effectively, strategically, and practically.[23]

---

[23] To its credit and to try to take the politics out of base closings, in 1988 Congress established the Base Realignment and Closure (BRAC) Commission. BRAC is bipartisan and covenes biannually (1991, 1993, and 1995). See footnote 55 ahead. In this process, the president submits to Congress a list of military facilities to be closed or reduced recommended to him by this Commission. The intent of the process was to provide a mechanism for taking politically difficult actions. Hence, the entire list can be accepted or rejected only as a whole. Assessment of the BRAC follows.

The change in the socio-economic structure of the nation is another factor that will affect how well or how badly defense downsizing occurs and is a corollary of the growing expense of both the overhead glut and the administration of the nation's needs. The comparisons in tables 12 through 14 and figures 5 and 6 illustrate the evolution of how national resources (GNP and GDP) have been allocated over time and how debt and its service costs have grown. It is these costs and expenses that ultimately will force defense spending down or require increases in the national debt.

Table 12. Allocation of GNP/GDP over time

	1850	1970	1990
GNP/GDP (1990 dollars)	$2.8 billion	$1,300 billion	$3,500 billion
Agriculture	20.5%	2.7%	2.4%
Sales, retail commerce	27.4%	16.4%	16.4%
Construction	5.3%	5.1%	4.9%
Manufacturing/industry	15.7%	26.7%	18.9%
Transportation, communications, public utilities	11.9%	8.6%	8.9%
Services	19.2%	11.3%	19.3%
Finance, insurance		11.2%	17.5%
Government		15.0%	11.7%

Table 13. Personal consumption—1970 and 1990

	1970	1990
Durable goods	13.4%	13.8%
Non-durable goods	42.2%	32.8%
Services	44.4%	53.4%

Table 14. Growth of U.S. debt—public and private and debt service[a]

	Fiscal year dollars		
	1970	1980	1989
GNP	990.2	2,670.6	5,151.3
Total debt (public and private)	1,596.9	4,657.8	12,389.1
Federal debt	380.9	908.5	2,866.2
Total interest paid as percent of GNP[b]	10–12%	20–22%	24–28%

a   All dollar amounts in billions. Taken from Federal Government debt (Budget of the United States Government, 1991).

b   Interest calculated using average of prevalent long- and short-term interest rates in the same proportion as the average life of the total debt.

Figure 5. Interest burden of nonfinancial corporate business (percent of cash flow)

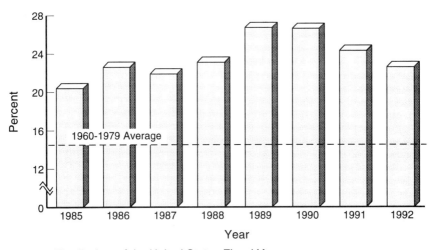

Source: *The Budget of the United States Fiscal Year*

Figure 6. Household debt payments (percent of disposable personal income)

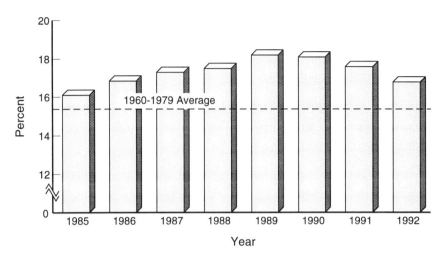

Year

Source: *The Budget of the United States Fiscal Year 1995*

This broader allocation of GDP is matched by the changes to the spending patterns and allocations of the federal budget. In the comparison of percentage of allocations by category over the past forty years, several trends hold obvious implications for future defense spending. First, non-discretionary or mandatory spending—that is, accounts the government is legally obligated to pay, such as entitlements and interest—have grown to about 70 percent of the $1.5-trillion annual federal budget. Of the remaining third of the budget that is discretionary, about 60 percent goes to defense and the remaining 40 percent goes to discretionary entitlement programs that are virtually all domestic in nature. Before the 1993 Budget Reconciliation Act froze discretionary nondefense spending programs, the rate of annual growth that reflects built-in cost escalators of discretionary social programs was running 30 times greater than the average annual increases in defense since the Carter-Reagan build-up began in 1979.

Second, the "walls" between and among domestic, defense, and international programs built in 1990 have come down. Although defense is being cut by about 5 percent per year in real terms, the inherent growth in other entitlement programs and the collapse of those budget walls mean that unless no attention is paid to restraining deficits, the only place from inside the budget where discretionary funds are available to meet other needs is the National Defense Account.

Third, the impact of the latest tax increases on the economy, on revenues for the government, and on the deficit has yet to be felt. Should these consequences exacerbate future budget deficits by declining revenues, defense is certain to absorb some of these fiscal shortfalls through large cuts.

Figures 7 through 9 portray the fiscal constraints to be faced. The implications of this survey of the state of the nation reinforce the concern that the process of downsizing defense is likely to evolve through inaction or deferral until such time that the unintended damage done to U.S. military might demands remedial action. Of course, it is not entirely impossible that a new, frightening threat could develop to coalesce public support for at least maintaining defense spending at or near current levels. But if the international analysis presented earlier is correct, this probability is so low as to be of no consequence.

Figure 7. Federal budget deficit (percent of GDP)

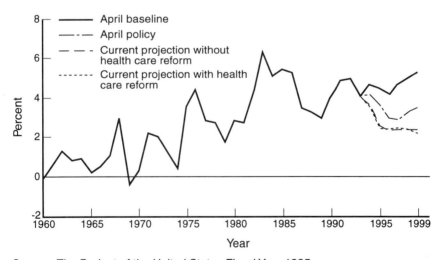

Source: *The Budget of the United States Fiscal Year 1995*

Figure 8. Federal debt (percent of GDP)

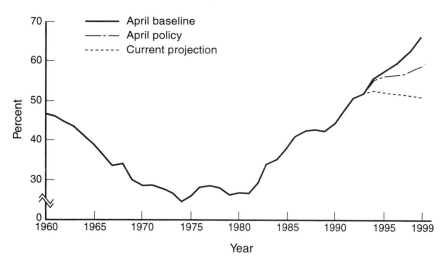

Source: *The Budget of the United States Fiscal Year 1995.* Note that although federal debt is expected to level out through 1998, its percent of GDP may not.

Figure 9. Net interest on the federal debt (percent of GDP)

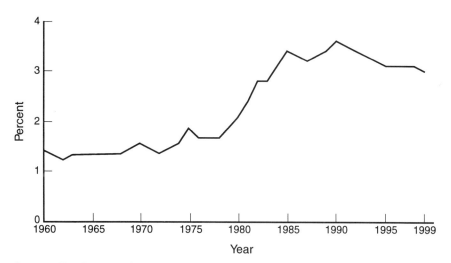

Source: *The Budget of the United States Fiscal Year 1995*

Certainly strong presidential leadership could force focus on the challenges to defense and avert any spiral of major decline. Emphasizing his responsibility and authority as commander in chief, the president could persuade the nation and the Congress to keep defense on a reasonable and adequately funded course. However, an enormous expenditure of political capital would be required to succeed in this effort. Because the issue of defense is overshadowed by far more pressing political, economic, and social priorities at home that consume the attention of the White House, there is little incentive or political pressure for any president to embark on this course, barring an extraordinary event. Indeed, the White House is likely to focus on those aspects of defense that have greatest domestic political significance, particularly jobs and "big ticket," highly visible weapons programs that directly affect the industrial base, and the pertinent social agenda, in this case expanding the role of women in uniform and ending discrimination against homosexuals in the service.

To the degree that defense might be insulated from the political and budget process much as the Base Closure and Realignment Commission sought to do, a powerful argument could arise citing this attempt as a means to bypass constitutional prerogatives. Even the warning about the dangers of a "hollow force," while inducing sympathetic rhetoric, is not strong enough to impel action. Hence, if the constitutional tensions of checks and balances cannot be reduced and if maintaining strong military forces is a national priority, the only means of avoiding these impasses is through creation of an incentive that is powerful enough to gain political acceptability without straining the Constitution. One such incentive follows in subsequent pages.

CHAPTER FOUR: GOVERNANCE AND THE FUTURE
COMMON DEFENSE

A traditional question that has shaped much of the post-war debate over national defense is, "How much is enough?" Implicit in that question was the requirement to defend against the USSR and a specific, highly capable strategic military threat. In this world of strategic uncertainty, the emerging question that should be central to a needed-defense debate is, "Defending against what?" Absent obvious, overt, highly credible specific threats and a substantive foundation for defining national security, this question will prove difficult to answer short of relying on theological determinations and explanations.

The differences between the Bush and Clinton administrations in articulating answers to "defending against what" are not great. This comparison should not be surprising because, political preferences aside, presidents tend to see foreign and defense policy through the same lens. The buffer effect of this continuity is appropriate if radical change is unwise and harmful if decisive alternatives are desperately needed.[24] Absent a specific threat, only so many generalities can apply to satisfying the rationale for defense.

As a result of the absence of a specific and dangerous threat, a principal and obvious objective for the nation's strategy and accompanying military power today is "reconstitution," that is, the ability to regenerate sufficient military capability in sufficient time to deal with a reconstituted Russian or other "Soviet style" threat. Depending upon subjective assessment of how and how quickly this reconstituted threat would emerge, the conclusions (or hunches) can be transferred to structuring U.S. forces. The dilemma is obvious: There is no objective basis for projecting whether any threat will ever be manifested by Russia or another contender. Hence,

---

24 Perhaps ironically, the best example of this continuity of presidential "lenses" is U.S. policy towards Somalia. The seemingly "liberal," once anti-Vietnam members of the Clinton administration have been taken to task for using many of the same arguments offered by the Johnson and Nixon administrations to justify enlarging the war in Vietnam as the grounds for shaping U.S. actions in Somalia.

the future range of possible U.S. military options for a reconstituted threat that has no certainty of arising is as broad as those individuals with views on what may or may not happen. This is not a particularly powerful foundation on which to base both resource requirements and full justification for funding defense.

The most useful cases for structuring U.S. forces deal with regional conflicts, crises, and contingencies. Intuitively, this is sensible; however, as both Bush and Clinton planners have discovered, developing scenarios for regional contingencies that are both plausible and politically acceptable is not easy. The Bush DOD was ridiculed for scenarios that envisaged U.S. forces reinforcing Poland against Russian attack. The Clinton DOD was criticized for allegedly succumbing to using slogans such as "win-hold-win" as surrogates for strategic concepts. But the real issue was producing a credible, threat-based scenario. Like the reconstitution issue, much of the debate was reduced to beliefs about what might or might not happen in this world of strategic uncertainty.

Thus, another Desert Storm-type operation is postulated on the basis that Iraq could rearm or Iran could intervene against its oil-rich neighbors in the Gulf. North Korea could attack South. Yet, for every scenario like these, to paraphrase Sir Isaac Newton, there is at least an equal, opposite force that will argue this planning contingency is either misguided or will not happen.

Similarly, both the Bush and Clinton administrations took strong views on preventing or countering the dangers of proliferation of weapons of mass destruction and the spread of advanced military technological capabilities. The Clinton administration has specified antiproliferation as one of the four major mission areas for the DOD. But translating this antiproliferation requirement from policy to programs and budget does not follow any easy mathematical formula or model. Indeed, it can be argued that preventing the use of these mass destruction weapons is a more important objective than preventing their proliferation. At the end of the day, short of using force, the United States has few policy tools that will guarantee success in stopping the spread of these weapons.

Finally, the Clinton administration has explicitly noted "democratization" as a fourth role for the DOD in promoting and assisting emerging democracies. Part of this formulation applies to assisting in the conversion of former Soviet military power to more benign uses. Part of this role responds to humanitarian missions and to new peacekeeping tasks in line with an expanding portfolio of responsibilities for the U.N. Yet, no matter how compelling the rationale is for this role, translation into specific forces and capabilities is exceedingly difficult.

As noted, the administration completed its Bottom-Up Review. From this review, strategy, policy, budgets, and force structure were put into a single, unified framework. Underwriting this strategic review is the defense budget. Clinton defense budgets were projected as shown in table 15.

Table 15. Clinton defense budgets (billions of dollars)

	FY 1993	FY 1994	FY 1995	FY 1996	FY 1997	FY 1998
Budget authority	274.3	263.7	262.8	253.8	248.4	254.2
Outlays	294.3	277.7	272.6	264.9	249.1	252.7

To appreciate what these projections suggest for the size and capability of future forces that can be supported, an understanding of where and how money is spent, what costs and expenditures may have been understated or mistakenly calculated, and where real savings can be made is essential. Note in table 16 how defense spending has changed across the major accounts.

Table 16. Changes in defense spending over time (FY 1994 constant dollars in millions of TOA[a])

	Personnel	Operations	Procurement	Research & development
1970	113,556	82,132	73,590	26,972
1980	86,112	75,386	58,449	22,706
1993	77,230	92,275	56,783	39,047
1997 (proj.)	71,250	86,494	55,521	34,704

[a] TOA = Total obligational authority.

In order to deal with the possibility of underfunding, Secretary Aspin directed the Defense Science Board to review the FY 1994–99 Bush Future Years' Defense Program with regard to five areas:

- The Defense Management Report Decision (DMRD) savings and their accuracy

- The realism of major weapons cost projections

- Adequacy of operations and maintenance (O&M) funding

- Adequacy of funding for DOD health care and environmental programs

- The possibility of any significant procurement "bow-wave" beyond the FYDP.[25]

The report (called The Odeen Report after the chairman Phil Odeen) concluded that the Bush FYDP was $12 billion to $15 billion underfunded. This did not include health care, environmental clean-up, and other areas to be covered in later reports.

The funding shortfalls noted below vary considerably with these earlier findings. The reasons for these differences are not necessarily the result of fault or error in either the BUR or Odeen Report. The BUR had been completed before Congress took final action on the FY 1994 budget that added further cuts and reinstituted a pay raise not planned for or proposed by the administration. And the results of program and force-level changes made by the BUR took time to register on the future funding projections. However, it also must be restated that the following figures (as well as those of the Odeen Report) are estimates. Because of the vast number of programs and different accounting systems in the Pentagon, exact and timely data are extremely difficult to find. Instead, the following data provide a qualitative view of what the shortfalls are likely to be. In practice, to the degree history applies, these estimates are more likely to understate the shortages than not.

Several existing miscalculations and underestimates for projected defense spending lurk within DOD budgets. Total funding

---

[25] See The Defense Science Board Special Task Force Report of May 1993.

for current service acquisition and readiness programs may already be short by $20 billion to $30 billion for the FYDP. Health care in DOD is at least $10 billion in the red. The BUR projects $13 billion more in spending than the president's top line permits. A major OSD program review in 1993 suggests that the larger service procurement programs are underfunded by at least $10 billion. The Office of Management and Budget (OMB) and the Congressional Budget Office (CBO) estimated that the defense budget for FY 1994 was already $3 billion underfunded in outlays due to differing assumptions on pay and benefits. The decision by Congress to approve pay increases adds an unplanned $20 to $30 billion in obligations that must come from within DOD's budget. The costs of defense conversion in the U.S. and FSU, as well as aid to the FSU, are now part of the DOD budget and are included under the defense spending cap. This $2.5 billion in current outlays, while funded by Congress in 1993, is now a DOD responsibility and a future competitor for DOD dollars. Furthermore, the services have based out-year planning on achieving large cuts and savings through the BRAC, estimates that are far more optimistic than the record suggests. This basing discrepancy is likely to run in the billions of dollars. The Defense Business Operating Fund (DBOF), the DOD "checkbook," is in disorder and underfunded by several billion dollars or more. Finally, DOD will not be fully reimbursed for contingency operations in Bosnia, Somalia, and Haiti that have already cost several hundreds of millions of dollars or more.

On other levels, likely cost overruns of current programs, inflation, the effects of the tax package and health care reform, and the costs of environmental cleanup of DOD sites are uncertain but are likely to exact a large or enormous price tag on DOD spending. All told, the current five-year budget is already over $100 billion underfunded in outlays. And that does not include any cuts likely to be made in future defense spending by the administration or Congress. Table 17 summarizes the known areas of underfunding.

As an additional indication of the magnitude of possible underfunding, over the past twenty years or so, the general rule of thumb was that maintenance of a well-trained force at consistent and high levels of manpower, readiness, and modernization required annual real growth of at least 3 to 5 percent. The reasons were increases in inflation for manpower, new and better weapon systems, and operational and maintenance costs. Certainly, this shorthand is inexact and subject to caveats, but, for the Clinton FYDP, if this rule applies, it would equate to a further $70 to $90 billion shortfall.[26]

Table 17. Areas of known underfunding[a]

Item	Estimated impact on underfunding during the FYDP
Military pay increase	$20–30 billion
DOD health care	$10 billion
Difference between the BUR and president's budget	$13 billion
Differences/discrepancies over BRAC savings	$1–? billion
Major procurement program shortfalls	$10 billion (and certain to rise)
Defense conversion and aid to the FSU	$5–15 billion
DBOF shortages	$3–? billion
Unfunded contingency operations	$1–? billion
Accounting and other discrepancies of reprogramming	$3–? billion
Environmental cleanup	$3–? billion (and could be huge)
Future cuts, inflation, other areas of underfunding, and the Exxon-Grassley Act that would assign defense a larger share of any future budget cuts	? However, barring a new threat, the most likely outcome will be further spending cuts of 2 or more percent per year—possibly a total of around 10 percent or more over the FYDP, or $50-100 billion.
Total underfunding	$120–$250 billion

a   Figures are taken from the public record and unclassified documents and material made available to the author by DOD personnel. Refer also to footnote 18 for other references.

---

26 A historical review of real cost growth in all DOD accounts since World War II is revealing. The cost of new weapon systems grew at about 7 percent per year. On a compounded basis, this means a doubling in costs, in real terms, every ten years. Manpower costs have increased by about 3 percent per year, and operations and maintenance have increased by 2 to 4 percent. As noted, health care, environmental cleanup, and regulatory enforcement have enormous and probably unknown costs associated with each category.

The magnitude of this cost growth problem is suggested by a single but telling comparison. In 1948, the first Annual Defense Report of the Secretary of Defense was published. It sold for 55 cents. In current dollars, 55 cents in 1948 is now equivalent to about $6.00 (or an annualized 7-percent rate of inflation). The 1993 Defense Report, printed on glossy paper and filled with well-prepared charts and photographs, sold for $15.00.[27] This equates to a real cost growth of 250 percent. And, the material in each report is comparable.

Against an annual defense budget of $250 to $270 billion and a five-year budget of $1.3 trillion, the impact of a $20 billion per year or a total five-year $100 billion cut in outlays would seem relatively small. Note that the Clinton five-year plan was a total of about $129 billion less than the Bush plan and would reduce forces by about 200,000. Reality is somewhat different. Because of the need to gain immediate savings to deal with outlay cuts, the only accounts that provide that fungibility are personnel, operations, and training. People can be cut, which frees up saving through salaries forgone. Operations and training can be cut, which permits savings by not replenishing fuel, ammunition, and other consumables that are expended on a routine basis.

Long-term spending for procurement and research and development does not provide a source for immediate savings if and when cut. Generally, outlay savings in procurement programs are minimal for the current year even if a huge program is eliminated. Savings occur in future years. Therefore, because of this bias towards equating outlay cuts with personnel and training accounts, these are the accounts that will suffer disproportionately to the outlay shortfalls.

For example, an outlay cut of $10 billion in one year, if applied to only personnel, would lead to a reduction of about 200,000 uniformed personnel, or nearly a seventh of the current base force of 1.4 million.[28] A cut of $20 billion would mean a personnel reduction of nearly

---

[27] We were unable to obtain sufficient information on how DOD or the printing office calculated this figure other than by dividing total costs by copies published.

[28] This assumes average savings of $50,000 per service person, which may be a bit high. If that is the case, more rather than fewer personnel would be cut.

400,000. That is in a single year. To be sure, those personnel costs would not be carried over into future years so that if the $10 billion outlay shortfall persisted, it would be largely covered by the manpower cuts. However, what this approximate analysis suggests is that to maintain a future force as ready and as well-equipped as today's, a steady-state active-duty count of about 1,000,000 men and women is perhaps the upper limit that can be sustained. Clearly, with future cuts in spending and cost overruns almost certain facts of life, optimism for a condition of unchanged U.S. military strength should not be high.

Under the Reagan/Bush defense plans, U.S. military forces topped off at about 2.2 million active-duty personnel distributed among 18 active Army divisions, 3 active Marine Corps divisions, 26 tactical fighter wings (TFWs), and 15 carrier battle groups (CVBGs). Included in the reserves were 6 Army and 1 Marine Corps division and 10 tactical fighter wings. The Bush "base force" planned to reduce the total numbers to 1.6 million active-duty personnel divided among 12 active Army divisions, 3 active Marine Corps divisions, 22 TFWs, and 12 CVBGs. The Clinton "base force" is projected at 1.4 million active-duty personnel, 10 Army and 3 Marine Corps active-duty divisions, 20 TFWs, and 11 CVBGs. For the time being, strategic nuclear forces will be determined by START agreements and headed towards a level of 3,000–5,000 warheads distributed among the SSBN, land-based missile, and land-based bomber forces.

The practice, thus far, has been to maintain a more or less consistent, overall level of U.S. commitment overseas. Although the number of troops stationed in Europe is likely to decline to 100,000 or less, the U.S. continues to maintain a robust series of worldwide operational deployments and substantial presence. In fact, given deployments to Somalia, the Persian Gulf, and the Adriatic and to support U.N. peacekeeping operations, the operational tempo and accompanying demands on service personnel have remained relatively consistent over the past decades even though the principal threat for which that presence was conceived and rationalized has disappeared.

Additionally, the Clinton administration has pledged not to return to a "hollow force" and has made readiness among its highest priorities. Then-Secretary of Defense Les Aspin established a special readiness task force in the spring of 1993. Consisting of former senior military officers of all services and chaired by former Army Chief of Staff General E. C. Meyer, who coined the term "hollow force" during his tenure as chief, the task force's purpose was to underscore the importance of readiness, giving the secretary and public an objective, outside assessment of the impact "downsizing" has had on the force's readiness to carry out its missions.

Although the panel concluded that today's readiness was "acceptable in most measurable areas," it found "pockets" of unreadiness. These "pockets" were sufficiently worrying for the task force to note: "However, we observed enough concern that we are convinced that unless the Department of Defense and the Congress focus on readiness, the armed forces could slip back into a 'hollow' status."[29]

For the time being, the significance of these administration actions is the intent to keep all or at least the bulk of the active-duty forces "ready." Thus, substantial funds will be required for training, operations, and maintenance of equipment to meet these standards of readiness. And recruiting quality personnel is no less a challenge even with a smaller force. That, too, is expensive. All of these expenditures fall into the outlay category, meaning they are the most sensitive to budget cuts.

If these budget and shortfall forecasts are correct, the Clinton administration is headed for a collision between an active-duty force too large for the budget and readiness requirements and actual capabilities far below expected and planned levels. Furthermore, the interaction among threat, strategy, force level, budget, and infrastructure must shift the bias increasingly against military power as domestic factors dominate or overwhelm strategic and operational arguments.

As the Bush administration conducted its downsizing and produced its base force and the Clinton administration completed its Bottom-Up Review, the four services were actively reassessing and refining their own view of what active and supporting forces were required and what infrastructure and industrial base capacities should be maintained. Although service efforts were conducted in coordination with and in subordination to OSD and JCS decisions,

---

[29] Report of the Defense Science Board Task Force on Readiness, Office of the Under Secretary of Defense for Acquisition and Technology, June 1994, p. i.

nonetheless, service actions and attitudes are crucial to making downsizing work. The services and service secretaries, by law, are charged with the training and equipping of the forces, and the military services constitute the organization for carrying out the directives of higher authority.

For several reasons, during 1992–1993, the Department of the Navy was the most visible of the services in responding to changed circumstances and, for better or worse, the service most visibly affected by the issues reflecting the current and new political landscape at home and abroad.[30] First, the disappearance of the USSR meant that U.S. interests would shift to the world's littorals and regions adjacent to the sea. This meant the Navy and Marine Corps, because of geography, the ocean medium, and their basic military capabilities and uses, were likely to be the forces of choice or the forces on hand in most crises or contingencies.

Second, a series of events shocked the Navy to its roots. Although the Navy was an active and important participant in the Gulf War to liberate Kuwait, it received little public praise and much media criticism for its performance. The Army, Air Force, and Marine Corps, with a stunning 100-hour victory over Iraq's ground forces, were popularly perceived by most Americans as the real war winners. The Navy was seen in a supporting role and not helped by frequent media reports of an apparent unwillingness and inability to participate in genuinely joint and combined operations. Thus, even though much of the criticism was off the mark, the Navy moved quickly to repair the operational and internal deficiencies that were exposed during that war.

Just after the war ended, the "Tailhook" symposium met in Las Vegas, Nevada, in the fall of 1991. Tailhook was the annual convention for naval aviation. Although a private association outside

---

[30] This in no way diminishes the steps the Air Force and the Army have taken in responding to the new era. Since 1991, the Air Force has streamlined its organization, cut back dramatically on officer personnel, moved to decentralize authority, drafted a new policy paper *Global Reach, Global Power*, and changed its uniform. The Army has reintensified and streamlined its organization to support the new battlefield requirements and made large cuts in its active and reserve structure. The Navy example is used because it is more recent and covers a broader range of issues.

government, Tailhook had the blessings and support of the Navy and was considered a quasi-official event. Generally understood to be raucous, the 1991 convention got out of hand. There were numerous charges of sexual assault, harassment, and conduct unbecoming officers. For better or worse, the Senate hearings on the nomination of Clarence Thomas as associate justice to the Supreme Court occurred that same October. Anita Hill and sexual harassment issues were thrust prominently into American society and public interest.

The Navy, unfortunately, was fated to mishandle aspects of Tailhook. Given the sensationalism of the Thomas hearings, sexual harassment took on a momentum of its own, putting the Navy in an untenable position. On the one hand, the behavior at Tailhook was unacceptable, intolerable, perhaps including possible criminal misconduct, and the incident was surely exaggerated by the Thomas–Hill affair. On the other hand, the Navy rightly wanted to keep the matter in-house and deal with Tailhook as discreetly and quietly as possible. A collision was inevitable. In the summer of 1992, after the DOD Inspector General had been summoned to undertake the investigation the Navy started and relinquished, the Secretary of the Navy was forced to resign when Navy Lieutenant Paula Coughlin, one of the attendees at Tailhook and a naval aviator, went public with her allegations of what transpired at Las Vegas and her charge that the Navy failed to act on her complaints and those of others.[31]

The effects of the Gulf War and the public perception of the Navy's ancillary role and the explosive aftermath of the Tailhook

---

[31] Regrettably for the Navy, the Tailhook affair refused to die. Coughlin herself is in a legal battle that includes sworn statements contradicting her allegations. In 1993, after reviewing the record, the new Secretary of the Navy recommended that the Chief of Naval Operations be dismissed on the grounds of responsibility for the mishandled investigation. He was overruled by the Secretary of Defense. In February 1994, a military judge ruled that the CNO had been untruthful in his testimony at a Tailhook military tribunal. Although the evidence very much supported the CNO, in the wake of all this turbulence, Admiral Frank Kelso elected to retire early. The debate in the Senate over whether to retire Kelso with four stars lasted six hours and ended with a small majority voting in favor of the higher rank. This incident perhaps will mark the end of the Tailhook affair, although the legacy and bad taste are likely to linger.

affair were profound. The most cathartic result was a Navy that realized times had changed and that it must change with them. Stung by severe criticism, the Navy also recognized another disturbing problem.

During the Reagan years, the Navy had relentlessly pursued its goal of 600 ships. To support those ships, a homeport and basing scheme had been approved to increase the number of these shore facilities accordingly. During the first two rounds of the BRAC in 1988 and 1991, the Navy fought to protect those shore facilities. Indeed, one of the early commissioners (and a former Navy Secretary) was extremely critical of the Navy's refusal to appreciate the drain the bases placed on the rest of the Navy and the Navy's "stonewalling" of the BRAC. By 1992, however, the Navy understood that its infrastructure was vastly in excess of both what was needed and what future budgets could afford. In fact, the basing structure was threatening the health of the forces and their readiness because of the resources it devoured.

By 1992, the cumulative effects of these events coalesced and led to a series of fundamental responses by the Department of the Navy (DON). The Navy and Marine Corps drafted a document called ...*From the Sea* in which the sea services adopted the primary mission of influencing and affecting events ashore in and around the ocean littorals. To that end, the Navy and Marine Corps began a serious and thorough integration of both services, focusing first on naval aviation. However, the depth of and commitment to this integration are deep and will be powerful factors influencing future budget priorities. At the same time, the Navy reorganized its staff in Washington and abolished the so-called air, surface, and submarine platform "barons." The significance of this reorganization cannot be understated, because, for the first time since 1945, warfare requirements rather than needs of the individual platform barons were to dominate budget priorities. This reorganization also coincided with the Navy's commitment to "joint operations" and learning from the errors of the Gulf War.

During the 1993 BRAC, the Navy took an extremely aggressive stance in recommending bases to be closed. In part, the Navy had little choice because of its refusal in the past to rid itself of excess bases. But, more importantly, the Navy recognized that this excessive infrastructure was harming operational capability and adversely affecting the Navy's ability to perform its missions. In social terms, although the disastrous effects of Tailhook may never fully heal until a younger generation of officers moves into senior ranks, the Navy has taken the lead in opening combat and seagoing assignments to women. Finally, the Navy has taken a hard-headed view of likely budget levels and, for the moment, set the size of the future Navy at about 300 to 350 ships, perhaps the most visible sign of understanding the new realities.

The irony in all this will prove striking. Although the Navy and Marine Corps have made remarkable progress in adapting to change and the realities of the post-Cold War world, that adaptation is likely to be only the first step. Less visible but certainly as profound actions are likely to be needed to deal with conditions that will be driven almost exclusively by the domestic political process and debate. Having taken measures that are fundamental departures from the past, instead of having the luxury of only refining those measures, the likelihood is very high that far more change will be needed. Reacting to and anticipating these future pressures, now that the more visible and overarching actions have been taken, could prove even more demanding intellectual and imaginative tests than those of the past several years.

Against this interplay among strategic change, budgetary reality, and future force structure is a political and decision-making process of great complexity and inefficiency. The growth of Pentagon and Congressional staffs is a well-known fact. But the issue is far deeper than staff bureaucracy or personalities. The issue at hand in determining how well or how badly this downsizing will be carried out concerns both constitutional and cultural prerogatives.

The conflict between Article I and Article II of the Constitution regarding the "providers" for the forces (the Congress) and the commander in chief (the president) remains. Given the need to make and stick by tough decisions with real life-and-death consequences for those forces sent into action, compromise is not necessarily the best or most effective solution in fielding the military.

Yet, if it is to function, the political system must rely on compromise. As a result, for those who view the military as simply an instrument for delivering or threatening to deliver decisive force and not as a social or welfare agency, the failure of the political process to cut overhead such as militarily unnecessary bases represents the worst extreme of this compromise. For those who view the military as an extension of society, bases and their link with the civilian community are important despite the fact that military readiness or capability may be impaired. And, for most Americans, since all "politics are local," when confronted with the choice of supporting a strong military or losing their jobs or income through a defense build-down, it is obvious which preference wins out. This dilemma remains persistent. As such, the effectiveness and efficiency of downsizing, from a military perspective, will be eroded.

To a degree, the same dilemma applies to the National Guard and reserve forces. The Constitution gives the states their own militia. Indeed, the Second Amendment guarantees the right of these militias "to keep and bear arms." (Note that this right does not extend to the people *except* through the militia.) Hence, the debate over active versus reserve force mix is not only emotional and economic, it has constitutional roots.

The political culture and current standards of so-called "political correctness" are other aspects of the process that are obstacles to enhancing effectiveness and efficiency. The legal restrictions and obstacles to entry into senior government service by civilians, ranging from full disclosure of family assets to forfeiting many rights to subsequent civilian employment on the grounds of potential conflict of interests, not only delay the selection and confirmation of senior appointees, they also discourage many of the best from serving. The fear of unwittingly being subject to the public microscope and the degree to which relatively minor or insignificant trespasses are magnified under this inspection are further restraints to public service. The Clinton administration has been criticized for failing to fill many senior appointments quickly enough, but the fact is that the entire process does not allow either speed or the full range of qualified personnel from which to choose.[32]

Where are we headed?

Barring an extraordinarily unlikely crisis, the DOD budgets projected by the Clinton administration are an absolute top line.

---

[32] The Clinton administration has a larger number of lawyers and former Congressional staffers than usual because both categories generally have fewer conflict-of-interest problems arising from past or future employment. Indeed, it would be interesting to see how earlier cabinets under Presidents Eisenhower or Kennedy would have fared under the current rules.

Analysis shows an underfunding shortfall of $100 billion and probably double or more will arise during FY 1995–1999. One can only guess at the size of future defense reductions to be imposed on DOD spending by the executive branch, Congress, or both. Those cuts will be determined by the state of the economy, the size of the deficit, and the popular perception of the balance between international and domestic priorities. But, if the tax and economic package passed by Congress and signed into law by the president in August 1993 does not close the deficit, it is virtually certain that the defense budget must be the primary target for expenditure cuts. By the end of the century, if no threat or genuine crisis emerges, total defense underfunding is likely to amount to $200 to $300 billion. This underfunding will be exacerbated by "cost creep," by inefficiencies in the process, and, as will be shown, by the prodigious appetite of infrastructure "tail" to devour military "teeth."

Determining the specific impact of as yet unspecified spending shortfalls and reductions in the defense budget on force structure is, at best, a first approximation. The largest consideration, after estimating the size and pace of spending cuts, is to determine the strategic prioritization among the many funding categories that support force levels, overseas presence and deployments, readiness, procurement, and research and development.

For example, the funding decision may be made to maximize the numbers of active- duty forces at the expense of readiness, procurement, and research and development accounts that would suffer the majority of spending cuts. Alternatively, the funding priority could be to maintain the readiness and capability of those forces already in service at high levels that would require compensating and major reductions in overall numbers and in procurement of weapon systems. Or, the priority could rest on the decision to identify a "core force" constituting a certain percentage of the overall force and ensure that this force is kept in suitably high states of readiness and modernization. The remaining forces outside this core force would absorb the necessary budget cuts and, in essence, would end up as a "force-in-being" or a strategic reserve at much lower levels of readiness. Table 18 summarizes the more likely prospects for U.S. military might later this decade. Note that only the best case assumes a combination of full funding and effective reforms.

Table 18. Prospects for U.S. military might

Case	Force levels	Budget	Readiness
BUR maintained (best case, assumes full funding)	1.4 million active	$270 billion	High. This assumes either full funding and/or imposition of effective reforms.
BUR not fully funded (most likely)	1.3–1.4 million active	$240–250 billion	The bulk of the force is "hollow." Morale will be low and maintenance and replacement backlogs large. This assumes effective reforms or corrective actions are not taken.
BUR not fully funded (worst case)	1.2–1.4 million active	$200–225 billion	The force will be "hollow" or worse. This is an unready, unhappy military probably in worse condition than anytime since World War II.

The most likely outcome, if history is relevant and negative practices in downsizing are repeated, is that DOD will wage a powerful rear-guard effort to resist cuts in spending, cuts in force levels, and cuts in readiness. It is very likely that spending among the services will continue to be prorated around current budget shares and that "balance" and "compromise" will be the policies on which resource priorities will be made. Should all this take place, U.S. military forces will atrophy over time. Force levels will be too large for likely budgets to sustain them at high levels of readiness and modernization.

The nation can avoid this condition in several ways if an unforeseen threat does not intervene to change the strategic equation or if spending is not increased to fund the full BUR force. First, the nation can simply be stoic and unworried by a lack of military readiness and capability. The argument and rationale for this position are clear. Given an absence of clear and apparent dangers and emphasis on domestic priorities, DOD would be directed to make do with those resources it was assigned without protest. From a strictly U.S. national security perspective, the world would not be viewed as a more dangerous place. In all likelihood, enough strategic warning time should be available to permit adequate action to be taken in the future. Even with an active-duty force of a million or less, armed with nuclear and advanced weapons, the U.S. would still have the most formidable military in the world. There are no genuine threats to the nation's actual survival for the foreseeable future. In this regard, if these arguments are accepted, the Truman demobilization provides the best model for downsizing in which forces were cut dramatically and, despite the Korean conflict, the nation still managed to survive quite well.

Second, the administration can provide sufficient resources to support the BUR force, which will require some combination of increasing defense resources. Spending increases are one means although the political chances of adding to the defense budget are realistically zero. Reforms could be imposed to free up resources already assigned to defense. The Clinton administration has promised reform. As of 1994, the results have not been significant despite the promise of the Federal Acquisition Streamlining Act of 1993 to impose some reform.

Third, the nation can revise and adjust its national security policy. Objectives, strategy, forces, and budgets, along with infrastructure, can be defined in keeping with the post-Cold War era. However, without reform, it must be repeated that the system and process will not permit the maintenance of a constant level of military capability without spending more money.

Unfortunately, each choice has certain flaws. The most likely outcome will be a much weaker and much less capable military force than needed to deal with future circumstances that remain unpredictable and uncertain. Hence, promoting the requisite support for that capability will prove elusive.

The decision to accept or tolerate an erosion in military power assumes that ample warning time will be available and that the nation will muster the capacity to act. Obviously, in this case, the attributes of high readiness and high probability of success in the initial stages of conflict are downgraded. That could prove politically unwise or disastrous.

The choices of freeing up resources and revising strategy have the decided disadvantage of depending upon future Congresses to honor and support any deal over time. Given the broad expansion of constitutionally imposed limits of appropriations to two or three years and the reality that new Congresses are not legally obliged to accept all agreements or arrangements made by earlier Congresses, legal and political issues of fundamental importance are at stake.

At the same time the fiber and muscle of the active forces will be tested by budget and political realities, the infrastructure will also be squeezed. The defense industrial base will continue to contract, and, as the Odeen Report observed in May 1993, "cost creep" will only worsen:

> *The rapid loss of the defense business base is likely to lead to significant increases in the overhead and [general and administrative] rates of defense suppliers. As demonstrated in the F-22 program last year, this could lead to unexpected and largely unavoidable cost increases in existing programs....*[33]

Indeed, F-22 could even be canceled due to budgetary reasons. All these factors beg for the need to invoke a public hearing on the future of defense. Although it is unprovable that deferring such a debate and examination will do absolute damage to the nation, there is no reason to take the risk. And, in the process, perhaps some good can be done by strengthening the way in which we do provide for our security.

---

[33] "Defense Science Board Task Report on FY 1994–99 Future Years' Defense Plan," May 1993, p. 2. On January 18, 1994, *Flight International* reported that even while cutting the buy of F-22s from 648 to 442, the total of the program costs was likely to grow and that at least an 11-month delay has been incurred for the first flight test. In the late summer of 1994, there were suggestions by OSD that the entire program might be delayed for fiscal reasons.

PART II: "AND THE GOOD SOUTH WIND STILL BLEW"

The evidence strongly suggests, but cannot irrefutably show, that defense faces a continuing downward spiral driven by funding gaps already in place, by the likelihood of greater reductions in future appropriated budgets, by the escalating costs of overhead and infrastructure that also exacerbate inefficiencies, and by the political reality in which decisions will conform more with domestic than with strategic or operational priorities. Concurrently, some of the supporting infrastructure, ranging from bases to the defense industrial network, will also contract. In dealing with the consequences and challenges of these trends and realities, the Department of Defense has several tactical alternatives it can follow in fulfilling its responsibilities.

First, DOD can accept without much protest whatever resources are allocated and do its best. The Bottom-Up Review, in this case, provides the general framework for force design and the intellectual structure for its rationalization. The BUR is, as its principal drafters noted, a "sporty track" with very ambitious plans for force improvement as well as substantial overhaul of the acquisition system as an objective. Clearly, force levels will shrink around the conceptual justification. Inherent in this policy choice is the realization that U.S. military power will contract; that the forces will become fewer in number and, if the earlier analysis is correct, less ready to carry out their tasks; and that the strategic environment will allow enough warning time to respond to new and powerful threats should they arise. Finally, the presumption could be that the stronger domestic economy that would result will provide the wherewithal to reconstitute those forces needed to deal with a future crisis.

Second, DOD can opt to resist these trends to the point of provoking a clash within government. Following the approach used by former Reagan defense secretary Caspar Weinberger, DOD can use all its influence and credibility to oppose any and all cuts to its basic programs. The problem with this approach is that DOD is likely to be beaten down and overwhelmed by a president or a Congress bent on bringing the department to heel. The risks would be possible draconian measures passed by Congress to cut or alter DOD priorities in fundamental ways.

Third, DOD can adjust and change. This tack includes the possibility of making sweeping changes to U.S. military posture to deal with the demands of likely resource realities, in part through imposing reforms to generate efficiencies and to leverage the economies of smart and lean program management. Change can be accomplished either around and within the framework of the Bottom-Up Review or through a new framework. However, as in the other tactical approaches, this one, too, has certain risks and problems and cannot be implemented within a vacuum or within only the domain of DOD. As the BUR suffered from the lack of White House guidance, any revision of U.S. strategy will be successful only if it is mandated and directed by the president and supported by Congress.

Part II examines the principal components of future U.S. military might and derives alternatives and options for consideration, debate, and implementation.

CHAPTER FIVE: STRATEGY

THE LEGACY

For nearly five decades, U.S. national security strategy remained remarkably consistent in its objectives, logic, basic assumptions, and identification of the principal enemy. To the degree there was a strategic debate, it was generally over means and not ends. The powerful and multifaceted threat presented by the Soviet Union ultimately was contained and deterred through a network of political, military, and economic alliances and instruments, including a large measure of foreign and military assistance, and assured by the strength and determination of the United States to act as the "leader of the free world" as well as the source of much of the globe's economic power.

The guarantee of Cold War deterrence ultimately rested on the threat of massive and presumably fatal nuclear and thermonuclear retaliation should the Soviet Union attack the United States or its allies, although mobilization offered an insurance policy if world war were to be fought only on the conventional level. Over the years, the original notion of nuclear deterrence was extended to include the concept of flexible response and other forms of military initiatives, many of which lay well beyond the nuclear boundaries, in order to match or counter new Soviet weapons, doctrines, and technologies. This societally threatening aspect of deterrence and, presumably, the unprecedented speed and certainty with which nuclear and thermonuclear weapons could devastate an intended victim's homeland made this Cold War relationship different from all others in history.

Furthermore, containment was manifested in a series of alliances among seemingly like-minded states to deter and encircle the USSR to prevent its ambitions from overflowing its borders. In NATO, for example, an attack against one member was viewed as an attack against all. Sustained and nurtured by a U.S. economy that appeared limitless in performance, that would be mobilized in war, and that maintained a technological supremacy that seemed insurmountable, the U.S. and its chief allies also assumed an almost spiritual belief in the superiority of democracy and capitalism over communism and autocracy. Hence, the combination of containment, thermonuclear deterrence, alliances, economic and technological superiority, wartime mobilization, and ideological optimism served to underwrite U.S. and Western security for four decades.

From these foundations flowed the operational planning factors that were central to strategy and force design. Warning and mobilization time were clearly critical factors because from them came the requirements for troops and material and deployment schedules to bring reinforcements to bear. The enemy order of battle was also critical, as was the amount of war materials (such as ammunition, fuel, and spares) to be kept on hand before mobilization kicked in new production. These criteria could change and could be debated, but they did perform the vital function of providing a measure, rightly or wrongly, of how much was enough.

The end of the USSR and, for all practical purposes, communism as a political alternative to democracy removed the basis for the world order that existed throughout the Cold War. As the post-Cold War world ages, the extent of the real and perceived consequences of the demise of the USSR will play out. Thus far, however, U.S. national security strategy has not changed profoundly, nor has the U.S. chosen to demobilize as it did after the end of World War I and World War II.

To be sure, the U.S. is determined not to fall into the trap of demobilization or excessive disarmament. That is a noble intent. But it is both puzzling and interesting that neither the Bush administration nor, so far, the Clinton administration has embarked on a profound review or reappraisal of U.S. security in this new era. Thus, where the U.S. may be at risk is in finding or inventing the new basis for its future national security and its national security strategy in a world no longer dominated by the bipolar nature of that earlier geostrategic era.

The objectives, logic, and assumptions that shaped the Cold War are unlikely to be relevant (or even helpful) in this different and strategically uncertain world. Without an intellectual or political basis for policy and strategy, sustaining both a consensus and even close to current budgets for U.S. military power will be extremely difficult. More to the point, the lack of rationale for defense mandates even further reduction in strategic and operational priorities *vis a vis* domestic needs.

In the United States, the classical and academic approach to determining strategy is no secret. First, the nature of the world and threats to U.S. security are identified or assumed. Second, U.S. interests are specified and threats to U.S. interests are matched against a range of protective instruments for which military force has been the ultimate arbiter. Third, the amount of military force deemed to be sufficient or necessary to protect the nation is determined by the judgment of the executive branch tempered by its assessment of the attitudes of Congress, the public, and relevant international actors. Finally, these judgments are presented to Congress through the annual budgeting process and thrust into the political debate over allocating national resources and determining national priorities.

The dilemmas of determining any strategy in this uncertain world, now driven increasingly if not entirely by domestic politics, are obvious when set in perspective. Identifying real or possible threats to U.S. security of a level of danger or risk remotely close to that posed by the USSR leads to a simple conclusion. There are none. Specifying U.S. interests that must be protected produces banal platitudes that, although no doubt valid in an absolute sense, seem less than relevant when matched against likely threats and possible dangers.

Thus, planning factors are difficult to create given ambiguous and uncertain threats, and no firm quantitative basis for rationalizing the strategy and forces is easily produced. Because of this uncertainty, lack of specificity, and an accompanying lack of universal planning criteria, arguments with more or less equal plausibility can be made for fielding military forces of the current 1.6 million level, for a level of 1 million, for a level of half a million, or virtually any number within this boundary. In other words, without a real threat, there may be no satisfactory strategic answer to the question of how much is enough.

These dilemmas extend to applying the intellectual basis of the Cold War strategy to the current and future worlds. The concepts of containment and deterrence were directed at a single and powerful threat. That threat straddled Eurasia and cast its shadow on a world in which the threat of nuclear war could not be eliminated from national policy considerations of either side in the Cold War. Geostrategy therefore mattered and a system of behavior was established along with "rules of the game." Both the U.S. and USSR and their allies could operate under these rules in the nuclear age without recourse to world war.

Current American rhetorical replacement themes for the threat of the former USSR echo the need to maintain "regional stability" and contain regional crisis or conflict. In other words, the implicit attempt thus far by the United States has been to transfer the geostrategic concepts and objectives of containment and deterrence to regional rather than global settings without fully determining whether these concepts fit. The current, unstated assumption appears to be that containing or deterring threats and regional instabilities is conceptually independent of the size or nature of the threat and independent of any serious threat of nuclear retaliation. That assumption is not necessarily relevant.

It can be argued that non-nuclear containment and deterrence have worked in the case of Libya's Qaadafi, seen as a direct threat to the United States. American retaliatory strikes against Libya in 1986, backed up by an embargo of sorts, have restrained Libyan actions against U.S. interests. On the other hand, despite what may or may not have transpired in the days just before Iraq's August 1990 invasion of Kuwait, containment and deterrence visibly failed against Iraq. Saddam Hussein disregarded the rituals of U.S. signalling before and during the occupation of Kuwait, and it took the force of arms to expel him. Bosnia seems an unsolvable tragedy immune to all forms of containment and deterrence. Furthermore, because containment requires at least consensus among a few states over who is to be contained, gaining that consensus is difficult when the terms *allies* and *adversaries* are often interchangeable.

Above all, deterrence developed from the nuclear realities of a bipolar geostrategic world and the power of technological superiority. The United States also believed that nuclear superiority over the USSR translated into political capital as well as into the offset to Soviet conventional numerical military strength. As the Soviet Union increased its nuclear forces, nuclear deterrence was extended along almost theological lines as this side attempted to exploit its qualitative technological advantages and the other side relied more on larger, more powerful warheads until its technology could close the gap. This deterrence was extended in non-nuclear areas and to such regions as the Middle East where formal alliances with either superpower did not exist.

Deterrence between the superpowers ultimately rested in the capacity of each to threaten the total destruction of the other's society. There is now only one superpower and the Cold War nuclear balance is behind us. The question for the future is whether classical deterrence and the threat of massive or complete destruction has relevance and application in conditioning the attitude and behavior of potential, non-superpower adversaries. For example, it is extremely unlikely that the United States would do to Iraq or Iran what it threatened and promised to its allies it would do to the USSR with nuclear weapons in the event of an attack. Even if a nuclear device were detonated on a U.S. target by a would-be adversary, the relevance of a nuclear-based scheme of deterrence and the total destruction of the offending society through the use of U.S. nuclear weapons seem doubtful or useful constructs.

On the other hand, if the use of U.S. conventional military force can be extended beyond the requirement of defeating an enemy's armed force to threatening or causing the destruction of the enemy's society with non-nuclear weapons, deterrence as defined in the bipolar nuclear age could be relevant. In other words, mass killing of a seemingly innocent society through use of retaliatory nuclear weapons may be out of the question. However, the ability to shut that society down without much loss of life to the enemy may have deterrent value. The example of the UN war against Iraq in 1990–91 may be instructive.

The evidence in that war suggests that the "instant thunder" air campaign of Operation Desert Storm eliminated or destroyed the electrical, communications, transportation, and other vital networks of Iraqi society, effectively shutting down that nation in a matter of hours. It may well be that less advanced and even economically backward states could be enormously vulnerable to conventional attacks against primitive and therefore highly vulnerable networks. If that vulnerability exists, a non-nuclear form of deterrence, in which the U.S. has the conventional capability to destroy an adversary's military and literally destroy or incapacitate the adversary's society for as long as the U.S. required, might have relevance. Whether the U.S. could muster sufficient political resolve or callousness to embrace this version of deterrence against the nearly certain backlash of international reaction remains an open question.

A subset of this post-Cold War variant of deterrence could also be relevant to addressing a current nightmare scenario of U.S. defense planners—the case where the U.S. has already intervened or is about to intervene militarily against an adversary possessing one or a few nuclear weapons either openly or covertly. The worst case in this scenario, as was the scenario of all-out nuclear war in the days of the East-West conflict, relates to a U.S. expeditionary force eviscerated under a nuclear cloud. How and why the U.S. would stumble into such a debacle are arguable questions, but the contingency of the U.S. being deterred itself by a nuclear weapon or two cannot be dismissed out of hand. A concept based on a conventional capability that can destroy an adversary's military power and also threaten destruction of that society may be worthy of further examination as either an explicit or implicit doctrine and strategy.

Of the other assumptions central to U.S. Cold War strategy, their application to today and tomorrow is as questionable as that of deterrence rooted in nuclear threat. Containment was maintained by a network of alliances. NATO, SEATO, the Rio Pact, ANZUS, CENTO, and the bilateral U.S.-Japan, U.S.-Korea, and U.S.-Philippines mutual defense treaties were products of that era.[34] The central questions for the surviving alliances are whether and how to maintain threat-based alliances after the threat has passed. NATO is the most obvious and most important case regarding the future role of alliances within or without a security context.

Through significant and unprecedented effort, NATO transformed its strategy and force requirements to respond to the collapse of communism. Catalyzed by German reunification and the failed Soviet coup in August 1991, the objectives of maintaining stability and containing crises were ratified in November 1991 at the Rome summit of NATO heads of state as the new rationale for the alliance. Yet, the difficulty of transferring these objectives into

---

[34] SEATO—Southeast Asia Treaty Organization; ANZUS—Australia, New Zealand, United States; CENTO—Central Treaty Organization.

practical actions was magnified by the civil war raging in the former Yugoslavia, and the decision by the NATO states not to take an active or interventionist role in resolving that conflict until 1994 severely hurt NATO's credibility. Critics carp that, without practical application, what good is this new basis for alliance? Without a good basis, what good is the alliance?

On the European side of NATO, there is intuitive and implicit strategic understanding for the need to maintain NATO. Explicitly, the Europeans want the U.S. engaged for many reasons. Transatlantic trade and economic harmony remain vital. U.S. presence reassures against possible instability in the East, whether civil war spilling over or resurgence of a Russian threat reemerging to challenge Europe. Furthermore, U.S. leadership is a nice balance to possible aspirations or ambitions of Germany, France, and the U.K. in which the U.S., as *primus inter pares*, can prevent future inter-NATO rivalries from getting out of hand.

On the U.S. side, there is little popular strategic appreciation for maintaining a viable NATO. The end of the Warsaw Pact for many Americans ended the *raison d'etre* for NATO. And, to these same Americans, any replacement or substitute threat for the USSR as the new basis for the alliance is a hollow exercise. Regardless of the future viability of NATO, the demise of the USSR certainly has challenged the United States' ongoing assumption of the need to maintain alliances as central tenets of a security strategy.

Korea is perhaps the one alliance where both a sense and reality of threat remains. Whether or not North Korea acquires nuclear weapons, most Americans agree with maintaining the commitment to guarantee South Korea's security through a military alliance. U.S. force levels in Korea will no doubt decrease, yet Korea is perhaps the one example rather than the general rule where the reality of a threat-based alliance exists.

Japan forms possibly the most complex test for the notion of alliance. The U.S.-Japanese Mutual Defense Treaty has been in place for nearly three and one-half decades. That treaty was based on the general proposition that nonaggression could be a permanent fixture of Japanese behavior and was in the best interest of both Japan and its neighbors. The United States accepted the role of guarantor and, indeed, of custodian of Japan's national security, principally against the USSR and China. And Japan pledged a national policy of nonaggression and self-defense, with its military forces purposely constrained by limits on defense spending of about 1 percent of GDP; by limits on the types of weapon systems acquired; and by limits on the overall command-and-control structure that made "offensive" operations literally impossible.

From the Japanese perspective, the implicit assignment of key Japanese national security responsibilities to the United States allowed that debate on rearmament not to take place within Japan, provided a credible reason to justify America's surrogate role existed—e.g., the Soviet threat. From the U.S. perspective, the strategic advantages of having Japan as the world's largest aircraft carrier directly athwart Soviet Pacific military power and the assurance that Japan had permanently foresworn the ambitions of the East Asian Co-Prosperity Sphere of the 1930s were enormous. As a result of geopolitics and geoeconomics, Americans and Japanese alike saw the U.S.-Japanese relationship as America's most important bilateral arrangement. And, there were no reasons to test that proposition as long as the Cold War persisted.

The end of the Cold War and of the USSR, growing economic disputes and differences between Japan and the United States, and enormous political corruption that has led to the electoral defeat for the first time ever of the Liberal Democratic Party are representative issues that are altering and challenging the U.S.-Japanese relationship. Concurrently, the demise of Soviet power does not end the entire threat to instability in the region, and the balance among and between the states of Northeast and Southeast Asia is by no means in perfect harmony.

The upshot of these factors is an enormous dilemma for the United States. On strategic grounds, a continued and viable U.S.-Japanese relationship is essential. Physical U.S. military presence and U.S. guarantees for Japanese security remain the best instruments for ensuring stability. The U.S. is an accepted (and perhaps expected to be) power for good, and the U.S. and strong U.S. presence are seen as vital by states in the region and with interests in the region. U.S. presence remains the best restraint on potential Japanese ambitions (even if there were no likelihood of revanchist actions), thereby serving as a vital strategic insurance policy.

On economic grounds, however, U.S. domestic critics have a valid point. If the Japanese can have both their security and economic cakes, as it were, why should they change their policies? Moreover, why should the U.S. accept a double hit in its GDP, underwriting both Japan's security and its economy? Hence, if strategic considerations obtain, U.S. policy is relatively clear. If domestic economic considerations obtain, new policies are likely. On a rational basis, balancing strategic and domestic considerations should be straightforward; however, given the nature of the U.S. political process, there is no certainty that rationality will win out.

Finally, the long-standing assumption and assertion that the U.S.-Japanese relationship is the most important bilateral partnership in the world must be questioned now that the joint threat has passed. The different conclusions reached by strategic and narrower economic analyses are evidence of the need to reexamine this question. How this relationship evolves could prove to be the largest uncertainty of them all.

In this review, the last international arrangement that can be categorized as a quasi-alliance pertains to the UN and its emerging roles in the world. The end of the East-West conflict removed one of the greatest constraints to the U.S. more actively soliciting UN involvement where force was required—namely, the Soviet veto. The example of a UN coalition fighting Desert Storm and forces under a UN mandate providing "peacekeeping-like" functions in Somalia and Bosnia are relevant. Certainly, from a U.S. perspective, international action by the UN in regions of crisis or instability provides certain political and strategic advantages, including the not insignificant values of political cover and alternatives for U.S. unilateral intervention.

In its first year, the Clinton administration looked to the UN for both multilateral action and political cover while keeping the option of unilateral intervention open. But the UN relies on a "lowest common denominator" approach, reflecting the need to obtain a Security Council resolution. This is not always in the U.S. interest. The commitment of international military force by the UN also implies, ultimately, an accounting to determine whether the UN can remain and be supported as the instrument of choice. The credit the UN received for Desert Storm and for a variety of peacekeeping operations has reinforced its credibility and authority. However, the tenacious and perhaps unresolvable problems in Bosnia, Somalia, and Rwanda have been debits to the value of UN intervention. Without some positive measures of UN success over the long term, the tendency to rely on the UN for these international roles pertaining to peacemaking, peacekeeping, and restoring stability is likely to be dampened and reduced. Hence, the potentially negative aspects of using the UN and international cooperation as a principal policy instrument must be well understood.

Against this Cold War background of containment, deterrence, and alliance-driven security considerations, the U.S. assumed that its economy was the engine of growth for the West and for the developing world. Implied in this assumption of economic dominance were unshaken beliefs in the superiority of U.S. technology and in the comfort that most problems could be overcome with money. American largesse in its many aid and assistance programs was made possible by this economic vitality. And, for three or four decades after World War II, this assumption and its supporting beliefs were verified by results. America was the world leader in virtually all technological areas. In the 1960s, both the Great Society programs for providing solutions to social ills and the Vietnam War were undertaken simultaneously on the grounds the economy could afford both. Foreign aid and assistance continued to be generous, but the economy could not stand up to these larger demands as, over time, the financial burdens grew and grew.

Domestically, the war against poverty and the larger programs of the Great Society put in place entitlement programs that would have appetites for growth beyond anyone's expectation. Internationally, the countries ravaged by the Second World War reconstituted themselves, and so the various Italian, German, French, and, most visibly, Japanese economic miracles came to fruition. The extraordinary economic advantage the U.S. possessed after World War II was impossible to sustain over the long term, and, as other states could simply grow at faster GDP rates, U.S. dominance had to erode.

In the early 1980s, the notion of supply-side economics and its ancillary policy of stimulating growth through capital expansion dominated official U.S. political and economic policy. And, while no doubt creating larger holders of wealth, both the private and public debts were multiplied. Spurred by a quadrupling of the federal debt in less than a decade from $1 trillion to $4 trillion, the total amount of public and private debt jumped to about $15 trillion in 1993.

The combination of powerful economic rivals, a general sputtering of world economies in the early 1990s, and a huge debt position of its own that siphoned away large percentages of GDP for debt service made it clear that the U.S. would have to take a more realistic view of its own economic strengths and limitations. Furthermore, as was shown earlier, the seemingly permanent imbalances in the structure of the federal budget, the inability to control either entitlement or mandated spending,[35] and the difficulty in stimulating economic growth have combined to dash the dream of perpetual American economic dominance. The future consequences are far from dismal provided the gap between American expectations over ever-increasing standards of living and the reality of likely long-term economic performance can be spanned.

Concurrently, the notion of U.S. technological superiority has been displaced as U.S. advantages have been narrowed or overtaken. As microelectronic technology has diffused worldwide and as the revolution in information technology has created and opened vast new markets, the U.S. is one of many competitors in these areas and not necessarily the leader. For the foreseeable future, however, the U.S. is likely to remain dominant in one sector—military technology.

The end of the USSR has removed the only power with the military resources and capacity to challenge the U.S. Although our NATO allies and Japan could match the U.S. on a selective or single military system basis, without the appropriate stimulus, there is no reason why any one state would seek to overtake the U.S. across the full spectrum of military technology. In all areas, from nuclear weapons to system integration, the U.S. has huge and probably near-permanent advantages. Indeed, one ability in particular is unmatched—the ability to integrate multidimensional and enormously advanced systems with sensors tens of thousands of miles in space

---

[35] Mandated spending refers to federal legislation that directs states and local authorities to pay for enacted programs without any funds from the Federal Government.

and linked to fixed and mobile earth-based surveillance platforms and targeting networks each, in turn, capable of directing precision-guided weapons through command, control, communications, computers, and intelligence (C^4I) technology from stealth aircraft to highly accurate cruise missiles and large numbers of tactical aircraft. Thus, even as America's relative economic position *vis a vis* other states declines, in the area of military technology, the rate of closure is vastly lower, if it indeed is closing.[36]

The final assumption on which U.S. strategy has been built was the perception of the superiority of democracy and capitalism over all rivals. On one hand, the evaporation of authoritarianism and communism as available and serious potential alternatives would prove the correctness of that assumption. On the other hand, the lack of relevance of liberal democracy to many or most of the world's states suggests that attempts to overlay the U.S. model will not work. Capitalism has defeated Soviet communism or, more precisely, outlasted it. Arrogance on America's part would not seem well-advised. Whether capitalism and democracy can really work in Somalia, Panama, or Iraq, for example, is another matter.

Given the demise or erosion in relevance of these Cold War assumptions, it is no surprise that planning assumptions for defense have also changed. While warning time, mobilization, and enemy orders of battle have been used in evaluating requirements for the MRCs in the BUR, these criteria are only as plausible as the scenarios they represent. Hence, these planning factors are unlikely to prove as enduring as in the days of the Cold War when there was but one large threat.

Because the principal assumptions that have underlain U.S. security strategy have been overtaken by current reality or made obsolete by Soviet Russia's demise, what foundations should form

---

[36] Futurists raise a caveat here. The long-term impact of "nanotechnology," which is based on the speed of information technology and the manipulation of subatomic particles to build complete structures and even systems, could, someday, conceivably produce a rival to the U.S. While this may seem like science fiction and not reality, it cannot be entirely dismissed.

the basis for future U.S. security? Or, given the uncertain and diaphanous nature of threats to U.S. security, can a specific strategy with specific objectives be fashioned that has enough credibility and plausibility to be taken seriously? If a specific strategy is unobtainable, can U.S. strategy be sustained on a broad, general basis? And, finally, does any of this strategic debate make a difference? As the sole superpower, engaged internationally by virtue of experience, tradition, economic or business, security, and humanitarian interests, is it reasonable to believe the United States could or would withdraw? If that is the case, then aside from a few generalities and basic objectives, does the United States really need a highly articulated or precise strategy? And, with or without a precise strategy, what level of military power will be needed and can be sustained?

As of 1994, the Clinton administration has chosen to defer the matter of developing an overarching, rigorous, and explicitly documented U.S. national security strategy and associated foreign policy. In a striking way, the similarities and continuities between the Bush and Clinton administrations are real and deep. U.S. strategy and policy towards the FSU, trade (GATT and NAFTA), Iraq, NATO, and China, among others, have remained remarkably consistent. And the DOD, under Mr. Clinton, aside from moderating explicit prohibition on permitting homosexuals to serve in uniform, has developed a plan that bears striking similarities to the "base force" advanced by Mr. Bush. The tendency of different governments in general and the executive branch in particular to maintain relatively consistent policies across administrations suggests the more likely case of how development of future strategy will play out.[37]

If there is no sweeping and real attempt to recast U.S. national security policy, other than through asserting that change has occurred, the United States is most likely to preserve the basic conceptual structure of the Cold War. This approach risks resisting or ignoring the many opportunities and alternatives created by the

---

[37] Restating the similarity of pronouncements and criticisms over U.S. engagement in Somalia or Haiti and the debate over Vietnam in the 1960s underscores this consistency and continuity within the branches of government.

end of the USSR, and, instead, replaces the specific threat of Soviet aggression with generalized worries about instability, regional conflict, proliferation, and terrorism. But, without a credible intellectual foundation for national defense, the chances are high that severe compression and contractions in military might are inevitable.

No matter what approach is taken in constructing a vital national security policy, the fundamental question that underlies the issue of strategic formulation is whether the United States can identify its major interests and objectives with sufficient precision, clarity, and plausibility to justify the strategy and budget that must follow. If that cannot be done, is there another means of determining what the public would support or tolerate in terms of general levels of military might on an instinctive or judgmental basis only? In other words, without sufficient threats or dangers to menace U.S. interests in a significant way, without specific reasons to show how force serves or advances U.S. objectives, or without explicit or implicit public support, any strategy risks being hollow or flawed.

We all know that, conceptually and practically, potential dangers to U.S. security mandate retaining substantial military force. However, in a different security context, that is why police forces and law-enforcement agencies are necessary as protective instruments. Yet, there is no "strategy" per se for police forces, and police chiefs need not wax eloquent on the need for a strategy. So, one answer to this strategic question is that, absent a specific threat or apparent danger to U.S. security, we need not get upset about lacking a carefully constructed strategy.

The obvious danger of a lack of strategic specificity is that it will not generate enough public support either to maintain the level of military capability that is likely to be needed or to provide enough political clout to administration officials to permit a sensible downsizing of military power to occur. Americans in general and Congress in particular have become so used to annual posture statements, elaborate testimony, and dependence upon a national security strategy statement that any recognition of the need to maintain forces just because it is sensible to do so will be lost in the public debate over defense spending. Yet, whatever strategy is produced is likely to fall short of the interests and objectives test just noted above.

WHAT NEXT?

A variety of strategies could be implemented, including ones that represent extreme change. One extreme case would be to abandon any overarching strategy or military rationale and simply allocate a certain percentage of GDP to defense. This approach would be the equivalent of having military power for an insurance or police-like role. Another extreme case would be for the U.S. to adopt a minimalist strategy in which we would largely demobilize, keep a small standing force, and perhaps pursue an aggressive R&D policy searching for new, leap-ahead systems that would provide us with permanent military advantage. Although selective aspects of these extremes are not entirely ignored in these discussions, there are only three realistic choices:

- Steady as you go (i.e., take no action)

- Fund the Bottom-Up Review force (i.e., free up the resources needed)

- Readjust and change.

"Steady as you go" maintains the objectives, strategy, and force structure set by the Bottom-Up Review. The requirements for winning two nearly simultaneous major regional contingencies and maintaining substantial military presence overseas remain the building blocks. However, the erosion in U.S. military capability that would be wrought by insufficient defense spending would be tolerated or accepted. The arguments supporting this choice are straightforward.

Even a force of 1.4 million active-duty personnel that was largely unready by today's standards would remain the most formidable military in the world. With dominant nuclear and advanced conventional weapons in place, the United States could still mobilize in time of crisis. Given a paucity of adversaries presenting mortal challenges to American interests, it would be a long time before a threat of that scale emerged. Hence, there would be a warning time.

The maintenance of constant objectives and strategy would be seen as reassuring to friends. The absolute decline in military power would be offset by a remaining capacity to use some level of force in a convincing manner. And, there would have to be a credible expression of commitment as well as action in responding to any new adversary in the future.

Defense spending would decline. Lesser resource demands by defense would relieve other pressures on the federal budget from competing domestic programs and from the need to redress the permanent annual deficit. The cumulative effects would, in theory, contribute to rebuilding and strengthening domestic capacity. Social as well as economic priorities and gains would fall into this category. Futhermore, since defense is viewed increasingly as a lesser important need, expenditure of political capital would be directed where the public wishes it—to domestic issues.

Little action would be required by the president or Congress. In the best of all worlds, the White House should recognize the military consequences of this choice and accept them. The argument that the international situation permits this focus on domestic issues may prove wrong in time, but it's a reflection of the attitude of most Americans.

"Fund the BUR force" means that both the construct and the resources to keep those forces at high levels of both numbers and readiness will be maintained. The resources necessary to this end could come from either more defense spending or through making major reforms that will free up an equivalent amount of money. The rationale for this choice is likewise clear.

Although there is no dramatic threat present, uncertainty persists. If the U.S. were to allow its military might to decay, there is no guarantee it would redress that condition when and if required by a future adversary. Furthermore, U.S. military power is seen as a stabilizing factor. Eroding this capacity could lead to an erosion in the structure underpinning international security.

Given a GDP in excess of $6 trillion, additional resources of even $50 billion a year for sustaining defense are economically affordable. Domestic programs will not be affected significantly, if at all, by a redirected expenditure of resources amounting to about eight-tenths of 1 percent of GDP. Hence, the domestic and economic arguments against this choice are based more on emotion than analysis. Whether reform could be imposed to gain this level of freed-up resources that would obviate more spending, however, is an unknown.

Finally, the U.S. can "Readjust and change." The arguments for choosing this approach rest on two propositions. First, the world has changed so significantly that the United States has the opportunity or responsibility to follow suit. Second, experience has shown that major imbalances between strategic and operational objectives and actual military capabilities tend to cause more instability than when there is better balance. Put another way, if the use of military force is to be effective when the time comes, the required capabilities must fit the strategic objectives of the exercise.

Before examining each of these choices further, it is useful to take a closer look at the components that make up the common defense. "Threat" has already been assessed, as have the economic and political aspects of the "budget" and the "strategy." This leaves force structure and its direct link with the budget, commitments and deployments, and, of course, infrastructure. From the many alternatives and options within each of these components, larger decisions relating to which of the broader choices to follow can be better informed.

Chapter Six: Force Structure and Budgets

Force structure means more than the design and organization of the forces, the basic building blocks from which they were derived, and the source or basis for generating this fighting power, such as tanks, ships, and aircraft. The qualitative and intrinsic values of morale, spirit, and tradition are inseparable yet difficult to measure. As John Paul Jones observed, "Men are more important than guns in the rating of a ship."

In the abstract, and independent of any strategic preference, the shape of future force structure encompasses a nearly unbounded universe. This universe contains countless combinations and permutations for force structure, considering the different variables and components that could bear legitimate scrutiny, such as:

- The Budget, i.e., different spending levels and how much or how little money goes to defense

- Different priorities regarding how forces are based on sea, air, land, and space

- Different weapon systems and constructs for organizing fighting power

- Different priorities between forward-deployed and home-based capability

- Different levels of readiness

- The degree of dependence on reconstitution, reserves, and mobilization

- Different emphasis on modernization

- Different rates of pursuit of advanced technology

- Different degrees of reliance on allies and other policy instruments, including international organizations.

Because none of these variables is all-exclusive or all-inclusive, another dimension or level of review is necessary that examines their interaction.

To narrow these boundaries that relate possible future U.S. force structure to national security policy and to the composition, organization, design, and capabilities of that structure, addressing (if not fully answering) three sets of questions is vital:[38]

- What forces are needed strategically and operationally; how does that structure incorporate the many independent and dependent variables of choice; and what are the assumptions and criteria underwriting each choice?

- What level of capability and what types of force structure are politically and economically sustainable and justifiable in this era of strategic uncertainty?

- How do we safely, sensibly, and affordably get from today's force structure and capability to that of tomorrow and properly balance the threat strategy, force structure, budget, and infrastructure relationships?

To determine where we might or should be headed in the future, it is generally useful to appreciate where we have been regarding force structure. In this case, the term force structure not only must include the fighting forces but also must be linked with and balanced against the logistical, supporting, and industrial infrastructure that produces and sustains the goods and services needed for defense.

---

[38] No one has put this issue better than Dr. William W. Kaufmann in his *Planning Conventional Forces 1950–80*, The Brookings Institution, Washington, DC, 1982, p. 24: "Do these difficulties mean that conventional force planning has been off on a wild goose chase for the last twenty years? It is all well and good to compare U.S., allied, and opposing tanks, antitank weapons, artillery pieces, helicopters, aircraft, and warships. But such comparisons are not a sufficient basis for force evaluation and planning or judgments about the military balance. *In fact, no one yet has devised a serious planning substitute for (a) the development and analysis for plausible but hypothetical campaigns in specific theaters, (b) the determination of the forces needed to bring about the desired military outcomes in those specific theaters, and (c) difficult judgments about the number of contingencies for which U.S. conventional forces should be prepared.* [Italics are mine.] What is more, when careful analyses are done and sober judgments are made, they strongly suggest that current conventional threats can be contained by conventional means at costs that are quite bearable to the United States and its allies."

There is a striking and highly relevant consistency pertaining to the "structure" and basic building blocks for military forces. Throughout history and despite the effects of technological, strategic, and operational revolution, the organization of military forces has remained remarkably consistent. And, over the past century, even the nature of the most important weapon systems has shared this consistency.

War and combat were restricted by science and gravity first to the dimensions and environments of land and sea and, in this century, to the atmosphere above. As a result, armies were fielded to wage war in the ground environment and, since Napoleon, have been traditionally organized around brigades, divisions, and corps or field armies. Navies fought on the seas and contiguous areas with key organizational units—the capital ship, battle group, and fleet. As air forces evolved, the medium of the air permitted access to the ground and sea environments as well as to strategic campaigns designed to destroy the will of the adversary and usually targeted against the homeland.

In part because of these obvious consequences of geography and physics, and in part because of the time and expense it took to field, train, and equip forces, changes in force structure had elemental bias toward evolutionary and not revolutionary alterations except when some profound external factor intervened. Thus, it comes as no surprise that the tank (and armored personnel carrier) and artillery for the Army, the capital ship for the Navy, and aircraft and helicopters for each of the services have been around for a long time and are likely to continue their roles, technology withstanding.

In the case of the United States, since the end of World War II and the highly traumatic implementation of the National Security Act of 1947, major or sudden change to U.S. force structure invariably took the form of numerical increases or decreases from the force levels then in being. Even given the impact of important technologies such as nuclear weapons and nuclear power, ballistic missiles, surveillance and detection from space, precision-guided munitions, and exponential advances in computational power, change tended to be incremental. There was never a serious *and* lasting attempt by either the White House or the Congress to overhaul or to revise the basic organization or design of U.S. force structure and the means to apply military force.

Nor was the divisive, bitter, and explosive debate over the "roles and missions" of the services reopened except on the margin after the shattering experiences of the late 1940s and early 1950s in which "unification" of the military establishment into a single Department of Defense, the creation and separation of the Department of the Air Force, and the internecine service warfare over air power and strategic bombing threatened to wreck the flesh and fiber of the forces.

Thus, despite the impact of nuclear weapons and associated delivery systems, the force structure under the Truman administration was simply a decimated version of the World War II design. Although Eisenhower's "new look" featured a "pentomic" (or penatomic) design for the Army and great emphasis on nuclear deterrence, that force was an evolutionary product bearing close resemblance in function and unit organization to the forces of 1945, even with the advances in weaponry and jet propulsion. Over the years, this consistency and continuity in U.S. force structure were maintained. The "roles and missions" endured the passage of time, and, as a partial result, more or less proportional and equitable division of resources among the services continued such that the Army, Navy, Air Force, and Marine Corps were never threatened by extinction or by complete absorption into a competing organization.

By the mid 1960s, force structure as viewed by each of the services became wedded to the demands of deterring and, if deterrence failed, prevailing in conflict against the Soviet Union. By the mid 1960s, the so-called "2-1/2 war" planning scenarios and the contingency of simultaneous conflict against the USSR and China and a "half war" elsewhere provided the basic yardstick for establishing and building or maintaining the force structure. Part of those measures included specific criteria that, depending on where the measure was set, held obvious consequences for force structure planning.

Each of the services responded to Title 10 requirements of the U.S. Code to conduct prompt and sustained combat operations within its warfare dimension. For example, in responding to the threat of Soviet and Warsaw Pact ground attack into Europe, the Army used warning time, that is, the amount of advanced alertment; mobilization time to reinforce, resupply Europe, and restart wartime production; the amount of prepositioned wartime materials and stocks to be on hand; and certain analytical models to evaluate force-on-force wargaming to permit identification of capabilities needed in Europe as the hooks or foundations on which plans for forces, logistics, reserves, support needs, and other contingencies rested and were related to the rationalization and justification of budget programs.

The Navy defined and built its force structure to deal with the demands of sea lane defense, sea control, and power projection ashore in the same type of war against the USSR. Depending upon the development of Soviet forces and the degree to which U.S. doctrine emphasized nuclear or conventional means, the Navy regulated emphasis on its wartime missions with conclusions for its particular budgetary programs. Indeed, the Navy force structure of 1994, for all its advances, bears striking resemblance to the design of the force in place in 1947. The Marine Corps planned on "forcible entry" through amphibious assaults *a la* World War II on the "flanks" of NATO and wherever else those capabilities were necessary.

The Air Force remained divided between its pursuit of strategic missions whether in nuclear war or in strategic bombing campaigns and its support for the Army on the ground through a mixture of air control or superiority, interdiction of the battlefield, and close air support.

In addition to using the scenario of war against the Soviet Union to drive military planning, the services also had to account for other tasks, including peacetime presence, forward deployment, and crisis response in which the USSR might or might not have been involved.

The transition during the Nixon administration to the "1-1/2 war" scenario that eliminated China as a military threat did not alter the earlier construct for defining force structure. Both the Carter and Reagan administrations maintained the same "1-1/2 war" scenario for identifying force structure, specifying that the "1/2 war" would be a Persian Gulf scenario, with the Soviets intervening to control access to oil. The Reagan administration expanded the "1 war" requirements and built up accordingly, including plans for a 600-ship Navy. But, in practice, the organization and design of "force structure" continued to be remarkably consistent over time, conforming with continuing reliance on tanks, artillery, capital ships, and aircraft as the basis for fighting power.

As noted, the Bottom-Up Review, while eliminating the Soviet threat, substituted the two major regional conflicts or contingencies as the basis for much of the planning for future forces. And, although the former USSR did not constitute the threat, ground and air campaigns were envisaged against Soviet-style adversaries (Iraq and North Korea). The Navy, because there is no real threat to controlling or commanding the seas, shifted to its new strategy of littoral warfare. Although in the Navy's case it can be argued that the end of the Soviet submarine threat translated into a dramatic reduction in antisubmarine warfare (ASW) capabilities—namely, reducing the U.S. submarine force by half or more and decommissioning a majority of ASW-only ships and patrol aircraft—the force structure is really only smaller and is still organized around capital ships, battle groups, and aircraft for projecting naval forces and power ashore.

A last point on this discussion of the evolutionary nature of changing force structure: analysis and modeling are helpful but are not authoritative. Paraphrasing Voltaire, "figures lie and liars figure." No model or analytical technique replaces good seasoned judgment. Analysis is indeed important, but is also limited in accuracy and predictability and should not be seen as a surrogate for decisions. Determination of any future force structure must recognize these limits. Finally, it is useful to summarize the basic assumptions and tools each administration used to produce the force structure of its time. Table 19 contains such a summary.

Table 19. Summary of assumptions and tools that each of six administrations used to produce its force structure

Administration		Comments
Truman	1945–1950	Small standing force of World War II design with emphasis and mobilization.
	1950–1952	Larger force to deal with the threat of Soviet aggression, mostly in Europe.
Eisenhower	1953–1960	The "new look" emphasized nuclear and thermonuclear weapons against the backdrop of massive retaliation; a "2-1/2 war" planning scenario was the general but unmeant guideline.
Kennedy/Johnson	1961–1968	Flexible response with both nuclear and conventional emphases. Greater use of analysis to support "2-1/2 war" planning scenario.
Nixon/Ford	1969–1976	Shift to the "1-1/2 war" planning scenario with increasing emphasis on "flexible targeting" for nuclear weapons.
Carter	1977–1980	As above, specifying the "1/2 war" as a Persian Gulf contingency.
Reagan/Bush	1981–1992	As above with the Reagan build-up to make more robust the "1 war" scenario against the USSR. In 1990, the base force was developed for regional contingencies.

To address the three sets of questions noted above that ultimately will provide the basis for any future force structure, the highly specific and often technical building blocks that cumulatively make up defense must be examined. These components, in fact, define the manner in which monies will be spent and priorities established to implement the broad planning implied by shorthand terms such as "2-1/2 war," "1-1/2 war," or "2 MRC" criteria. Because these specific components are so interactive, no attempt is made to rank their importance *vis a vis* the others:

- *Budget*—Clearly, the amount and rate of reduction or addition to defense spending will hold great influence over future force structure both in terms of the quantity or numbers and the quality or actual combat capability of the forces. Four long-term, stable levels for annual defense spending set this boundary: what it will take to fund the BUR force fully (about $270 billion); $250 billion, which is the current Clinton plan and represents the ceiling; $200 billion, which is a possible mid-term and sustainable long-term level; and $150 billion, which is the lowest level likely to be politically plausible and below which it is virtually impossible to see defense budgets drop this decade.

- *Near-term and long-term readiness*—The readiness of the forces to fight is a complicated matter that includes not only the level of preparedness of active-duty forces but the degree of reliance on reserve forces, on mobilization, or on reconstitution and how these factors are balanced. Additionally, the active-duty forces can be structured at different levels of readiness in which, for example, a "core force" is kept at a permanently high condition of readiness; a "tranche" at a lower condition requiring an arbitrary period of time x to be brought back to operational standards; and a third tranche requiring a time 2 or $3x$ to return to fully operational status. Supplies of spare parts and ammunition can be included as part of this category.

- *Manning*—As a corollary to readiness, manning can determine force structure through emphasis on active or reserve and mobilization forces and on whether to continue the all-volunteer force or to return to some form of draft and required military service. Also, manning can be a surrogate or short-hand for aggregate capability. In the various choices offered, three aggregate levels of manning will be examined: 1.4 million active duty, or the BUR; 1.0 million; and 750,000. This boundary of 750,000 to 1.4 million is likely to cover the future range of manning. Similar ranges for reserve forces are also offered.

- *Modernization and technical innovation*—The pace of and degree to which weapon systems are updated or replaced and the rate of reliance on technological innovation form another category that affects both the qualitative and quantitative aspects of force structure. On one extreme, policy could be to withhold modernization in favor of awaiting the technological breakthroughs that "leap ahead" and make current systems obsolete. The other extreme could be a policy for more rapid but incremental modernization.

- *Functional assignment and balance of forces*[39]—In the past, U.S. practice has generally been a proportional or equitable and balanced distribution of resources and capabilities among the services and naval, ground, air, and space-based forces. That balance can be continued. Or, priority can be placed on naval forces, with appropriate reductions in other capabilities to fit budget constraints, or on land-based or "garrison forces," with ground and air capabilities cutting other forces appropriately. Last, there is the reconstitution option that gives low priority to standing forces and emphasizes remobilization and reconstitution. A subset of this category is to reexamine and possibly redefine roles and missions.

---

[39] It is tempting to cast this category as redefining roles and missions, particularly as Congress has mandated a commission on this very issue. Because the roles and missions debate will focus principally on tactical aviation and its relationship to strike, air defense, and ground support and on the balance between the Army and Marine Corps, my organization is broader. However, roles and missions are included as a subset.

- *Basing and presence*—Force structure could be designed on the degree of priority given to home or overseas basing and to presence. Although this category could be a subset of functional balance, the geographic determination of where to station forces and in what numbers could be a means of choosing force structure beyond which types of forces would be preferred. The role of allies and alliances and reliance on both form a further subset for choice.

- *New missions*—Force structure could also be modified by pursuit of new missions that require reshaping of the force. Peacekeeping and peacemaking are two of the more widely debated roles for military forces. But as the domestic focus increases, missions that are more civil in nature to include policing-like functions, drug control, nation- and city-building, and education could be advanced as grounds for redefining force structure.[40]

- *New organization*—Force structure can be revised on the basis of changing the organization and assigned equipment down to the unit level. Because the aggregate capability of U.S. fighting power has increased considerably in both relative and absolute measures, the notion of reducing the size and equipment levels of military units bears review. For example, the Navy long held to the position that the carrier air wing should number about 80 to 90 aircraft. The new air wing will number about 50 to 55 aircraft. An Air Force fighter squadron (or wing) might be similarly reduced, as well as an Army tank or artillery battalion. In other words, to the degree quality counts, cannot quality be proportionally affected?[41]

---

[40] Although I am opposed to this approach and advise caution in adopting many of these "newer" roles, it would be a mistake to ignore these tasks.

[41] To be fair, the opposite view, namely, increasing equipment such as in a supercarrier with 300 to 400 aircraft, should be investigated. At the same time, reducing the size of troop strength in a division from today's 20,000 to what was seen in World War II as the optimum size of 12,000 to 14,000 should also be reviewed.

A final aspect of these force structure considerations deals with the pursuit of "flexibility" on the basis that, particularly in an era of strategic uncertainty, this flexibility allows coping with surprise and the unexpected. All things being equal (perhaps the exception rather than the rule), military commanders will invariably seek flexibility in capabilities as a high priority. The reason is clear— war and the outcome of battle are uncertain. Inherent flexibility enables forces to deal with the unforeseen even though the costs of obtaining flexibility do not usually come cheaply.

The aircraft carrier is among the best examples of how flexibility can apply to both changing strategic and operational applications as well as to the pressures that lead to evolutionary change. The destruction of "Battleship Row" at Pearl Harbor was the final and unexpected event to signal the carrier's ascendancy, even though the operational virtues of sea-based airpower were understood years earlier. But, from that day in December 1941, the aircraft carrier became the centerpiece of U.S. naval power and arguably remains more so today.

In the nearly fifty years since the war ended, U.S. strategy has evolved from variants of "massive retaliation" and the threat of nuclear strike, to "flexible response" with a balanced conventional and theater and strategic nuclear emphasis, to the "countervailing" and "horizontally escalating" notions of the 1980s in which imaginative uses of military force were meant to deny the Soviet Union certain wartime military and geographic advantages. In the strategy of "massive retaliation," the principal role of the aircraft carrier was to deliver nuclear retaliatory or "second" strikes against the USSR and its Warsaw Pact allies. As the doctrine of "flexible response" was established, the carrier resumed more traditional roles of sea control, protection of sea lanes, and conventional strike. Vietnam and Desert Storm were clear examples of using carriers in these more traditional roles and in this type of strategy.

In the late 1970s and throughout the early 1980s, the notion of "maritime superiority" became a driving phrase in naval strategy. Translated into English, this meant that the U.S. Navy would be required to defeat or neutralize Soviet maritime power even in Soviet homewaters. The term *homewaters* was crucial because it authorized the Navy to plan on conducting certain offensive wartime tasks that were central to designing its force structure.

First, the countervailing concept of threatening the Soviet ballistic missile submarine (SSBN) force was legitimized. This task demanded that U.S. forces, nuclear submarines (SSNs) in particular but aircraft carriers for defensive cover and support of submarine operations as well, would have to operate inside Soviet bastions against enemy SSBNs. Second, the aircraft carriers would have to be able to survive for days at a stretch under continued assault from powerful Soviet attacking forces operating near their homeland. Fortunately, the strategy was never put to the test, but the strategic and operational flexibility of aircraft carriers enabled these forces to fill many roles, a number of which were far different from when these hulls were first launched.

To the degree that an understanding of "strategic uncertainty" can be translated into the actual design of weapons, flexibility would seem an essential characteristic for shaping a substantial part of future U.S. military might to include both qualitative and quantitative criteria. But, as in the case of the aircraft carrier, the expense of obtaining flexibility is likely to lead to buying fewer numbers of more capable, expensive platforms and, if readiness remains a priority, of fielding fewer well-trained forces.

The method for deriving future force structure choices is clearcut. First, answers to the three broad questions are bounded by the fiscal and political realities. These constraints in turn bound the realistic and practical universe for choice.

Second, within these boundaries, a range of options and alternatives within each set of the eight components of force structure can be identified. Specific options and alternatives can be married up and matched across all eight components. Depending upon which priorities and preferences are set, the products can be combined into separate force structures.

Third, these separate force structures can be analyzed on a cost-benefit, risk-reward basis. Part of this analysis must include not only what missions or tasks can be successfully undertaken and at what costs, but also what missions must be forgone, diminished, or ranked as uncertain.

The strategic and operational rationale for force structure can be sensibly based on a combination of historical experience and the assumptions of the Bottom-Up Review. During the Cold War, the United States waged three "hot wars," all in concert with at least a few allies. In Korea in 1950, Vietnam during the late 1960s, and the Persian Gulf in 1991, the United States deployed about half a million active-duty personnel. With the demise of the USSR, it is logical and commonsensical to assume that any crises for the foreseeable future will be regional and that deployment of a half million or so troops seems an upper limit. The BUR specified two nearly simultaneous crises for planning purposes. For the moment, whether the U.S. could or could not "win" such a simultaneous requirement is a secondary issue. For example, depending upon the necessary military power to achieve the aims of the campaign, a second crisis could be tied to mobilization, the commitment of allies, and some form of Congressional action authorizing those steps. Hence, in this view, the criterion of half a million troops or less and some means, either direct or indirect, to deal with a second crisis offers a starting point for defining force structure.

The level of capability and force structure that is politically and economically sustainable and justifiable is principally a function of the level of defense spending the nation will pay either grudgingly or willingly given its other priorities. This amount is a political expression reflecting the general perception of external threat and the economic consequences of the budgetary and fiscal state of affairs of the nation. Even if large deficits persist indefinitely, the economics of GDP and the budget suggest that a certain level of annual defense spending will be sustainable. Common sense suggests the same logic applies to maintaining some military capability. The public understands that the nation needs substantial military forces. It also appreciates that defense spending has already been cut nearly in half from the Cold War level—one of the only federal programs to endure real spending reductions and not just limits to the rate of growth. For the moment, the Clinton administration assumes (as did the Bush administration) that the public will support defense spending at no more than the 4-percent range of GDP. This suggests that $150 billion to $250/270 billion (in 1994 dollars) per year in defense spending is an appropriately realistic and likely future boundary for defense, assuming no crisis intervenes.

A further measure of this spending boundary is derived from the implicit and inherent judgment of the public and Congress about how much military might is needed. Too low a level, as in the late 1970s, and the public will register its concern. Too high a level and the public will not support that amount of might, absent a crisis. Bush determined a base force of 1.6 million; Clinton selected a force of 1.4 million. Since 1990, a number of polls and public samplings have attempted to construct how little military might the nation would tolerate and what general level it would support. In line with the other criteria, these findings suggest and reinforce spending of $150 billion to $250 billion per year, or about 2.5 to 3.5 percent of GDP.[42] However, the choice of fully funding the BUR must also be considered as the upper boundary.

From this fiscal boundary of annual spending levels and, depending upon the force structure selected, as noted, an active-duty force structure of between 750,000 and 1.4 million personnel seems a plausible, affordable, and realistic range for further assessment.[43]

Against these fiscal and manning boundaries, alternative division of resources among sea-, land-, air-, and space-based forces and among the eight specific, technical components can be analyzed and set. Because several of the eight criteria can be used as further subsets of the broader force structure choices, to avoid a circularity in analysis, the most relevant start point is to set the "functional assignment and balance of forces." This can crudely be called the degree to which we choose between or balance garrison or land-based and maritime or sea-based forces.

There are four basic approaches to force structure. First is a continuation of the BUR force structure as prorated among the services, called the BUR force extended. The structure is predicated on responding to the MRCs, as is the current plan. Second is a "garrison force," largely land based in the United States and, selectively, overseas. These land-based forces, mostly Army and Air Force, would be deployed out of their garrisons in Europe, the Middle East, and elsewhere in times of crisis. A smaller Navy and

---

42 These measures were first documented in my book *In Harm's Way: American Seapower in the 21st Century* (Bartleby Press, 1991, p. 280).

43 Part III addresses the third question, regarding the safe and and sensible transition from today's force structure to that of tomorrow.

Marine Corps would be required and used in a supporting role as there would be minimum threats to sea lines of communication, and the prospect of large-scale amphibious assault would be replaced by friendly and secure land-based facilities into which to deploy land forces. Strike against the shore could be handled primarily by the Air Force and advanced precision weapons, with the Navy largely in a supporting role.

The fundamental shortcoming of the garrison force is inflexibility. Permanent land-based deployments to new or other regions would require an extensive and expensive infrastructure, certainly well above what is currently available in Europe, the Persian Gulf, and Korea. If emphasis on "heavy" land forces continued, combined with land bases likely to be exclusively within the United States, a "muscle-bound" garrison military dependent on these bases could easily result. For critics who wish to prevent future administrations from succumbing to the evils of misapplying military force, a "muscle-bound" garrison might make sense. However, if military power is to serve as a real policy tool, this type of inflexibility would probably not be in our interest. Hence, a posture that creates and exploits flexibility seems preferential.

The third approach is the maritime force with principal reliance on naval forces supported by land-based forces. The flexibility of maritime forces, their independence from many of the umbilical cords of shore basing, the likelihood that many or most crises will not occur in areas where substantial numbers of land forces are based or can be swiftly inserted, and the prospect that the uncertain future will not and should not require the U.S. to deploy much more than a full corps (100,000 personnel) constitute the principal arguments for this option.

The maritime force, while perhaps more logical and intuitively obvious given the changed circumstances of this era of strategic uncertainty, would require major changes within DOD in reallocating priorities. This could lead to a stifling interservice rivalry and pernicious results for the nation.

The fourth force structure is based on reconstitution. In this case, the U.S. would retain a smaller or even residual "base force" with limited capability but sufficient to deal with most crises on a consecutive or one-at-a-time basis. Larger or multiple crises would require mobilization. The arguments for this choice rest on the grounds that the likelihood of one or even two major future contingencies occurring is slim, there is likely to be sufficient warning time, and the savings that would accrue from defense would provide a larger amount of public good to the nation.

The reconstitution choice could be seen as an example of American retrenchment. Geostrategically and geopolitically, the consequences would tend to exacerbate uncertainty and possibly instability with the demise or decay of U.S. leadership.

An additional variant is noted although, for reasons that follow, is not recommended. Analysts have suggested that the U.S. posture a significant part of its forces for peacekeeping and related tasks. In other words, if a 2 MRC scenario were maintained, the second MRC could entail peacekeeping functions. Given the enormity of those tasks if Bosnia, Haiti, and Rwanda required U.S. forces, the total numbers of U.S. troops involved could reach into the hundreds of thousands.

Little discussion, thus far, has focused on nuclear force levels. The reason is straightforward. The United States has so many nuclear weapons and systems in place that the question is not one of numbers. The nuclear issue rests in maintaining a nuclear production facility for sustaining current and future systems and in dismantling large numbers of unnecessary systems. The subject is best handled as part of the industrial and technical base.

Within these boundaries of budget, numbers, and assignment and balance of mission and forces is the broader issue of readiness. There are three basic approaches to readiness. The first is to continue to keep high levels of readiness across most of the active-duty forces and, selectively depending upon mobilization assumptions, in reserve units. The notion underlying this policy is that high readiness throughout creates a more effective force. Operationally, forces are better trained and can be replaced or rotated with minimum negative effects. *Esprit de corps* and morale would be enhanced by the knowledge that there is only a first team. And, from experience, this has been an effective way to ensure the best operational return from the forces.

The major problem with maximizing readiness is that budget realities and constraints are likely to make this outcome the most difficult to achieve. Force levels are unlikely to be cut enough to pay for maximizing readiness, and an ever-tightening spiral of reductions exacerbating reductions could follow.

The second approach is a "staggered" readiness system in which forces are made selectively ready depending upon operational tasking. In this case, for example, a third of the forces would be close to fully ready. These forces would be both deployed and immediately deployable. A third or so would be at the 50- to 75-percent level requiring three to six months to be brought to full readiness. These forces would constitute an immediate strategic reserve. The last third would be at only low levels and require six to twelve months for rejuvenation. After twelve months, the reserves would be called on.

This concept of staggered readiness has a further variant. From within the active forces, a "core force" could be established. The definition for this force is the absolute minimum below which military leaders would not go in terms of having an operationally deployable and effective force. The remaining forces outside the "core" would be kept at whatever levels of readiness the budget would afford and therefore form the "fiscally flexible" part of the force that would absorb shortfalls in spending.

Staggered readiness, although highly rational, would require extraordinary planning and incentives to overcome the rigid system of high readiness imposed on the ethos and psyche of the forces.

Third is to adopt a reconstitution strategy that would pursue a "force-in-being" in which the overall readiness levels are kept fairly low with a few exceptions for emergency or rapid-reaction situations. A larger force and infrastructure could be maintained under this option. Reconstitution is feasible only if and when there is no sense of danger and the nation is prepared to accept fewer forces in favor of such a strategy.

Finally, "roles and missions" requires serious examination. The "roles and missions" issue has a long, highly controversial, provocative, and emotional history within the Department of Defense. In Congress, however, given the end of the Soviet threat, "roles and missions" provides both a sensible framework on which to assess the merits and demerits of a proposed defense budget and a bureaucratic means of attempting to impose control over the future direction of DOD. The areas within roles and missions that have usually evoked the greatest difficulty and debate have been strategic bombardment, tactical aviation, air defense, and the distinctions between the Army and the Marine Corps. A common criticism of Congress, notably echoed by Senate Armed Services Committee Chairman Sam Nunn, for example, is the charge that the U.S. really has four air forces—one each for the Army, Navy, Marine Corps, and, of course, the Air Force.

As General Colin Powell noted in his report to Congress on reviewing roles and missions in 1992, complementarity should be preserved and redundancy eliminated. In other words, if air defense over the battlefield is necessary, it makes little sense to change the uniforms of the personnel whose job it is to achieve that mission. If the fleet requires air defense at sea, what is the value of keeping that mission but assigning it to another service? At the time of this book's publication, Congress has directed the establishment of a roles-and-missions commission to offer recommendations for continuity and for change.

While restructuring roles and missions will have the most profound implications for force structure, that approach is not used here. First, the disciplines required in assessing force structure based on choices favoring garrison forces, maritime forces, and reconstitution forces and on budgets at $200 billion and $150 billion per year will resolve many of the possible redundancies that may exist in roles and missions but from a different perspective. Second, in my judgment, the roles-and-missions review is best served by close examination of the requirements of the battlefield and of crisis situations. If large or smaller sectors like air defense or forcible entry can be reduced or should be strengthened, those findings are relevant to determining what will be funded and what will not. As will be shown, this appears to be a more realistic means of implementing an effective and affordable force structure.

Taken together, the results of the earlier analyses show the range of possible force structures measured against funding, manning, readiness, and basing alternatives, as shown in table 20.

Against this table and the range and boundaries of choices and realities, the levels or rates of sustainability, modernization, forward deployment, and dependence on international organizations or alliances will be injected. This will provide a comprehensive and integrated set of options and alternatives that ultimately will form whatever future force structure results either by choice or default.

Table 20. The universe of future U.S. military might

I. BUR force fully funded at $270–280 billion per year (current dollars)

1.4 million active-duty force (approximate numbers)

• Army	450,000	15 divisions
• Navy	420,000	12 carriers, 340–350 ships
• Marine Corps	179,000	3 expeditionary forces
• Air Force	400,000	20 tactical fighter wings and up to 184 bombers

---

II. Alternative Choices and Budgets

Annual budget:	$150 billion		$200 billion		$250 billion	
Active forces:	0.75 million		1 million		1.2 million	
BUR force extended	• Army	225,000	• Army	310,000	• Army	370,000
(assumes	• Navy	220,000	• Navy	290,000	• Navy	350,000
maximum	• Marines	90,000	• Marines	130,000	• Marines	140,000
readiness)	• Air Force	215,000	• Air Force	270,000	• Air Force	340,000
Garrison force	• Army	280,000	• Army	400,000	• Army	450,000
(assumes	• Navy	180,000	• Navy	220,000	• Navy	250,000
maximum	• Marines	50,000	• Marines	80,000	• Marines	100,000
readiness)	• Air Force	240,000	• Air Force	300,000	• Air Force	400,000
Maritime force	• Army	180,000	• Army	220,000	• Army	290,000
(assumes	• Navy	280,000	• Navy	400,000	• Navy	450,000
maximum	• Marines	120,000	• Marines	150,000	• Marines	180,000
readiness)	• Air Force	170,000	• Air Force	230,000	• Air Force	280,000

- **Staggered readiness** For each of the spending levels, forces would be placed in one of three categories: fully ready; partial; and reserve. For example,

  Fully ready: 50% of the force

  Partial readiness: 25% of the force
  (i.e., 3–6 months to bring to full readiness)

  Reserve readiness: 25% of the force
  (i.e., more than 6 months to bring to full readiness)

  or some combination of the above

- **Reconstitution** Since the bulk of the force structure would be dependent upon reconstitution, no attempt is made to show a quantitative assignment of forces to any categories either by service or degree of readiness.

Several initial conclusions flow from the above and the interaction between and among these defense components. First, perhaps the most vital is identifying what each force structure can reasonably expect to achieve operationally and what it cannot. Indeed, in this decision-making process of defining a future force, it is strategically wisest to focus first on determining both the ability and inability to conduct tasks. From that consideration, one can work back to the appropriate force structure.

Second, in all cases of the garrison and maritime forces, assuming the "core force" concept applies, there would be sufficient capability to respond to a single Desert Storm, MRC type of action. Depending upon the magnitude of a second contingency and the degree of simultaneity required, the maritime force at *all* budget levels provides more capability, with one exception: if the garrison force has stationed forces in large numbers where the second contingency occurred, the outcome is about the same.

Third, the differences among these four force options are clear. The BUR force extended makes the most sense if the assumption is to preserve the traditional balance and distribution of resources among the services. The garrison force makes greatest sense if the guess is correct and forces are predeployed to the regions of crisis. The maritime force fits the era of strategic uncertainty best when flexibility in responding to crises is paramount. The reconstitution force fits best when warning or lead time is great and when the nation is prepared to respond over the long term.

Finally, these force structures must be matched, mixed, and compared against the other ingredients that make up the threat, strategy, force structure, budget, and infrastructure balance.

CHAPTER SEVEN: COMMITMENTS, DEPLOYMENTS, AND PRESENCE

Commitments are the obligations of any state, tacit or otherwise, to make good on protecting, demonstrating, or advancing its interests. Interests are usually defined by need, tradition, declared doctrine, law, and treaty, and broadly encompass matters of national security and foreign policy. Deployments are the physical means of sending or stationing forces abroad either on a permanent or part-time basis as required by commitments or the broader national interest. Presence is the principal military mechanism for demonstrating, underwriting, and symbolizing these commitments. While requiring the physical deployment or stationing of forces "overseas," the success or failure of presence generally depends on perceptual and even metaphysical measures of how well or badly political and military influence are exerted or neutralized.

During the Cold War, the commitments of and by the United States were defined by the broad concepts and accompanying collective security arrangements designed to deter and contain the threat and spread of communism. Technically and legally, these security alliances and the establishing treaties could not bypass Congress and automatically commit the United States to war in the event of direct Soviet or communist military attack. A formal and legal declaration of war by the U.S. Congress was still required. However, the American commitment symbolized by the presence of U.S. forward-based and deployed military forces was a compelling guarantee and assurance that more than compensated for any lack of automaticity in going to war.[44] The challenge and dilemma for policy, then and now, continues to rest in converting commitments into credible and appropriate physical guarantees and terms that can be expressed in the currency of military force.

There never has been and never will be any formula to convert these commitments and obligations into absolute guarantees or precise numbers of troops or military capabilities. The process for making this conversion is therefore inexact, normally arcane, and often circular as interests, commitments, and force requirements

---

[44] Given what happened in August 1914 when a series of secret treaties automatically made war inevitable through guaranteed declarations to fight, this was not a bad arrangement.

become interchangeable and, more frequently, drive each other, sometimes in conflicting directions. The absence of a major threat or any single basis for establishing national security needs is the greatest limitation to using interests and commitments as yardsticks for defining appropriate levels of necessary military force.

In the United States, the responsibility for converting many of these commitments into specific requirements for forces, force structure, and overseas deployments and presence begins with the major military commanders in the field. These commanders in chief must estimate their wartime needs—today measured against abstract or nominal threats rather than the more formidable and concrete Soviet order of battle—and set peacetime requirements to deal with routine and contingency operations, all against the background of what the political realities in Washington might accept or reject. These operational requirements are passed through the Joint Chiefs of Staff, the Chairman, and Secretary of Defense and coordinated with the other pertinent departments, including State, Justice, and the intelligence community. The White House may formally interject itself to change or set particular needs, such as ordering more naval ships into the Indian Ocean after the Tehran embassy had been seized in 1979. Normally, however, the Defense Department determines the forces needed to meet the commitments. In any event, the annual defense budget becomes the ultimate and *de facto* approval mechanism for the commitments by funding or not funding the level of forces for carrying out these operational responsibilities.

It is useful to note in snapshot form how U.S. commitments, deployments, and presence have varied over the years. Between July 1, 1948, and June 30, 1949, about 252,000 Army personnel were stationed overseas and about 400,000 were stationed in the U.S. (tables 21 and 22). Twenty years later, and obviously affected by the war in Vietnam, U.S. military overseas presence and deployments were as shown in table 23.[45] Table 24 shows deployments and overseas presence during the past decade.[46]

---

[45] SecDef Annual Report 1968, p. 514.
[46] SecDef Annual Report 1949, p. 142. Naval forces were also forward deployed at about the same ratio.

Table 21. A comparison of major tactical units of the Army as of July 1, 1948, and June 30, 1949[a]

July 1, 1948	June 30, 1949
10 divisions (7 overseas)	10 divisions (5 overseas)
3 infantry regimental combat teams (2 overseas)	5 infantry regimental combat teams (3 overseas)
5 infantry regiments (all overseas)	2 infantry regiments (both overseas)
1 armored cavalry group (in U.S.)	4 armored cavalry regiments (3 overseas)
1 engineer special brigade (in U.S.)	1 engineer special brigade (in U.S.)
13 antiaircraft battalions (11 overseas)	43 antiaircraft battalions (14 overseas)
United States constabulary (in Germany, Austria)	United States constabulary (in Germany, Austria)

[a] No formal alliance outside the western hemisphere and the Rio Pact was in place, and presence was largely through the occupation of the defeated enemies during the process of democratization. The most important major changes were the build-up of the General Reserve, the movement of troops within and from the Far East command, the reorganization of the constabulary, and the designation of United States Forces, Austria, as a separate command.

Table 22. A comparison of major tactical units located in the continental United States as of July 1, 1948, and June 30, 1949

July 1, 1948	June 30, 1949
82d Airborne Division	82d Airborne Division
2d Infantry Division	11th Airborne Division
2d Armored Division (1 combat command only)	(less 1 regiment)
7th Infantry Regimental Combat Team	2d Infantry Division
3d Cavalry Group	3d Infantry Division
2d Engineer Special Brigade	2d Armored Division
2 antiaircraft battalions	14th Infantry Regimental Combat Team
	3d Armored Cavalry Regiment

Table 23. A comparison of military personnel—June 30, 1967, and June 30, 1968 (percentages listed in parentheses)

	Department of Defense	Army	Navy	Marine Corps	Air Force
Shore activities:[a]					
June 30, 1967	3,027,902 (89.7)	1,442,498 (100.0)	410,505 (54.6)	277,405 (97.2)	897,494 (100.0)
June 30, 1968	3,277,018 (91.0)	1,570,343 (100.0)	452,108 (59.1)	299,717 (97.5)	904,850 (100.0)
Continental U.S.:					
June 30, 1967	1,868,339 (55.3)	766,414 (53.1)	317,689 (42.6)	170,144 (59.6)	614,092 (68.4)
June 30, 1968	2,029,079 (57.2)	890,546 (56.7)	345,562 (45.2)	193,622 (63.0)	599,349 (66.2)
Outside continental U.S.:					
June 30, 1967	1,159,563 (34.4)	676,084 (46.9)	92,816 (12.3)	107,261 (37.6)	283,402 (31.6)
June 30, 1968	1,197,939 (33.8)	679,797 (43.3)	106,546 (13.9)	106,095 (34.5)	305,501 (33.8)
Afloat and mobile activities:					
June 30, 1967	348,978 (10.3)	—	341,114 (45.4)	7,864 (2.8)	—
June 30, 1968	320,884 (9.0)	—	313,349 (40.9)	7,535 (2.4)	—
Total:					
June 30, 1967	3,376,880 (100.0)	1,442,498 (100.0)	751,619 (100.0)	285,269 (100.0)	897,494 (100.0)
June 30, 1968	3,547,902 (100.0)	1,570,343 (100.0)	765,457 (100.0)	307,252 (100.0)	904,850 (100.0)

[a] Includes Navy activities temporarily based ashore.

Table 24. U.S. military personnel in foreign areas—FY 1981 to FY 1992 (in thousands)

	81	82	83	84	85	86	87	88	89	90	91	92[a]
Germany	248	256	254	254	247	250	251	249	249	228	203	168
Other Europe	64	67	70	73	75	75	73	74	71	64	62	58
Europe, afloat	25	33	18	25	36	33	31	33	21	18	20	17
South Korea	38	39	39	41	42	43	45	46	44	41	40	39
Japan	46	51	49	46	47	48	50	50	50	47	45	47
Other Pacific	16	15	15	16	16	17	18	17	16	15	9	8
Pacific, afloat (including Southeast Asia)	25	33	34	18	20	20	17	28	25	16	11	16
Latin America/ Caribbean	12	11	14	13	12	13	13	15	21	20	19	20
Miscellaneous	27	23	27	25	20	26	27	29	13	160[b]	39	20
Total[c]	502	528	520	511	515	525	524	541	510	609	448	393

[a] As of March 31, 1992.
[b] Includes 118,000 shore-based and 39,000 afloat in support of Desert Storm.
[c] Numbers may not add to totals due to rounding.

In general, these deployments, certainly since the late 1950s, reflected U.S. commitments to deal globally with the USSR and Chinese threats and conformed with the alliance arrangements shown in figure 10.[47] This chart dates back to 1959. Although the ANZUS Pact and the treaty with the Republic of China are no longer in force, U.S. commitments have conformed with and continue to conform with this structure of the Cold War.

Figure 10. United States collective security arrangements

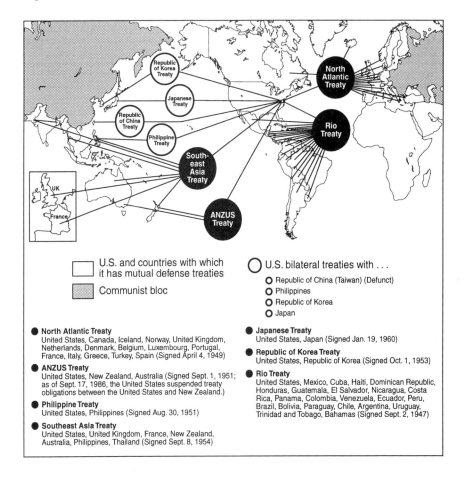

Figures 11 and 12 and table 25 show the number and location of major overseas U.S. bases since World War II and serve as an approximation of the quantitative extent of U.S. commitments,

----

[47] SecDef Annual Report 1959, p. 80.

deployments, and military presence over those years.[48] The last charts in this series (figures 13 and 14) show the location of major U.S. units that follow from the BUR.

Figure 11. Base site establishment dates: Europe

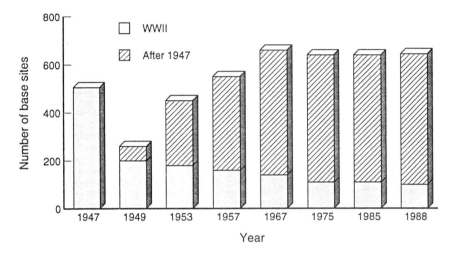

Figure 12. Base site establishment dates: Asia/Pacific

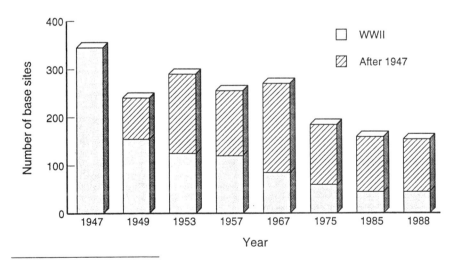

[48] James R. Blaker, *United States Overseas Basing*, Praeger, New York, 1970, pp. 40 and 41.

Table 25. DOD defense military installations and properties used by U.S. forces in foreign areas, September 1991

	Army	Navy	Air Force	Marines	Total
Australia	0	1	1	0	2
Belgium	1	0	0	0	1
Bermuda	0	1	0	0	1
Canada	0	1	0	0	1
Cuba	0	1	0	0	1
Diego Garcia	0	1	0	0	1
Germany, Federal Republic of	15	0	8	0	23
Greece	0	0	1	0	1
Greenland	0	0	1	0	1
Iceland	0	1	0	0	1
Italy	2	2	2	0	6
Japan	2	6	3	3	14
Korea, Republic of	4	0	2	0	6
Netherlands	1	0	1	0	2
Panama	1	2	1	0	4
Philippines	0	3	0	0	3
Portugal	0	0	1	0	1
Spain	0	1	1	0	2
Turkey	2	0	4	0	6
United Kingdom	1	3	10	0	14
Total	29	23	36	3	91

Figure 13. Location of major Navy and Marine Corps units (as of Oct. 1, 1992)

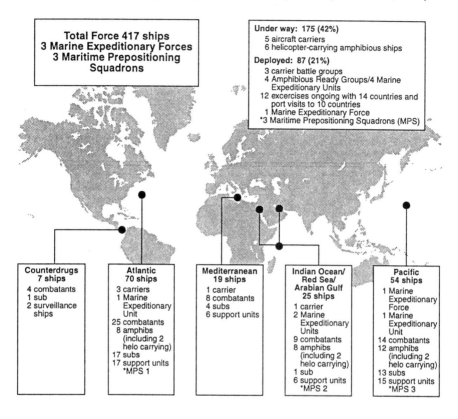

Figure 14. Deployment of U.S. divisions (as of January 1, 1993)

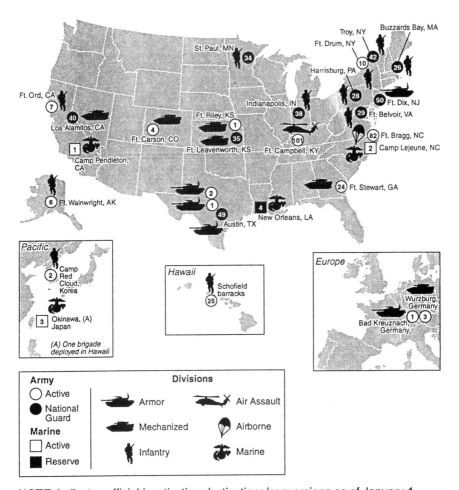

NOTE: Indicates official inactivations/activations/conversions as of January 1, 1993.

One consequence of the current regime of commitments and the resulting operational requirements for deployments and presence is the enormous demand on the forces to fill these requirements. Even though the USSR is gone, the "operations tempo"—that is, the time units are deployed or are on active service away from home bases—is about as high as any time during the Cold

War outside of specific crises. This pace of operations can have debilitating effects of the first order on morale, retention, and "hollowness" as personnel are frustrated, bored, or worn down by spending so much time away from home without the obvious reason as to why such demands are vital to defending the country. Hence, the current high tempo of U.S. operating forces is a symptom of a progression to a future condition of "in irons." Using the Navy as an example, and recognizing that the size of the Navy is shrinking, the days under way per quarter (120 days) over the past 20 years are an indication of these operational demands (table 26).

Table 26. OPTEMPO history by fleet (days under way per quarter)

FY	2nd (East Coast)	3rd (West Coast)	6th (Mediterranean)	7th (Pacific)
75	26.0	27.0	40.0	45.0
76	26.0	24.0	44.0	45.0
77	28.0	27.0	45.0	45.0
78	31.1	27.0	47.8	45.0
79	28.5	27.0	47.8	48.3
80	30.2	27.6	57.1	55.8
81	31.0	25.9	61.0	53.9
82	31.0	27.0	61.1	54.1
83	28.8	25.2	59.9	51.0
84	30.7	25.2	67.4	52.6
85	29.7	25.1	52.9	54.2
86	26.1	27.6	50.6	50.4
87	28.1	25.9	52.8	53.5
88	28.6	24.4	51.8	54.7
89	28.7	27.5	53.8	53.4
90	29.1	27.2	55.1	53.3
91	30.4	27.3	58.7	54.9
92	28.7	30.1	51.2	55.8

Fundamental questions and issues must be addressed in defining future requirements for U.S. commitments, deployments, and presence. Strategic uncertainty and the end of the USSR have circumvented the sharpness and clarity of earlier rationale for establishing the criteria for the numbers and location of U.S. forward-based forces. Without a threat as powerful and obvious as the FSU, new security frameworks embraced by such slogans as the "new world order" and the "dangers" of regional instability have thus far proven hollow in advancing a politically acceptable rationale for national security. The reasons for this disconnect between strategic rationale and policy action extend beyond the absence of a single, plausible threat.

First, the rationale for national security and accompanying military needs built on only an implicit (or commonsensical) basis will simply not be either credible or acceptable unless there is adequate public support and consensus for those conclusions. The public and Congress intuitively question the need to maintain what appears to be a largely Cold War posture now that the Cold War is history. Indeed, even within the two most recent U.S. administrations, many have voiced concern over the level of U.S. commitments, deployments, and presence. And, as events in Bosnia, Somalia, and Haiti have underscored, U.S. military presence in those regions is unpopular both here and there and is not flush with stories of success.

Second, geostrategy and power politics mattered in the Cold War. Because of the breadth of the Soviet threat and its vast military capability, U.S. geostrategic responses could not ignore Russian and Warsaw Pact numbers. The size of any response counted, and the U.S. reckoned that commitments, deployments, and presence had to be both large enough and seen as such by allies and adversaries alike to be credible deterrents to Soviet ambitions. Rarely, as in the British experience of the 19th century, would a single gunboat suffice when, perhaps months after a misdeed, the full force of the fleet could be brought to bear on a miscreant. Furthermore, the realities of geography that placed Russia astride Europe and Asia and made America distant from its allies shaped the nature of U.S. commitments, deployments, and presence. Thus, many Americans were stationed and deployed overseas during the Cold War. But those days are over.

Third, in the post-Cold War world, there is neither the popular consensus yet for defining specific commitments, deployments, and presence nor political agreement on how much or how little military capability is necessary and credible to underwrite a future regime for U.S. military overseas activities. Continuation of the Cold War order and security structure but with fewer U.S. forces appears to be the policy. Thus, NATO has been "redefined and refocused," and U.S. military forces stationed in NATO countries cut from 300,000 or 400,000 during the Cold War to 100,000 or less. Whether that level is politically and strategically sustainable and what U.S. commitments and force levels are needed in other regions remain open questions. The relevance of military force in resolving inherently non-military or immediately unsolvable problems further confuses the attempt to define U.S. commitments, deployments, and presence in a politically or strategically satisfactory manner.

During the Cold War, the U.S. commitment to protect and defend friends and allies ultimately meant war if direct Soviet aggression or attack took place. Today, where is a U.S. commitment leading to war likely to occur? To be sure, a rejuvenated Russian military threat could return NATO to its earlier *raison d'etre*. And an attack by North Korea into the South most certainly would involve the United States in that conflict. However, the ultimate commitment by the U.S. to a real war as opposed to a military intervention seems to be decidedly less relevant or likely in a world without a Soviet threat. The question of whether the U.S. might or might not go to war to prevent or contain nuclear proliferation is perhaps the single caveat, and North Korea could prove to be the test case.

Deployments, of course, conform to national commitments. Permanent deployment of ground and air forces (even though troops are rotated in and out) and robust deployment of mobile forces—usually maritime, but, as in the case of the annual NATO reinforcement exercise "Reforger" and the "Bright Star" exercises in the Middle East, sometimes including ground and air forces—were givens during the Cold War. Commitments set the general requirements for war and peace and were manifested through these permanent and rotational deployments culminating in presence. This physical presence was meant to demonstrate and symbolize intent and interest while possibly exerting or denying political influence. Indeed, the Clinton administration has explicitly set "presence" as one of the major requirements to be met by U.S. forces.

The ideas behind military presence are not obscure. Physical presence is meant to be reassuring to friends and, up to a point, frightening to adversaries. The symbolism of presence and whatever advantages accrue from having forward-deployed forces ready and available for the unforeseen remain central supporting components of this argument. With forces present on station, in general terms, a quick-reaction response to problems either in or near the region is available. And military force has often been used by the United States in many so-called post-war "crises" or instances where U.S. forces had been pre-deployed. However, despite these advantages, the costs of maintaining forward presence are not small. Among these costs are the domestic political considerations of convincing a majority of Americans that overseas presence is as good a use or an even better use of dollars that could be spent at home.

The Clinton administration has explained that U.S. foreign policy is one of "engagement" and that it is based on extending "partnership" arrangements to new and old friends, particularly in the FSU. What these terms will mean in practice is uncertain. Current U.S. foreign policy remains largely an extension and continuation of the Bush foreign and security policy that, despite the "base force" and "bottom-up" reviews, still retains much of the structure of the Cold War.

Commitments, deployments, and presence must be regulated by the larger strategy and strategic choices and, obviously, by the resources and force structure that are provided for and are available to the nation's defense. It is demonstrably unwise to maintain an extensive set of commitments unrelated to strategy and unconnected to the forces necessary to honor those commitments. On the other hand, too much silence on the issue of commitments, even with overwhelming force available, does not always lead to good policy.[49] Because it is entirely unlikely and impractical for the United States to retreat into a "fortress America," U.S. commitments and capabilities must rest on careful and purposeful balance of interests, strategic objectives, and available resources.

The three broad choices posited earlier are useful departure points for defining future requirements for commitments, deployments, and

---

[49] It can be argued that Secretary of State Dean Acheson's public statement in January 1950, which did not specifically mention Korea within the U.S. security shield, provided the wrong message and signal to the North Korean government in its deliberation of whether to attack South Korea.

military presence. "Steady as you go" and "Fully fund the force" will demand a future security structure and deployment pattern with emphasis on Europe, the Middle East and Persian Gulf, and the Pacific. At this stage, it is too soon to know whether and how NATO membership will be extended east, thereby extending U.S. commitments. Also, the Clinton administration does not seem particularly anxious to reduce overall U.S. commitments, and, under the UN mantle, there may be more rather than fewer U.S. military personnel involved, particularly if thousands of U.S. troops are required as part of a peace settlement in Bosnia. However, meeting these commitments under the funding shortfalls that will occur either will be impossible or will impose fundamental changes elsewhere.

The "Readjust and change" choice could lead to a wholesale reexamination of U.S. commitments, deployments, and military presence. One possible extreme is for the U.S. to assume a "minimalist" posture. In this regard, the United States would retain its bilateral and multilateral treaty arrangements, but, in the post-Cold War world, it would reduce the overseas bases and forces it maintains on deployed status. In Europe, a minimalist posture would mean the United States could reduce its forces in NATO to a symbolic and "trip-wire" level measured in the tens of thousands. So too, large-scale presence in Japan and Okinawa would be reduced. Korea could be the subject of negotiations with the North in order to link substantial U.S. military withdrawal with assurances for stability and perhaps even more urgent movement towards unification or denuclearization.

A second possibility in making change is for the United States to pursue a selective posture for its commitments and deployments. In this case, unlike the minimalist posture that leads to reductions everywhere, selectivity would be used to emphasize the most important and vital U.S. interests. If the Pacific region were viewed as increasing in priority, NATO forces could be reduced to maintain what is presently in place or required in Asia. A Eurocentric vision would reverse that priority. Should the U.S. see its interests increasing in South America, the Middle East, or under UN mandates, downsizing other commitments would follow to support those of higher priority.

Finally, a changed strategy could still call for an aggressive posture of "active engagement." In this regard, U.S. commitments could expand to include a NATO with North Atlantic Cooperative Council members and peacekeeping tasks in Bosnia or in the Middle East as part of the Israeli-PLO peace agreement, and the U.S. would expand overseas deployments and presence even at the expense of downsizing forces based at home. The logistics of supporting and maintaining a policy of "active engagement" would mandate the restructuring and redesign of forces as well as changing the stationing policies if a larger percentage of U.S. forces were to be sent abroad. The rotation base, that is, the personnel for relieving deployed with non-deployed forces, would be reduced, thereby lengthening service abroad. The members of Congress would have to be convinced to support expanded overseas presence while decreasing U.S. basing and spending at home.

If a policy of default occurs and fully funding the BUR force proves impossible, the U.S. faces an inevitable reduction in its military might. In this case, the questions that must be addressed deal with balancing future commitments, deployments, and military presence with fewer forces and forces perhaps deployed differently. This leads to three possibilities:

- Downsize commitments, deployments, and military presence to fit the resources

- Downsize the forces, leaving gaps with the current requirements

- Innovate or change.

In the first possibility, both the operational requirements for and the commitments themselves would be downsized to fit the forces. At the end of the day, this means that fewer U.S. military personnel will be stationed abroad on a routine or permanent basis.

The second possibility is to cut the forces and leave the current commitments, deployments, and presence requirements in place, depending on mobilization or reconstitution to fill these gaps. However, a series of unchanged requirements reflects permanent objectives and, therefore, offers plausibility and assurance as the size of the response is tailored to meet a smaller or larger threat.

Third, perhaps the most interesting and most difficult possibility is that of innovation or change and, of course, is applicable to each of the three broader choices. Innovation can cover parts of the minimalist, selective, or active engagement postures noted. Among the prospects for innovation are alterations in how we consider the nature and modality of deployments and presence (i.e., whether they are permanent, part-time, or flexible); the means (i.e., the types of land, sea, or air forces to be used); and new regional frameworks and structures for building military cooperation in training, exercising, communicating, and perhaps peacekeeping or crisis-management tasks. With the exceptions of future peacekeeping missions perhaps in concert with the Israeli-PLO peace arrangement, Haiti, and Bosnia, it is unlikely that new, permanent commitments for future deployment and presence requirements will be needed. Hence, part-time or flexible grounds for innovation appear the most fertile.

For example, the Sixth Fleet in the Mediterranean and the Seventh Fleet in the western Pacific could be operated and organized around a series of staggered or flexible deployments that are variable both in duration and in the composition of the deployed units. This notion of flexible deployments is not new. Alternating or rotating the deployment of sea, land, and air forces is another possibility.

Suppose a carrier battle group or naval units had been deployed to region A for duration Y. In turn, they could be replaced for a period of time by a squadron or wing of aircraft operating from appropriate facilities and supported by a company or battalion of land forces. In this case, the type of force deployed may be less important than the fact that some form of military force is being used. If the "threat," for example, is seen largely as that of a ballistic missile, assignment of a defensive counter like Patriot might provide an appropriate sign of commitment and presence. The logistics and difficulties in implementing this type of flexible option cannot be ignored, but are not grounds for discarding the concept either.

Regional frameworks and structures also provide opportunities for innovation. For example, in NATO, the successful standing naval forces squadrons for the Atlantic and on-call for the Mediterranean could be replicated within the various NATO regions. These standing forces could, in essence, be no more than permanent staff and unit organizations into which actual forces could be rotated. Presence would be maintained through assignment of personnel to these staffs and the actual, though less frequent, rotation of sizable forces. The key will be in reducing the size of all NATO staffs first and then introducing additional tasks.

In the Pacific or elsewhere, bilateral or multilateral training staffs could be created for the same purpose. On a regularized and more frequent basis, forces could be deployed or rotated through these regions principally for training but also as nascent peace-keeping forces in which military cooperation and attendant communications would be precursors for actual use or for creation of a more formal regional structure. The types of forces to be used in this training or exercise structure are far less important than the existence of these structures.

The modalities of alternating or rotating deployed and presence forces must finally rest on an examination of what presence can and cannot actually achieve and what presence is meant to achieve. For years, particularly in naval circles, presence has had a semi-mysterious quality that has been viewed as inherently and inarguably useful. In 1970, for example, presence was elevated by then head of the Navy Admiral E. R. (Bud) Zumwalt to equal status with the Navy's other three primary missions—deterrence, sea control, and power projection. And, in 1993, reinforcing these views on presence, the Bottom-Up Review defined the need for forces for the presence roles above those required to conduct two MRCs.

In an era of strategic uncertainty, the qualities of presence may or may not prove to be national advantages. Presence provides on-scene forces, access to regions of crisis, basic familiarity with these regions, certain perhaps preconceived expectations on the part of U.S. decision-makers, and attitudes or reactions of states in the region to this presence that may or may not exaggerate the role the U.S. would assume in crisis. Surely, access and regional familiarity are usually positive factors. However, the presence of on-scene forces may still be insufficient for military purposes in time of crisis and could lead to or provoke a military failure; presence may require or precipitate a political response simply by virtue of forces being there when a response may not be necessary; presence may generate expectations of usefulness in the minds of political leaders beyond what is possible; and presence may provoke as well as reassure local states.

There is no formula to prove or guarantee the utility or risk of presence in advance, but representative instances of presence and crises suggest the range of what might be expected in the future regarding utility and risk. In January 1968, North Korea hijacked USS *Pueblo*, then on patrol in international waters off the Korean coast. Though conceivably an act of war and with U.S. forces present in large numbers nearby in South Korea and Japan but preoccupied by the Vietnam imbroglio, no firm action was taken and the presence of U.S. forces provided little value. In May 1975, the American-owned ship SS *Mayaguez* was seized by Cambodian gunboats off the Cambodian coast. U.S. forces in the region were quickly summoned, and two days later, with substantial loss of American lives, a U.S. Marine force successfully recaptured the ship and freed the crew. Initial U.S. air strikes had convinced the Cambodian government to liberate the ship but, sadly, not in time to forestall the recapture operation.

From October 1979 through January 1981, the United States increased its presence in the Persian Gulf and Indian Ocean in retaliation for and because of the seizure of the U.S. embassy in Tehran. It is doubtful this presence had much salutary effect on Iran and the Khomeni leadership. On the other hand, in January 1991, Somali rebels were threatening the capital of Mogadishu, and evacuation of the U.S. embassy was ordered. In a daring night rescue, U.S. Marines and Navy Seals from U.S. units distantly present in the region as part of Operation Desert Shield flew nearly 500 miles to effect this evacuation.[50]

These three examples are broadly representative of more than 200 instances of the use of naval force in response to international events and crises since 1946 and suggest the limits of what presence can and cannot achieve. Because the U.S. was unwilling or unable to apply massive use of force either to recapture or liberate *Pueblo* and its crew or American hostages in Tehran, presence provided

---

[50] For a review of all incidents of this type since 1986, see Adam B. Siegel, *The Use of Naval Forces in the Post-War Era: U.S. Navy and U.S. Marine Corps Crisis Response Activity, 1946–1990* (Center for Naval Analyses: Alexandria, Virginia, Feb 1991). This most useful publication describes 207 instances of naval use.

no leverage or utility. In relatively small or minor actions like *Mayaguez* and the Somali evacuation, the presence of U.S. forces created additional options for the U.S. Government to consider. However, the U.S. casualties and the negative public reaction to the *Mayaguez* raid were indicators of the risks and costs that can multiply quickly if military and operational success is not convincingly achieved. Regarding Somalia, despite the skill with which the evacuation was made, had no U.S. forces been present, it is arguable that other, perhaps more risky escape routes still existed. The point is that presence is no guarantor of success, and the occasions in which presence really counts in crisis and in the first stages of crisis are relatively few. On the other hand, when the stakes or risks are large, the use of forces immediately on hand through presence is almost certainly tempered by caution, and, in most cases, there will be time to consider options and to bring other forces to bear.[51]

On a routine basis, an argument can be made that presence as reassurance is useful. Training, exercises, and port visits no doubt can serve positively as adjuncts to presence, but the actual ability of presence to exert the intended influence is more difficult to determine. Without concrete proof of either merits or demerits, the debate over presence becomes a debate over advocates who assert or assume benefit and critics who assert otherwise or question the value presumed.

On top of these considerations, the double dilemma posed earlier by domestically driven criteria in using U.S. force and the potentially non-military or inherently unresolvable situations where force

---

[51] Proponents of presence will cite other examples as better and more representative demonstrations of its utility. The presence of the Sixth Fleet in the Mediterranean, it can be argued, makes the case, and a large number of past instances can be used as evidence. For example, in the 1980s, presence permitted the U.S. to take a number of forceful actions in situations ranging from retaliating against Libya in 1981 and 1986 to capturing the hijackers of the cruise ship *Achille Lauro* in 1985. In most of these cases, a combination of enough time to react and other alternatives provided compensating weight to the need for continued presence. On the other hand, as Napoleon remarked about wishing to have generals possessing luck, good fortune is entirely unpredictable.

might be used as a last or only resort will complicate the presence issue. Thus, three policy actions should be taken regarding presence:

- First, we should understate the explicit and crisis utility of presence, focusing instead on the more easily understood necessity of presence to underwrite or symbolize U.S. commitments. This approach makes no promises on what presence may or may not achieve outside this primary role of representing U.S. commitments.

- Second, the U.S. no doubt still needs great regional understanding and familiarity as the world grows no less complex a place and more, often newer, actors play larger roles. Presence is extremely useful in this regard. The consequence is that area specialists will be needed with education and training on more countries and on more cross-cutting issues that migrate from geostrategy to geoeconomics than were needed during the Cold War when there were relatively few potential adversaries and those were largely conditioned and constituted by the East-West conflict.

- Third, a major analytical effort, using as much data and as many viewpoints as is responsibly possible, should address the issues of what advantages and utility come of presence; what the disadvantages and risks are; where presence might be effective or ineffective; and what the grounds and assumptions are for making these evaluations.

A more useful concept in shaping future considerations for presence relates to access. Access is the ability to gain and sustain entry either peacefully or forcefully. To obtain access, as an alternative or complement to presence, a network of access "enablers"—basing and landing rights, overflight rights, communications and logistics systems, and pre-positioned supplies—needs to be established and maintained. The use of the Indian Ocean island base of Diego Garcia as a means for enabling access is an example of the type of structure needed. And, being able to use these networks when and where necessary without obtaining someone else's approval is likewise vital.

For example, during the October 1973 Arab-Israeli war, fearing a retaliatory Arab oil embargo, America's NATO allies refused landing rights for U.S. resupply flights to Israel. The U.S. was able to conduct its resupply by air with great difficulty and cost occasioned by extensive rerouting and inflight refueling, and probably could have forced the allies to change their minds if the crisis and response demanded. During the 1990–91 Gulf War and build-up, had NATO states not permitted and not actively helped with the flow of war materials through and over their various borders, deployment of the necessary UN forces and equipment to Saudi Arabia would have been virtually impossible.

This establishment of access enablers as an important policy component has direct relationship with and perhaps lineal descent from the Cold War. The United States purposely maintained the strategic nuclear umbrella, the overhead intelligence collection, strategic command-and-control capabilities, and strategic lift assets for the alliance—in other words, the critical networks or strategic sinews that could not and need not be duplicated by other partners. Access can be approached in the same way. The United States would continue to assume the role of keeper and provider of these networks and sinews that enable the maintenance and exploitation of access where and when that may be required.

Access is not a new concept; it has served as the basis for prior policy action. However, as U.S. overseas military presence contracts, as U.S. commitments to stability and global security continue, maintaining sufficient access to ensure timely insertion of forces as may be required is essential. To that end, contingency planning must continue to test and identify strong and weak points in the ability to generate access and, within resource limits, to ensure that supporting steps are taken to reinforce the necessary basing, landing, and overflight rights, and that other logistical and communications capabilities are in place.

The most useful way to relate these choices is to identify the objectives that underwrite the various commitments and the accompanying levels of deployments and presence; tables 27 through 29 address these issues for central Europe and the former USSR, the northwest Pacific, and globally.

Table 27. Central Europe and the former USSR (objectives, commitments, deployments, and presence)

Objectives	Commitments	Deployments	Presence
	Current		
Support democratization and open market reform	SALT, ABM, CFE START, INF treaties	N/A	N/A
Support aid and assistance	Funding	—	—
Reduce nuclear and conventional armaments	Advisory personnel	—	—
Defense conversion	"Partnership"	—	—
	Alternatives and additions		
Extend NATO "partnership"	Defense of FSU, Central Europe	U.S. forces	Part-time (?) Low-level
Extend NATO membership	Defense of FSU	U.S. forces	Full-time
Extend economic partnership	Treaties, agreements, funding	—	Low to medium level
Peacekeeping in Bosnia	Impose peace	U.S./NATO forces	Up to 25,000

Table 28. Northwest Pacific (objectives, commitments, deployments, and presence)

Objectives	Commitments	Deployments	Presence
	Current		
Assure U.S. engagement	Treaties (U.S.-Japan; Korea)	Seventh Fleet	All U.S. military forces
Promote stability		U.S. in Korea	
	Peace		
Promote trade, economic development	Security and stability	U.S. in Okinawa	Full-time Robust
		Exercises	
Reduce grounds for conflict	Troop presence		
	Restraining N. Korean nuclear proliferation		
	Alternatives and additions		
Broaden security framework through CSCE-type mechanism	As above	Greater military cooperation and exercises	Probably larger
Seek arms control agreements	Treaties	?	?
Seek alliance, nonaggression treaties	Treaties	?	?

Table 29. Non-regional/"global" issues (objectives, commitments, deployments, and presence)

Objectives	Commitments	Deployments	Presence
Current			
Promote democratization and open market reforms	GATT, IMF, international agreements	In concert with other objectives	In concert Selective
Free/fair trade		Selective, i.e., Kurdish, Somalia relief	
Antiproliferation	UN		
Antiterrorist	MTCR; non-proliferation treaty	?	
Promote human rights			
Promote humanitarian actions	Maintain access "enablers"		
Alternatives and additions			
Provide a UN force/make the UN the ultimate arbiter of international disputes	To subsume national authority and autonomy to UN decision	?	?

Against this backdrop of choices, certain preliminary conclusions can be drawn regarding commitments, deployments, and presence. At the outset, it is imperative to identify the basic objectives of national security, defense, and foreign policy that are to be translated into commitments and the deployment of forces. However, identifying objectives that can be achieved, sustained, and credibly matched by appropriate force requirements is not simple. Otherwise, this process would have been more effective.

Commitments are founded in national obligations, intentions, and interests. They are expressed both in concrete terms of military forces, signed treaties, and other documents with the authority of law and in less concrete terms marked by declaratory statements, mutual trust and confidence, and implicit actions that may not require demonstrable uses of physical and visible instruments but nonetheless signal a certain message and meaning.

From these commitments, judgments about appropriate levels of military force for underwriting these obligations are made and become the basis for operational or military requirements. However, the lack of a universally acceptable measure to show that one response is more effective or more appropriate than another must be addressed by logic, strategic design, or some other plausible analytical means.

The absence of specific and massive threats suggests that qualitative rather than numerically driven responses have more relevance. For example, the commitment to defend NATO from Soviet attack required a plausible and reasonable military response. But, today and into the future, ensuring European stability does not necessarily have any quantitative military solution. In other words, numbers of troops above a certain level may yield no real advantage.

Finally, as requirements regarding future U.S. commitments and accompanying military needs are considered, access, as a key criterion and determinant and an end in itself, may provide a formidable means of defining and fashioning policy tools and instruments for dealing with the demands of strategic uncertainty.

Chapter Eight: Infrastructure

Of all the major defense-related issues, perhaps none is more politically charged, highly complicated, and less conducive to solution than that of infrastructure. Defined in this book as the vast, supporting network of facilities that provide vital services for the military forces, infrastructure includes: the bases and facilities to house, train, homeport, and sustain the military; the Reserve and National Guard components; the civilian and military defense industrial base; the technology base where it may differ from the defense industrial base; and the acquisition process. Because of the nature and composition of infrastructure, it falls squarely between the executive branch and Congress in terms of responsibilities and authority—a situation inherently and explicitly laden with the best and worst characteristics of the political process.

Because the infrastructure is both so vast and so extraordinarily complicated, no attempt is made to conduct highly detailed and specific analysis, which is probably beyond the capacity of any single individual. Instead, through historical and first-principle types of analyses, the largest issues and choices are abstracted to as broad a level as possible for the express intent of laying out an appropriate range of future options. Also, the caveat applies that for every general rule or proposition regarding infrastructure, no doubt large numbers of specific exceptions exist that contradict, or at least appear to contradict, the broader view.

Few issues are in as much inherent conflict and tension as that of the infrastructure reflecting the collision of prerogatives and responsibilities between Congress and the White House. The president and his DOD are concerned with obtaining the best defense for the nation at large. The criteria of matching strategy and forces, of maintaining high levels of operational capability, and of achieving efficiency and effectiveness in program management are fundamental objectives for defense. No Congressman would argue against the general efficacy of those criteria. But Congress views its responsibility for assuring national well-being side by side with representing constituent interests.

The budget is the mechanism for dealing with competing national and local claims on defense resources. Employment, the flow of funds and federal spending into local districts, and natural disagreements between Congress and the president are major forces at work. Any steps necessary to improve either the efficiency of managing the infrastructure or its downsizing will meet some natural resistance from Congress. In many cases, this interaction has led to cuts in or skewing of the defense budget to sustain or protect much of that infrastructure.

Base closings, shrinking of the industrial base, reductions in reserve and guard forces, and other actions seen as mandatory by DOD to preserve military fighting power are likely to be resisted by Congress to protect jobs and to reflect legitimate arguments to sustain specific portions of the infrastructure that may not otherwise serve a useful military purpose. Rarely has Congress moved on its own to cut fundamentally or substantially the interests of the constituents it rightfully represents. Nor is it obvious when or where the DOD was prepared to sacrifice military capability on the grounds of protecting local, non-defense interest except when or where politics provided no other option.

The Clinton administration, through the Bottom-Up Review, defines infrastructure as the "foundation on which our military strength is built," and estimates its total costs for FY 1994 as $160 billion, or about 59 percent of the DOD total obligational authority. Figure 15 shows the breakdown of these costs.

Figure 15. Infrastructure categories (percentage of $160 billion in FY 1994 budget)

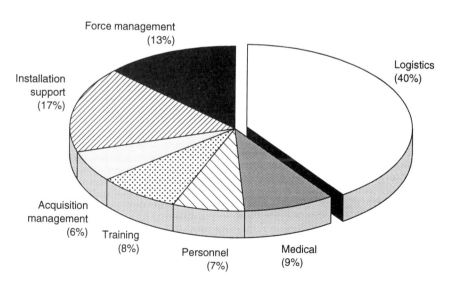

As will be shown, from 1989 to 1993 and including the actions of the first three Base Closure and Realignment Commissions, the defense budget has been cut by nearly 30 percent in real terms, force structure by about 35 percent, and the infrastructure by less than 17 percent. Because the infrastructure still included many facilities that date back to World War II, these reductions and realignments have been modest at best even though the political pain and consequences have been quite high.

In terms of infrastructure, figures 16 and 17 depict graphically, how the DOD budget has shifted over the past four decades in terms of actual spending. Although funding for strategic forces has dramatically and understandably declined from the build-up of the early 1960s, categories that are generally representative of infrastructure have shown the opposite tendency. The future trends depicting the growing disparity between "teeth" and "tail" take into account the actual and projected savings made through the BRAC process.

Figure 16. Infrastructure drain 1962-1980

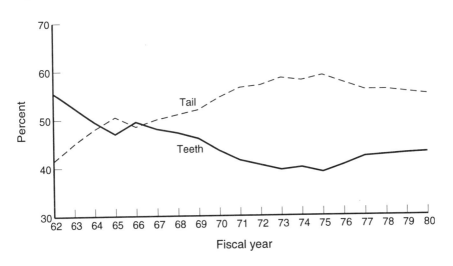

Note: All figures taken from Office of the Comptroller, the DOD, May 1993, pp. 62–63. "Teeth" included strategic and general-purpose forces, and air- and sealift. "Tail" included the other accounts.

Figure 17. Infrastructure drain 1980-1998

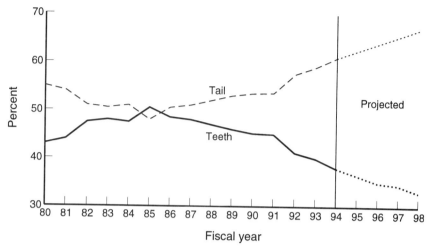

Note: All figures taken from Office of the Comptroller, the DOD, May 1993, pp. 62–63. "Teeth" included strategic and general-purpose forces, and air- and sealift. "Tail" included the other accounts.

- "Teeth," measured by strategic and general-purpose forces, have shrunk from about half of the budget to less than two-fifths. The trends between "teeth" and "tail" are diverging rapidly in favor of infrastructure.

- Intelligence and communications funding has increased, in real terms, by more than double.

- Air and sealift funding has increased by nearly half.[52]

- Guard and reserve funding has increased by nearly two-thirds.

- Research and development funding has increased by almost half.

- Training, medical, and administration have increased, particularly in relation to the reduction of one million active-duty service members since 1962.

---

[52] Lift clearly contributes to fighting power as well as parts of other budget accounts, but it is the size of the differential that is suggestive of the trend.

Bases and Related Infrastructure

The need for military bases is more than obvious, but reducing bases that have become redundant or obsolete is a difficult and often painful process. From the early 1960s and through the 1970s, various secretaries of defense initiated actions to close relatively large numbers of bases and installations dating from the war in order to obtain economies and to reduce overhead costs. In 1977, anxious to protect constituent interests and base-related constituencies, Congress enacted a statute requiring DOD to notify Congress when and if an installation became a candidate for closure or realignment. The law also required time-consuming environmental impact assessments that effectively blocked further closures.[53]

By the late 1980s, an increasingly bloated base structure threatened the readiness of the forces and, in turn, collided with the politics resistant to closures. The result was the first Base Realignment and Closure Commission or "BRAC" created in 1988.[54] In 1990, when Secretary of Defense Dick Cheney announced further base closings, Congress protested that process, charging it was "politically influenced." In its stead, Congress created an independent, five-year Defense Base Realignment and Closure Commission to meet in 1991, 1993, and 1995.[55] This BRAC was to provide an independent review of closures proposed by the secretary of defense and forward its recommendations to the president. The president either approved or disapproved the entire list without exception and forwarded the package to Congress. Congress then passed or rejected the recommendations without introducing any changes or riders.

Base closings and realignments took place in 1989, 1991, and 1993. The next and last commission under present law will convene in 1995. The achievements of the first three commissions are

---

[53] See Section 2687, Title 10, USC and p. 3-1, *Defense Base Closure and Realignment Commission 1993 Report to the President*, dated July 1, 1993.

[54] *Ibid.* The 1988 BRAC recommended closure of 86 facilities and realignment of 59 others.

[55] See Public Law 101-510, as amended, under Title XXIX USC. Even though the title of the law reverses "closure" and "realignment" from the 1988 statute, the commission is still called the BRAC.

important, principally in the political acknowledgment that bases must be shut or reduced. The law provided a mechanism that bypassed the normal political process by requiring one up or down vote in each house on the entire package and by barring all amendments and riders to the basic bill. On the debit side, the first two BRAC commissions encountered resistance among the services, and, therefore, the first rounds of cuts were not sufficient to offset the decline in force levels and spending, creating even greater overhead costs in infrastructure.

The 1993 BRAC was more ambitious, but the total reductions made to date in infrastructure are less than a fifth of the bases and facilities in service and proportionally much less than the cuts in manpower and budget levels. It is also likely that the savings projected for the first three rounds of BRAC will greatly exceed what dollars are actually saved—although the value of achieving savings should be lower in priority than reducing the drain on budgets imposed by this infrastructure. Finally, because Congress must approve all money for base closings, failure to fund these accounts fully will delay or prevent the actions of the BRAC. Hence, the impact of this infrastructure drain has not been compensated for and still poses an enormous problem for maintaining a ready fighting force.

Table 30 gives an idea of what each BRAC achieved. Note that little or no distinction is made in the size of the base or facility affected.

Table 30. BRAC achievements

Year	Bases affected		Projected savings[a]	Percent of domestic bases affected
	Closed	Realigned		
1988/89	86	16	$500–700 million per year	3
1991	34	48	Long-term $1.5 billion per year	5
1993	130	45	Long-term $2.3 billion per year	8

[a] In 1989, the commission projected long-term annual savings of $500 million. In 1991, net savings of $2.3 billion and recurring savings of $1.5 billion after a one-time cost of $4.1 billion was projected. In 1993, a one-time cost of $7.43 billion was projected, with about $3.8 billion in savings from 1995–1999 and $2.33 billion in annual savings thereafter.

At the same time that it is obvious that the basing structure must be substantially reduced not only for reasons of economy but also because that structure is absorbing scarce resources at the expense of military capability, many vital facilities and functions that would harm military muscle if shut have migrated to or are located on these bases. Hence, realignment and downsizing of bases rather than outright closing may be an appropriate response. The Philadelphia Navy Shipyard is a good example.

The Navy argues that the Philadelphia Shipyard is no longer needed for ship construction or repair, but three essential facilities collocated there provide essential services the Navy cannot lose. Relocation would prove expensive. These facilities are the large-ship propeller manufacturing and repair facility vital for aircraft carrier maintenance; the boiler and gas turbine laboratory vital to supporting all the Navy's propulsion systems; and the reserve or mothballed fleet facility. The propeller facility is the only one of its kind and therefore crucial to the maintenance, repair, and construction of aircraft carriers because there is no alternative source for these propellers. The boiler and turbine laboratory represents about $500 million in investment—a unique and vital asset. As long as ships are kept in mothballs, relocation would be expensive. Thus, while much of this shipyard could be shut, there are strong arguments for retaining specific facilities. This situation applies to each of the services and large parts of the basing structure.

To a large degree, there really are no distinct "choices" for dealing with the basing structure. Failure to rationalize and reduce basing will prove excessively costly and militarily wasteful. The issue is over the pace and timing of these realignments and reductions. One useful alternative is to embark on major consolidation and collocation of forces at a few "megabases." In the case of the Navy and Marine Corps, establishment of one megabase on each coast (and Hawaii), with major reductions to that end, and retention of smaller, satellite facilities that possess unique functions or are required by logistical, operational, and practical reasons provide a model for further consideration.

The Reserve and National Guard Component

The reserve component of the armed forces is as old as the republic and has formed an integral part of American military tradition and might. Designated in the Constitution as the militia and protected by the Second Amendment as "necessary to the security of a free state," the purposes and functions of the reserve have naturally evolved over time. However, no serious challenge to the existence of the reserve and guard has been mounted despite the operational and budgetary realities that might suggest the efficacy of such an approach.

Up until the end of the Second World War and except in time of emergency, the United States maintained a small standing Army and Navy. The National Guard fell under the authority of the individual states and their governors unless summoned by the Federal Government "to execute the laws of the Union, suppress insurrections, and repel invasions." The notion and mystique of the "citizen-soldier," answering the call to arms in crisis and tending to business and work in peace, were embedded in the social fabric of the United States.

For the post-Cold War period, U.S. military might in time of war was ultimately dependent on mobilization and recalling reserve and National Guard forces. To be precise, these mobilized forces included the Army and Air Force National Guards under the normal, peacetime authority of the 50 states, and the Army, Navy, Marine Corps, and Air Force Reserve. Typically, these forces have numbered in total from post-war highs of about 1.8 million in the 1950s to the current levels of about 900,000 (table 31).

Table 31. Components of the Selected Reserve[a]

	Fiscal year											
	83	84	85	86	87	88	89	90	91	92	93	94
ARNG	417.2	434.3	440.0	446.2	451.9	455.2	457.0	437.0	441.3	426.5	422.7	344.5
Army Reserve	266.2	275.1	292.1	309.7	313.6	312.8	319.2	299.1	299.9	302.0	279.6	230.2
Naval Reserve	109.1	120.6	129.8	141.5	148.1	149.5	151.5	149.4	150.5	142.3	133.7	117.2
MC Reserve	42.7	40.6	41.6	41.6	42.3	43.6	43.6	44.5	44.0	42.2	42.3	36.9
ANG	102.2	105.0	109.4	112.6	114.6	115.2	116.1	117.0	117.6	119.1	119.2	118.9
Air Force Reserve	67.2	70.3	75.2	78.5	80.4	82.1	83.2	80.6	84.3	81.9	82.4	81.9
Total	1004.6	1045.9	1088.1	1130.1	1153.9	1158.4	1170.6	1127.6	1137.6	1114.0	1079.9	929.6

[a] In thousands.

Each reserve component has been designed to support the active forces but in different ways peculiar to the needs of each service. The Army, with about a half-million reserve component, has assigned vital functions of combat support and combat service support that are largely logistics related to the reserves. The Air Force Reserve are organized around squadrons; they are well trained and can be recalled to active duty with relatively little training. The Navy Air Reserve is similar to that of the Air Force; a number of ships, mostly frigates and minesweepers, are in the Naval Reserve and manned by Reservists. But in general, the Navy, Marine Corps, and Air Force depend less on reserves than does the Army. Army Reserve forces, on balance, would require the longest time for mobilization.

Indeed, Army force structure after the 1970s was purposely designed to be highly dependent on reserve forces for understandable political reasons. Mobilization would be required for major contingencies. Hence, future Vietnam-like conflicts could not be waged by the Army without reliance on reserve forces. The president was authorized by Congress to mobilize up to 200,000 Reservists in crisis. Beyond that point, Congressional approval is mandatory. This role of the reserve and guard forces meant that political consensus would be and still is required to send large numbers of U.S. forces into action.

Four main points continue to define the debate over the guard and reserve. The first point is the constitutionally protected right of the states to maintain a militia. The existence of the National Guard is therefore nonnegotiable, although the size, the shape, and the matter of who pays for it are not constitutionally fixed. Second, the notion of "citizen-soldier" is as old as the republic. The guard and reserve fill this function and properly use this tradition as legitimate justification for existence. The third point is the role of the guard and reserve, the relationship or mix with the active forces, and the degree of dependence of one on the other. Fourth, and finally, is the level and quality of the readiness and capability to be required of the reserve component.

Of the first two issues, the only significant question that can be addressed is how much the federal and state governments should each pay for the guard and reserve. The Federal Government bears the costs for the reserve and 95 percent of the costs of the guard.

Given that the states administer the National Guard in peacetime, there is an argument to be made that the states should bear a greater financial responsibility, especially for disaster or crisis relief. Despite the potentially explosive nature of this question as it would play out in Congress, which is the natural ally and supporter of the reserve and guard in representing the states, it is still one that should be addressed in the context of serving as the incentive for producing change.

Regarding the two other issues, before his departure as secretary of defense, Les Aspin began reducing the size of the reserve component and focused its attention on two principal missions: preparing for major conflict in support of the active forces and assisting in domestic disasters and crises. There is, however, one basic set of choices for the reserve component relating to size and responsibilities. As the active force is reduced, the fundamental issue is the degree to which the reserve and guard components will share in those reductions or in augmentation and reconstitution if a strategy of regeneration is selected. Table 32 reflects the possible options against the range of force structure choices presented earlier if we continue to do business as usual.

Table 32. Reserve/guard choices vs. force structure choices

Force structure	Reserve/guard choices
BUR continued	Reduction in kind with selected augmentation to replace or complement active force
Garrison force	Reduction to support active force or greater emphasis on naval reserve (i.e., more naval capability in reserve)
Maritime force	Reduction to support active force or strengthening of reserve component of garrison forces
Reconstitution	Enlarged reserve component

It is also appropriate to evaluate objectively the benefits the guard and reserve actually contribute to the nation in terms of supporting combat operations for the resources expended. Making an objective evaluation will be very difficult for the reasons cited earlier dealing with tradition, mystique, and the close relationship with Congress. But, given the reality of the resource constraints ahead, it would be less than responsible not to consider a military posture with minimal reserve and guard capacity.[56]

THE DEFENSE INDUSTRIAL BASE

Among the most vexing infrastructure issues is the industrial base question. In an environment within a free market economy that has but a single customer for products and that customer is the government, the conditions are ripe for uncertainty, confusion, and, indeed, chaos. In the United States, substantial government ownership of the industrial capacity for producing armaments and related services has been eschewed for economic, political, and ideological reasons. Private-sector ownership, whether through publicly traded or privately held companies, must therefore deal with the uniquely difficult problems posed by a system in which government is the absolute customer and regulator. The conflict between this inordinately regulated defense economy and an otherwise free enterprise system poses problems that can be fundamentally unresolvable.

For example, when there is no market-driven mechanism to set price, profit, and supply and demand, the substitute criteria are often value- or belief-driven standards set by government. The government sets profit margins and imposes a huge regulatory regime that is distinct from the civilian economy and requires distinct and separate rules, accounting systems, personnel, and standards. Indeed, one side of this regulation, compounded by government actions to eliminate the scandal of "waste, fraud, and abuse," has been the growing criminalization of misdeeds and mistakes. Errors and violations of the civil code have led to attempts at, and successful, criminal prosecutions.

---

[56] This may prove the most controversial statement in the book. Despite the strongest rhetoric in support of the reserve and guard offered by every administration and the quality of their personnel, the nation must look seriously at whether we can continue to rely as heavily on this capacity in the future as in the past. A largely negative answer would mean a dramatic reduction in the reserve and a return of responsibility for the guard, especially funding, to the respective states.

Furthermore, there can be no long-term arrangements to set some modicum of certainty or incentive for the manufacturer or contractor to stay in business for the long haul. Finally, competition, or at least the goal of ensuring or managing competition, has become enmeshed and insinuated through legislation particularly well represented by the 1984 Competition in Contracting Act. But when there is only one customer and trends toward industry consolidation and growing numbers of single or dual producers across the defense sectors become obvious, competition can become fiction although the law demands it.

As a result of these factors and impelled by declining budgets, appropriate levels of defense industrial base capacity are often argued for in terms of national security needs. Rather obviously and logically, some form of self-sufficiency is required to sustain unique and irreplaceable production capabilities that, if lost, could jeopardize national security. The shipbuilding, aircraft, ordnance, electronics, and nuclear industries, among others, have often been accorded this national security label of protection. And, Congress' representation of the defense industrial base intensifies the politics and difficulty in addressing these important issues.

To be sure, there are certainly areas where national security demands autarky; nuclear weapons production is one such area. But the number of areas where national security would indeed be jeopardized by the elimination of a production capacity or asset needs serious review. At the same time, the criterion of competition and the reach of antitrust and monopoly prevention laws also must be examined if any rational solution to the industrial base issue is to be reached.

There are three basic choices regarding the defense industrial base. First, there can be a policy of *laissez-faire* in which the market determines the winners and losers or the survivors and victims through a form of economic Darwinism and the survival of the fittest. Second, there can be a strict government industrial policy in which significant and even dominant government intervention determines the survivors and victims in the private sector. Third, government can elect to nationalize the defense industrial base or at least a significant portion of it.

The *laissez-faire* choice assumes the market is the ultimate mechanism for adjudicating the industrial base, which means the fittest generally will survive, and the fittest are usually the largest. Competition in the broadest sense can be squeezed out, particularly as consolidation forced by less and less defense spending continues. The result can be a situation with concurrent monopsony and monopoly with one buyer and one seller and where value for spending would be determined not by market factors but by the state of affairs between industry and government. Given the merger between Northrop and Grumman and the proposed merger between Lockheed and Martin-Marietta, consolidation is a timely issue and one to be examined in subsequent pages as it may affect competition.

Industrial policy requires the government to make difficult and far-reaching decisions about winners and losers. In this regard, the Janus-like quality of divided government does not assure that a single, coherent industrial policy follows. Nor does an industrial policy necessarily guarantee that an efficient or effective industrial base will follow.

Nationalization of the defense industrial base would put all or most private ownership in government hands. Nationalization would be hugely expensive, certainly initially, as substantial compensation would be mandated under virtually all conditions. And, if history is a guide, many of the efficiencies and economies of scale of private companies would be lost.

In the past, because of the robustness and redundancy of the industrial base, the U.S. Government has had the luxury of deferring tough choices and of using variants of these choices concurrently. Administrations have adopted a formal *laissez-faire* policy at the same time they pursued limited forms of industrial policy (that subsidizes or underwrites noncompetitive industries) and policy variants of nationalization in which the government continues to own certain means of production. A good example is that of the government simultaneously maintaining private shipyards, Navy shipyards, and a public-private mix of nuclear shipyards.

For nearly two centuries, shipbuilding capacity has been argued for on the grounds of national security. The country, as an island and seagoing nation in this argument, could not allow itself dependence on foreign sourcing for either commercial ships or warships. Foreign sourcing could always be cut off. Thus, the U.S., as with other great powers, elected to build both its own warships and its own merchant fleet. The need for autarky in warship construction was obvious. Construction of merchant ships was another matter.

For private shipyards to stay in business building and selling merchant ships, government-paid construction subsidies were required to keep up with the costs of production and to keep the price of commercial ships competitive. Indeed, the Jones Act of 1920 mandated that all shipping used in domestic U.S. waters had to be U.S.-built, U.S.-owned, and U.S.-flagged. Shipbuilding and shipping (i.e., merchant marine) were generally lumped together in the single category of maritime industry even though the first was really heavy construction and the second transportation.

In 1981 and impelled in part by ambitious plans for the 600-ship Navy that would give warship construction work to many private shipyards, theoretically reducing the financial pressure to build ships for civilian use, the Reagan administration ended the construction differential subsidies that the U.S. Government had provided to U.S. commercial shipbuilders in order to maintain competitive price equivalence *vis a vis* foreign yards for merchant ships. The argument then (and now) was that foreign yards had government support as well as lower hourly wages in building merchant ships.[57] Without federal subsidy, the U.S. commercial shipbuilding playing field was never "level." National security rationale formed the basis for having a strong merchant marine and commercial shipbuilding industry, as well as autarky in constructing men-of-war.

In fact, those Cold War national security arguments relating to the merchant marine were largely hollow. There were plenty of commercial ships of all types in service, and many were owned and operated by NATO allies. To believe in wartime that our allies who would be fighting with us in their own backyards would not make their commercial ships available for transportation, resupply, and sealift strains credulity. Whether the U.S. had both the capacity to build merchant ships and to own and operate substantial numbers

---

[57] Current trade negotiations are attempting to eliminate government shipbuilding subsidies in the U.S. and European industrial states.

of its merchant fleet was not relevant. More than enough ships were available through allies or through direct impressment to meet any wartime exigencies. Even in conflicts that were fought outside the alliance, such as Vietnam or Desert Storm, lack of shipping was never a limiting factor.

As a result of these business and political factors, both the U.S. commercial shipbuilding and shipping industries have rapidly contracted from the heydays of the 1960s. U.S. shipbuilding is now virtually on a military footing. Even with operating subsidies, the U.S.-flag fleet remains quite small. The point is that from a national security perspective, this contraction in maritime capability has been neither unhealthy nor an economically bad thing to have happened to the nation at large despite the pain to those in the industry. The same parallel can be extended to other sectors of defense-related production.

This analysis and review lead to an obvious conclusion if strategic and economic rationality are dominant considerations. The size of the required defense industrial base should be singularly determined by the level and direction of federal defense spending. Should defense companies choose either to market abroad or to expand their business through so-called "dual-use" products that have both military and consumer application, that is the choice of the private sector and should be independent of the Federal Government. This assumes all laws and government regulations are correctly followed in these sales.

From a political and economic perspective, another conclusion can be reached. Defense corporations can rightly argue that they and their employees have loyally served the national security interests of the United States as well as their shareholders. Because experienced and qualified people are vital to these defense industries and because there is no obvious and easily accessible market to which these employees can rapidly migrate during budget drawdowns, the government must assume some responsibility for and therefore share the expense of minimizing these peaks and valleys between hirings and layoffs. This argument, which carries great weight in Congress, translates directly into some form of government funding or subsidy that will underwrite these industries during periods of defense reduction.

Figure 18 and table 33 show the historical progression of the size of the defense industrial base measured by employment.

Figure 18. Defense employment as percent of total labor force

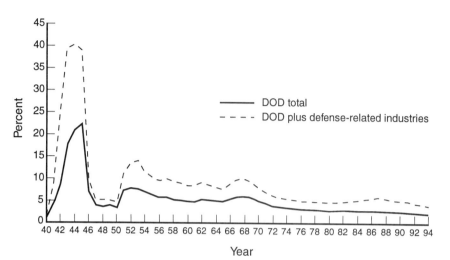

Table 33. U.S. employment and labor force (endstrength in thousands)

FY	Military active duty	DOD DH civilian work force[a]	Total DOD manpower	Defense-related industry employment	Total defense-related employment	Total labor force
1940	458	256	714	314	1,028	55,890
1941	1,801	556	2,357	2,500	4,857	56,855
1942	3,859	1,284	5,143	10,000	15,143	58,880
1943	9,045	2,193	11,238	13,361	24,599	62,470
1944	11,452	2,239	13,691	12,600	26,291	65,300
1945	12,056	2,628	14,684	11,000	25,684	65,670
1946	3,025	1,416	4,441	1,168	5,609	63,135
1947	1,582	859	2,441	786	3,227	60,956
1948	1,444	804	2,248	958	3,206	62,132
1949	1,614	821	2,434	732	3,166	62,197
1950	1,459	710	2,170	713	2,883	63,548
1951	3,249	1,201	4,551	2,400	6,851	62,505
1952	3,636	1,308	4,944	3,600	8,544	63,020
1953	3,555	1,304	4,859	4,118	8,977	63,898
1954	3,302	1,183	4,485	2,975	7,460	64,178
1955	2,935	1,160	4,095	2,500	6,595	65,461
1956	2,806	1,151	3,958	2,500	6,458	67,886
1957	2,795	1,132	3,927	2,850	6,777	68,258
1958	2,600	1,069	3,668	2,800	6,468	68,875
1959	2,504	1,049	3,553	2,700	6,253	69,704

(Continued on next page)

Table 33. (*Continued*)

FY	Military active duty	DOD DH civilian work force[a]	Total DOD manpower	Defense-related industry employment	Total defense-related employment	Total labor force
1960	2,475	1,018	3,493	2,460	5,953	71,460
1961	2,483	1,012	3,495	2,600	6,095	72,464
1962	2,808	1,039	3,848	2,725	6,573	72,071
1963	2,700	1,019	3,719	2,550	6,269	73,398
1964	2,688	997	3,684	2,280	5,964	74,901
1965	2,656	986	3,641	2,125	5,766	76,335
1966	3,094	1,093	4,187	2,640	6,827	77,629
1967	3,377	1,235	4,612	3,100	7,712	79,021
1968	3,548	1,233	4,781	3,174	7,955	80,088
1969	3,460	1,275	4,735	2,916	7,651	82,357
1970	3,066	1,161	4,227	2,399	6,626	84,051
1971	2,714	1,093	3,808	2,031	5,839	84,968
1972	2,323	1,049	3,372	1,985	5,357	88,055
1973	2,253	997	3,250	1,850	5,100	90,414
1974	2,162	1,013	3,175	1,860	5,035	92,547
1975	2,128	989	3,117	1,800	4,917	94,013
1976	2,082	959	3,041	1,690	4,731	96,115
1977	2,074	938	3,013	1,730	4,743	97,684
1978	2,062	935	2,997	1,765	4,762	100,838
1979	2,031	916	2,947	1,860	4,807	103,374
1980	2,063	916	2,979	1,990	4,969	107,261
1981	2,101	940	3,041	2,085	5,126	109,910
1982	2,130	945	3,075	2,290	5,365	111,446
1983	2,162	980	3,142	2,415	5,557	112,884
1984	2,184	1,000	3,184	2,735	5,919	114,701
1985	2,206	1,043	3,249	2,980	6,229	116,689
1986	2,233	1,027	3,260	3,315	6,575	118,947
1987	2,243	1,049	3,292	3,665	6,957	121,088
1988	2,209	1,010	3,219	3,450	6,669	122,927
1989	2,202	1,037	3,239	3,295	6,534	125,046
1990	2,143[b]	997	3,140	3,150	6,290	126,343
1991	2,077[b]	974	3,051	3,125	6,176	126,730
1992	1,880[b]	945	2,825	3,000	5,825	128,200
1993	1,705	915	2,714	2,725	5,439	129,500
1994	1,611	876	2,565	2,500	5,065	131,700

a   The DOD direct hire (DH) civilian work force figures include both U.S. and foreign national direct hires. Foreign national indirect hire (FNIH) employees that support DOD forces overseas are not included.

b   The FY 1990 active-duty military includes 25,652 National Guardsmen and Reservists activated pursuant to sections 673b, Title 10 U.S.C. FY 1991 active-duty military includes 17,059 National Guardsmen and Reservists, and FY 1992 active-duty military includes 954 National Guardsmen and Reservists activated pursuant to sections 672 and 673, Title 10 U.S.C., in support of Operation Desert Shield/Desert Storm.

The Clinton administration made a preliminary decision on industrial policy as it relates to defense by choosing to protect national nuclear shipbuilding capacity. Electric Boat in Connecticut was awarded a construction contract for another ship in the new class of submarine, the SSN-21 Seawolf, and Newport News in Virginia was awarded a construction contract for another nuclear aircraft carrier. These awards will keep both civilian shipyards in service at least for a few years. The latest SSN-21 award is also considered as a "bridge," that is, the last ship in this class while the Navy designs a new, smaller, less expensive ship to deal with the non-Soviet threat.

These first policy actions focus the key issues on the debate over the industrial base. There is no question that the United States must have nuclear-capable shipyards for repair and overhaul of the large nuclear fleet, a fleet that will remain in service for decades. However, given that antisubmarine warfare is a low naval priority today (and probably for a long time to come) and that the Navy's current and planned submarine fleet is very young and inordinately more capable than that of any potential foe, the question of why new nuclear submarines are needed immediately must be addressed. Arguments for sustaining both the nuclear design and production capability have obvious merit. However, maintaining the bare minimum of necessary nuclear skills without the need to construct a new submarine every year or so does not seem to be an insurmountable policy alternative.

Furthermore, regarding the new nuclear aircraft carrier, given that the Navy has 12 to 13 in service already and that most of these ships still have years of life left, the need to build another replacement at this juncture is not clear. Indeed, an alternative could have been to consolidate nuclear construction and repair at a single private yard—in this case, Newport News as that is the only yard that can construct both CVNs and SSNs—and let Electric Boat wind down. It should also be noted that both Britain and France have maintained a small but sufficient nuclear shipyard capacity to support a handful of nuclear warships, a lesson not to be ignored by the United States.

The fundamental considerations that underlie these issues and pertain as well to the other components of the industrial base concern the degree of autarky to be obtained or foregone; where reliance on a single production source without competition is satisfactory; and at what rate the exploitation of technological superiority should be pursued. From a strategic, operational, and national perspective, it is on these considerations that the future industrial base should rest. Based on these factors, in 1994, Congress added $150 million to the defense budget for the purpose of maintaining B-2 "Stealth" bomber construction capability for another year.

Regarding the degree and balance of autarky and competition, there is one potential solution to overcoming the short-term focus of the annual debate on the defense budget in which rational or economical choices are not always taken. At some stage, the executive branch should propose a plan specifying those defense sectors that can be autarkic and where competition can be lifted or put on a different footing through some type of incentive for single-source suppliers. In fact, the DOD initiative to repay contractors some costs of merger and consolidation from future savings that may realized is an excellent incentive. Futhermore, although "dual-use" products and technologies with potential in defense and private markets are useful concepts to pursue, with certain specific products such as munitions, tanks, missiles, advanced combat aircraft, and warships, there is no civilian or commercial application other than military sales to foreign customers. From this starting point, Congress can choose to deal with these recommendations annually or possibly in a manner similar to BRAC that would avoid a permanent and ongoing debate while downsizing is completed.

Another attempt at reconciling the dilemmas and conflicts within debate over industrial policy has been the notion of "roll-over." "Roll-over" means that companies would perform only the research and development and prototype production phases for a given system. Full-scale production would be deferred indefinitely unless or until needed. The advantages of "roll-over" reside in maintaining the cutting edge of industry and in developing new designs. The disadvantages are in costs or subsidies necessary to sustain an advanced base where profit has been in production and not R&D; making the transition to this newer system with these inappropriate profit incentives and their associated accounting systems; and the costs of retooling in crisis. As such, the disadvantages of "roll-over" seem far greater than the conceptual attraction.

The rate and pace of pursuing advanced technology, however, is a separate issue that may be prime for alternative policy choices. The seemingly urgent call to exploit technology on an immediate basis has been a simple and universal objective for U.S. defense planning. The exploitation of technology and technological superiority, implicitly as a high priority, has been seen as a sensible, supposedly less expensive and operationally attractive way to offset the prowess, strength, and advantages of U.S. adversaries. The Truman administration was the post-war pathfinder for many of these arguments and policies. And, American technology has been extremely impressive.

The major weapon systems of the late 1980s and 1990s—the M1A1 main battle tank; the Aegis cruisers and destroyers; the SSN fleet; combat aircraft from the stealthy F-117 and B-2 to the F/A-18 and F-16; precision-guided munitions; and the command, control, targeting, and intelligence networks extending from the far reaches of space to the depths of the ocean—are all in classes by themselves when compared with competing systems. But none of these systems came free of charge. Given the relative and absolute advantages created for the U.S. lead in weaponry by the end of the USSR, the U.S. is and must be seen as the strongest, virtually unrivaled military power in the world with the world's best-performing weapons.

Because of these absolute and relative military advantages, the urgency or rate at which the United States deploys and develops advanced technology is surely subject to review and change. It would be folly to abandon exploiting technological superiority on the grounds of our current and projected future advantages, and no serious analyst would suggest that. On the other hand, it would be nearly as unwise if the opportunity to alter the scale and scope of this exploitation were ignored in this post-Cold War world.

At the same time, because U.S. weapon systems carry such advantage over most competing systems, this might be the opportunity to assess how many systems should be assigned to operational forces and individual units in their equipping. For example, when the U.S. Army replaced the M60 series tank with the M-1 series, the number of tanks per battalion was reduced from 63 to 55. But, in the same way that the Navy has reduced the size of its carrier air wings from about 90 to about 55 aircraft, does the actual combat superiority of the M-1 mean that its numbers per unit can also be reduced? Those reductions in platforms per unit would be reflected in aggregate totals that could also be reduced while leaving the number of formations and units unchanged. And, in the case of tanks, the surplus or remainder not needed by this new equippage standard could be assigned to a reserve or cadre status in the event reconstitution were needed.

The United States can certainly afford to reduce the urgency and rate of exploiting technology. While achieving "leap-ahead" results remains a worthy objective, economies, efficiencies, and emphasis, and obtaining value for money spent should become higher priority criteria. Given the superiority of U.S. combat systems, there also may be excellent potential in scaling back the amount of equipment per unit to reflect these advantages.

The Defense Technology Base

Sectors of the defense technology base extend beyond only the "defense industrial base." Of principal concern is the defense nuclear establishment needed for the design, testing, production, maintenance, storage, and security of atomic and thermonuclear weapons. The United States is physically losing the ability to produce nuclear weapons. Facilities both for the production of fissile material and for construction and maintenance of weapons are being closed. The reasons for many of these closures are related to laws and regulations that protect the "environment" and people from the consequences of nuclear radiation and hazards and have been impelled by the collapse of the strategic competition with the USSR. Remediation of contamination and destruction of fissile materials and weapons now have higher priority than production and maintenance.

As the U.S. is moving to reduce and consolidate this nuclear capacity, the ability to produce tritium and deuterium, the hydrogen isotopes necessary in enhanced or boosted fission weapons and central to thermonuclear weapons, is disappearing. Thus, at some point in the future, the U.S. could unilaterally reduce or eliminate its own nuclear capability simply by losing the ability to produce the necessary components.

In the past, to ensure competition in designing nuclear weapons, the United States established and maintained two separate national design laboratories: Los Alamos National Laboratory in New Mexico and Lawrence Livermore Laboratory in California. In addition, the United States maintained a vast complex of laboratories and facilities vital to the production, overhaul, and testing programs for nuclear weapons. These facilities were managed by the Department of Energy and funded under the national defense account.

The allegations and accusations of mismanagement, contamination, and other abuses have been epidemic. But, regardless of the merits or errors in these allegations, the U.S. still spends about $15 billion a year on the nuclear weapons complex.[58] Given that the demands for nuclear weapons have been vastly diminished, consolidation and downsizing of the nuclear base must be a wise move. Reexamining the premise that two design labs are necessary is an excellent beginning for this consolidation.

INDUSTRIAL BASE SUMMARY AND CONSEQUENCES

Against the specific industrial base choices that include *laissez-faire*, explicit industrial policy and nationalization, and means to alter the pace of and dependence on urgent exploitation of advanced technology, the Congressional Office of Technology Assessment offered a menu of policy options in 1991. Table 34 reproduces those options.[59]

---

[58] In 1993, the Department of Energy was authorized $17.3 billion, of which $12.1 were designated for "atomic energy defense activities." DOD spent another $3–4 billion on related areas. *Budget of the United States Government for FY 1994*, p. A-81.

[59] *Redesigning Defense: Planning the Transition to the Future U.S. Defense Industrial Base*, Office of Technology Assessment, July 1991, pp. 14–15.

Table 34. Options for change in the Defense Technology Industrial Base

		Tiers of the base		
		Prime	Subcontractor	Supplier
Research and Development	Current base	Emphasis on systems development for production	Subsystem R&D funded through production contracts from primes	R&D generally driven by civil requirements
	Desired future base	Emphasis on technology demonstration, prototyping, and potential production	Subsystem R&D funded through government or commercial development	Same as above
Production	Current base	Excess capacity, rapid production to field new systems and minimize unit costs	Respond to subsystem requirements from primes for new platforms	Extensive integration with civilian base, concern over increasing internationalization of the supplier base
	Desired future base	Reduced overall capacity, low rates of production to maintain warm base and and personnel skills	Respond to subsystem requirements for retrofit of current platforms and new platforms	Rationalize supplier base to protect against potential vulnerabilities
Maintenance	Current base	Essential but limited involvement in maintenance	Maintenance of subsystems	Not applicable
	Desired future base	Increased involvement in maintenance	Same as above	Not applicable

(Continued on next page)

Table 34. (Continued)

			Ownership	
		Private	GOCO[a]	GOGO[b]
Research and Development	Current base	Scaling back on investment in R&D	Isolation from civil sector	Fragmented lab structure, lack of R&D strategy
	Desired future base	Explicit government funding of military-unique R&D; greater access to dual-use technologies	More integration of commercial technologies and technology transfer	Consolidate labs to become world-class developers of specific military technologies
Production	Current base	Largest element; operates competitively in a relativelyhigh-risk environment	Limited competition and reduced capital requirements; government moderates risk by providing some facilities and tools and gains efficiency of private management	Preserve unique military technologies that would be too costly or risky to produce in the private sector
	Desired future base	Reduced risk through multi-year contracting and more rational application of competition	Relatively more reliance on GOCOs as a result of reduced peacetime production requirements and to meet surge targets for theater conflict	Same as above
Maintenance	Current base	Essential but limited involvement in maintenance	Maintenance of nuclear weapons primarily	Major element of maintenance base, now undergoing consolidation
	Desired future base	Increased involvement in maintenance to maintain production capability	Increase use of GOCOs to reduce business risk, provide greater management efficiency	Relatively reduced use, with sufficient depots to maintain core capabilities

[a] Government-owned/Contractor-operated.
[b] Government-owned/Government-operated.

Source: Office of Technology Assessment, 1991.

(Continued on next page)

Table 34. *(Continued)*

| | | Industrial sectors | |
		Defense electronics	Combat vehicles
Research and Development	Current base	Commercial sector dominates	Military-unique, geared toward production
	Desired future base	Greater use of commercial developments	Greater use of prototype development that may or may not lead to production
Production	Current base	Strict military requirements and specifications have isolated defense from civil sector	Tremendous overcapacity, anticipated trough in production
	Desired future base	Modified requirements and changed procurement procedures to allow increased use of civil sector	Size plants for smaller, more realistic production rates
Maintenance	Current base	Maintenance performed mainly by services	Maintenance performed mainly in service depots
	Desired future base	New designs decrease maintenance requests	Competition between service depots and private sector

(Continued on next page)

Table 34. *(Continued)*

		Industrial sectors		
		Shipbuilding	Aerospace	Ordnance
Research and Development	Current base	Defense sector dominates, commercial sector not competitive	Robust, but largely focused on system development for production	Military-unique, geared toward production
	Desired future base	Same as above	Shift in emphasis toward a more deliberate development strategy and use of technology demonstrators	Greater use of prototype development that may or may not lead to production
Production	Current base	Inadequate demand to maintain competition among shipyards	Overcapacity, anticipated trough in production	Overcapacity, including mothballed munitions plants, yet questionable surge capability in many systems
	Desired future base	Increased reliance on single sources for production of warships and submarines	Less frequent modernization, with retrofits and upgrades of existing platforms	Reduced capacity, improved surge capability for selected items
Maintenance	Current base	Maintenance performed in both public and private shipyards	Maintenance performed mainly in service depots	Maintenance performed mainly by services
	Desired future base	More private sector maintenance	Increased competition between service depots and private sector	Same as above

The Defense Acquisition Process

Perhaps no single area within the defense establishment, and that includes Congress, is in need of more sweeping overhaul than the process by which the government obtains the goods and services for providing for the common defense.[60] That process is a mess that costs far too much, takes far too long, and imposes too many unnecessary roadblocks to reform.

Acquisition spans items from ice cream to intercontinental ballistic missiles. Although the basic issues central to the acquisition process are simple—namely deciding what to buy and how to buy it—few other sectors of enterprise are as overregulated, excessively managed, and scrutinized by layers of oversight as defense. Clinton's second secretary of defense, Dr. William J. Perry, has suggested that the cost of all this regulation and oversight amounts to about $20–30 billion a year.

That the United States has become laden with an extraordinarily complex, overly regulated, costly acquisition process is no accident. The public wants U.S. forces to be equipped with the best weapons at a fair or reasonable price. However, ensuring value for money, including the effective testing and operation of these systems has been an elusive objective. The consequences have been a permanent contest between government and business that unfortunately has led to the current condition of super-regulation, oversight, and excessive expense. Literally hundreds of "horror" stories provide anecdotal evidence about the nature of the process. Six-hundred-dollar toilet seats and many-thousand-dollar coffeepots were representative of the 1980s and allegations of DOD mismanagement. In truth, these two items were billed as required and demanded by the cost accounting system and not instances of fraud or illegality, even though attempts to criminalize these anomalies have grown. Regrettably, the system itself has been responsible. And the system has not improved.

---

60 For perhaps the most comprehensive examination of this topic, see *U.S. Defense Acquisition: A Process in Trouble*, Center for Strategic and International Studies, 1987.

During the Desert Shield portion of the Gulf War, the Army had an immediate operational need to buy 6,000 handheld radios. Because of the 1984 Competition in Contracting Act, DOD would have had to seek a competitive bidding process for the radios. As there was no other manufacturer, one would have had to be created. Thus, the radios would not have been legally procured within months, let alone in time for the war. Instead, the Japanese government bought the radios and donated them to the United States. The list of these tales is endless.

Today, the resulting process is one in which the time it takes to field weapon systems grows longer and longer. Time and money are directly proportional, and procurement costs continue to escalate above inflation. Oversight and regulation have increased dramatically. The tendency to prosecute mistakes under the criminal code has intensified. To avoid criticism of any program, fault-free or zero-defect procurement standards have been set that have complicated the process and have not worked. For example, during test and evaluation when an objective is to push systems to the limit and beyond to make them fail, that failure can be cited as evidence for ending the system. Hence, the very essence of test and evaluation can be corrupted by the politics of the process.

In addressing the "what to buy" question, the Department of Defense has increasingly relied on and formalized joint requirements established by military commanders in the field to determine program selection, particularly on those systems with application across the services such as command and control, targeting, and advanced munitions. By and large, the services have had the lead for service-specific systems such as ships or armored vehicles. Obviously, the secretary of defense retains the responsibility and authority for ultimate approval.

In 1986, the President's Blue Ribbon Commission on Defense Reform, named the Packard Commission after its chairman and former deputy secretary of defense, recommended that an under secretary of defense for acquisition be established. Through that under secretary, acquisition would be managed across the services, with responsible program executive officers reporting ultimately to this person. Whether this organizational change has helped or hindered the process is subject to debate, but certain realities must still be addressed regardless of organization:

- First, operational needs and requirements must be translated into actual weapon systems. In this translation, if the specifications for the system are relatively sparse, the theory is that industry can be more efficiently and less expensively tasked to develop an appropriate program. If the specifications are detailed, government theoretically has more control of the program even though the costs associated with ensuring the detail is obtained can be vast.

- Second, as the defense budget declines, fewer and fewer major systems are being acquired. For the first time in nearly 70 years, for example, the Navy has not a single new-design aircraft in the development or production stage.

- Third, with the collapse of the USSR and even with the requirement of the MRC as a foundation for planning, the availability of plausible and realistic scenarios for evaluating operational requirements and needs leading to system acquisition is problematic.

- Fourth, the time it takes from concept inception to program production continues to increase, generally increasing costs.

- Fifth, despite all the attempts at acquisition reform, improvement has been marginal at best, and, thus far, all attempts to bring Congress into any solution for reform have failed.

The "how to buy" aspect of acquisition is perhaps in more serious difficulty than the "what to buy" aspect. Part of the problem includes a vast, overly complicated, and often contradictory regime of acquisition laws, rules, and regulations. Reform of these regulations, despite many attempts by many administrations, has failed even in the executive branch. The vice president's commission on "reinventing government" produced many useful recommendations on this account. However, in 1993, when the DOD tried to raise the threshold of contract bids to alleviate micromanagement, the Labor Department successfully intervened on the grounds that such a step, while producing efficiencies, would run counter to the Davis-Bacon legislation regarding minimum wage and therefore could not be sustained.

To get value for dollar and to protect taxpayers, a huge system of oversight and inspection has been put in place. Armies of auditors, accountants, and quality-control personnel were unleashed by government and had to be matched by industry to create an appropriate interface for all this regulation and oversight. The result has been a huge increase in the cost of doing business.

There is no single accounting system in government, and the cost accounting standards, particularly in addressing overhead charges, have led to erroneous pricing. Hence, many products in the commercial world costing a few dollars have been priced in the hundreds and thousands of dollars. These pricing anomalies have contributed to beliefs about the extent of "waste, fraud, and abuse" in defense contracting, even though virtually every example of these excesses was done as required by the rules.

Each type of contractual arrangement, whether a version of firm fixed-price, in which the price is agreed to in advance, or cost-plus, in which any legitimate increases are borne by government, has certain advantages and disadvantages. These contractual realities must be understood and the proper vehicle used. For example, a firm fixed-price contract, i.e., when the price is set and fixed by both the buyer and seller, makes sense when the product is well established and efficient production rates can be achieved. Research and development and new programs where uncertainty abounds are generally the worst candidates for fixed-price contracts. The Navy's A-12 stealth attack fighter, which was canceled by Defense Secretary Cheney, suffered in large measure from a fixed-price contract that guaranteed failure by ensuring underfunding. On the other hand, political sensitivity to cost overruns makes this type of contracting quite attractive to government.

In cost-plus contracting, the government pays the costs of design, development, and construction plus a certain percentage fee to the contractor. The "plus" is the profit. Although there are ranges of incentives and measures to control costs and regulate the "plus" or profit accordingly, the problem is that the government does not have the same guarantee of setting a spending ceiling in advance as with a fixed-price contract. These basics aside, if a program is badly managed or technically cannot meet performance specifications, the type of contract is not relevant.

The inherent irony of the test and evaluation process was noted earlier. Weapons need to be tested and pushed to the limit; however, failure even in testing can be controversial or fatal to the program. Explaining this irony in simple political terms is not easy.

Finally, Congress bears fundamental responsibility and accountability for its role and actions in the acquisition process. As noted, Congressional involvement and oversight have expanded dramatically. The reasons for this involvement are both good and bad and understandable. The net result has been an enormous cost and price imposed on the process. If any efficiencies of a substantive nature are to be achieved, Congress must become part of the solution.

Even though all prior attempts at acquisition reform have had few positive and often negative results, the Clinton administration embarked on an ambitious program to reverse this impasse. During the first year and despite strong rhetoric for reform based on dual-use technologies, commercial specifications, and privatization where feasible, change has come slowly. The resignation of Secretary Aspin and the installation of Secretary Perry have not changed this rate of progress yet.[61]

There is no alternative to pursuing effective acquisition reform. The costs are simply too great to continue unchecked. Specific recommendations follow in Part III.

---

[61] See Les Aspin's memo of November 16, 1993, on acquisition reform. He outlined twelve specific actions. However, Congress' failure to undertake Congressional reform and the abandonment of that reform effort suggests a rough road lies ahead for acquisition reform. (Aspin's first reform recommendations included: socio-economic and small business and simplified acquisition thresholds; commercial items; defense acquisition pilot program; military specifications and standards; contract formation; contract administration; major systems and testing statutes; defense trade and cooperation; intellectual property rights; contracting for commercial activities; service-specific acquisition laws; and standards of conduct.)

FINAL THOUGHTS ON INFRASTRUCTURE

Downsizing any large organization from General Motors to the Department of Defense presents the most enormous difficulties that span economic, emotional, political, and personal considerations. That DOD is the largest business in the world was put in perspective years ago by Herman Kahn. To paraphrase Kahn's views, he brooded that the defense business was the only corporation in the world with 535 highly independent directors [the Congress], many with agendas inimical to the CEO and COO [President and Secretary of Defense]; whose budget was formulated usually at the last minute and good only for a year at a time; and whose success or failure was measured at the time, place, and choosing of a competitor who would break into our shops, stores, and outlets, kill as many of our employees as possible, and then proceed to loot and pillage.

The underpinnings for this business are the infrastructure, and the infrastructure, constructed initially for the Second World War and then for the Cold War, is far in excess of what is needed for support of fighting capability and is far in excess of what can be sustained by future budgets if military muscle is to be maintained. Ideally, a single plan for downsizing this infrastructure would seem sufficient. Unfortunately, the political process has had great difficulty in addressing an issue of that magnitude in a single forum. Thus, the first step must be selling the need and urgency for a comprehensive approach and solution.

During the 1980s when trust and confidence among the branches of government and the defense industries were at a low ebb, reform of acquisition was next to impossible to achieve because of the suspicions and animosities that aroused this mutual mistrust. In fact, public sentiment was so distrustful that criminalization of any wrongdoing became an expected outcome. The spectacular results of Desert Storm, combined with efforts by the Pentagon to downsize and a progressive reduction in defense spending, have cleared away some of the bad atmosphere that had poisoned relations through this period of intensified mistrust.

In the 1990s, the mood is different. Opinion polls continue to show the public's negative and cynical view toward Washington and the inability of Federal Government to take effective action in redressing the basic problems this nation faces. No doubt the public still wants a strong defense and views its military with favor, but reductions to the infrastructure that are vital to keeping a strong defense directly attack local pocketbooks. Downsizing will intensify the need for good and better stewardship of resources. Errors and wrongdoing will become even less tolerable and more conducive to criminalization charges as this atmosphere worsens.

Above all, jobs and economic security and well-being are threatened. Thus, the key in making sensible and necessary reductions in the infrastructure while dealing as fairly and humanely as possible with those who will be hurt in this process demands that appropriate and sufficiently attractive incentives are created to this end. Without such incentives, the effort to pare back the infrastructure in keeping with a ready force will not work. Sounding alarms about "hollow forces" and desiccated military morale, in light of possible base closings and job losses, simply will not carry the day. Thus, one of the principal recommendations of this book addresses the critical need for proper incentives to facilitate this process of downsizing and to make it work.

PART III: SOLUTIONS—"WITH A GOODLY COMPANY"

Within the spectrum of responsible political opinion, it would be difficult to find any Americans, outside of determined pacifists, who would take issue with the proposition that the United States needs a strong military capability. Indeed, a large majority of all Americans believes that the United States still requires the best or most capable military force in the world. But, beyond that basic belief and this broad consensus view, there is far less understanding of and agreement on what should constitute "best" or "most" and how much money is required to buy, maintain, and support the necessary level of military might.

Part I examined the record of earlier post-war defense build-downs, including the current and continuing effort to reduce U.S. military power in an orderly and rational manner. It identified and analyzed the principal challenges and risks to the U.S. national security using three broad categories—strategic uncertainty, domestic introspection, and the extraordinary expense of the process. The practical consequences of these categories as they will affect defense will be to unbalance badly the new threat, strategy, force structure, budget, and infrastructure equation.

The alarm was sounded that, without adjustment, the current U.S. defense program will prove fiscally unsustainable. The consequences of this impending fiscal mismatch will lead to a military force insufficient to meet the demands of the strategy, too large to be adequately supported by the budget, and devoured by the resource claims of a surviving and excessively large infrastructure. In all likelihood, although that force may be declared the world's most formidable, it is certain to suffer more than only "pockets" of hollowness, and its aggregate capability could be a third or so less than it was in 1994.

Part II used the three broad policy choices of "Steady as you go," "Fund the force," and "Readjust and change" to establish the boundaries for examining the more specific components that make up defense. It then identified and assessed a comprehensive set of alternative military capabilities. These alternatives were derived from different mixes of the strategy, force structure, budget, and infrastructure components. From this examination, plausible and realistic boundaries for defining future defense capabilities were established.

Part III conducts a cost-benefit analysis of the three broad choices. It then proposes specific solutions to deal with this seemingly inevitable spiral towards less and less military power. In general, these solutions will apply to the implementation of any or each of the three policy choices, although the most interesting and unusual case is that of readjustment and change. In all cases, however, the solutions will redress the imbalances between and among threat, strategy, force structure, budget, and infrastructure.

The proposed solutions will, in the first instance, demand strong and enduring presidential leadership, action, and commitment if they are to succeed. But, because defense is only a small fraction of both the nation's current priorities and allocations of GDP, political reality will be to force the focus on the issues making up the other 96 percent of the budget. Should the president be unwilling, unable, or unpersuaded to take a strong stand in forcing action regarding defense, Congress becomes the court of last resort. But Congress is not designed or organized to replace the chief executive. Despite the inherent problems with a Congressionally mandated response to the issues of defense, without strong presidential leadership, there may be no alternative, even if the record of Capitol Hill taking charge of issues of importance is far from perfect and this attempt could also fail.

The recommended actions also include an expanded and reengineered set of strategic alliances and relationships applicable no matter which choice for defense is taken. Consolidation of the infrastructure is vital if any significant efficiencies are to be achieved and if an affordable steady state of military capability is to be realized. Finally, if the choice of readjustment and change is made, successful implementation will require sufficiently attractive incentives to strike the right balance and match among threat, strategy, force structure, budget, and infrastructure. This new and future balance could be set so as to assure the best and most formidable military that is kept highly trained but at lower total levels of manning and at lower levels of defense spending. The incentive necessary to achieve this new balance is likely to be measured in terms of hundreds of billions of dollars that can be saved. Any lesser measure is unlikely to work

But, no matter which of these paths is ultimately taken, there is one highly irresponsible outcome, namely that the future condition of U.S. military capability could be left to chance, deferral, or default. That unhappy condition, which will lead to "in irons," must not be allowed to happen, especially without full recognition and understanding of the consequences.

CHAPTER NINE: THE CHOICES EXAMINED

For reasons that are analytical and commonsensical, future U.S. military might will be defined by one of the three choices. Each choice has risks and rewards, advantages and flaws. Each choice also will benefit from the proposed reforms and recommendations that apply regardless of policy preference. In fact, in all cases, real reform is essential if an affordable, steady-state level of military might is to be maintained.

The most likely outcome will be "Steady as you go," probably through a path of least political resistance. Regardless of how this choice occurs, the objectives, strategy, and foundation specified by the Bottom-Up Review would be largely maintained. Defense spending would not keep up with the needs of the forces. The result would be a continuing and, at some stage, perhaps debilitating erosion in U.S. military power. Because this hollow condition will not be fully manifested for several years and may not then prove catastrophic, complacency over these future consequences now is not without certain appeal.

There is no dangerous, mortal threat to the nation that demands immediate attention. Despite the occasional specter of a second Korean war or some other international event becoming a flashpoint, the United States will concentrate predominately on domestic matters. Because it may be several years before the signs of military decay become unmistakable, this hiatus allows time for the U.S. economy to improve, meaning that more resources may be available when future remedial action is taken.

Because downsizing both infrastructure and defense must be achieved through the political process, the prospect of major conflict between the White House and Congress is real. Issues such as health care and crime that are perceived as, and may be, more significant could be held hostage to the process of negotiating defense drawdowns and base closures. Thus, taking tough or unpopular steps to protect or reform defense could lead to unhappy consequences in these more politically visible or important matters. Given the general paucity of political capital, the smarter tactical decision could be to leave well enough, meaning defense, alone.

The choice of "Steady as you go" has three major weaknesses and flaws even if it is undertaken with full recognition of the consequences for military power. First, a degraded military posture may in fact prove harmful to the national interest. This possibility is unprovable in advance and may not occur. It is still a risk.

Second, the opportunity for imposing change or reform may be wasted, dissipated, or simply lost. If the international realities were such that undertaking a major readjustment made great strategic and economic sense now and no action were taken, it may be extremely difficult to exploit a similar condition in the future if it continued. Indeed, it could be shortsighted to expect significant change would not occur.

Third, failure to act or even to recognize these disturbing trends could be irresponsible in fact and seen as such as military might degraded. This failure could further delegitimize the authority of government as far as the public is concerned. Trust and confidence would be shaken and weakened. Although measuring the psychological impact of declining credibility and authority of government is a difficult or impossible task, it should not be assumed that no damage will be done.

To summarize, the virtues of "Steady as you go" are that this choice follows the path of least political resistance; it emphasizes the primacy of domestic issues as seen by the electorate; and it is likely that some period of grace will be available for future corrective action to be made. The weaknesses of "Steady as you go" are largely conjectural. There is no evidence that even a significant decline in military power will matter. If no crisis intervenes, nothing much may have been lost—except the opportunity to shift substantial resources from defense elsewhere to other problems.

Alternatively, there is the choice to "Fully fund the BUR force." Funding, in this case, means spending more money or imposing reform that frees up additional defense resources, or some combination of the two. The advantages of this choice reside in the degree to which stability and peace are assured or guaranteed by maintaining current levels of U.S. military strength, along with commitments and overseas presence. If there is a direct correlation between U.S. force capability and future security and stability, a failure to fund to that level will result in negative consequences. The amount required to correct the shortfall would be between $20 billion and $50 billion per year, moving toward the larger figure in later years; in any case, the total could be in the hundreds of billions of dollars before this century ends.

The difficulties associated with this choice are principally political and economic. These difficulties are directly opposite to the virtues of "Steady as you go." By not precipitating political controversy over defense, other agenda items may be protected. By forcing debate on defense, these other and perhaps more important priority issues may be put at risk.

Third is the choice to "Readjust and change." The risks and rewards are a magnification of those associated with the second choice. The principal advantage is seizing the opportunity to size U.S. defense capability by bringing threat, strategy, force structure, budget, and infrastructure into a new balance. Like the other choices, this choice will benefit from reform and indeed is dependent on reform. Another and singular major advantage of successfully administering this choice is the possibility of freeing up a substantial amount of resources, perhaps upwards of hundreds of billions of dollars over time, and using these resources to resolve other problems.

Aside from generating intense debate, there is the question of whether less U.S. military power, no matter how rationally achieved, is in the country's best interest. Those who favor the Bottom-Up Review force will argue that this is the level of military power below which the United States cannot and should not descend. As noted, however, the BUR force has substantive strategic and conceptual problems worth repeating.

If the earlier analysis is correct, the Bottom-Up Review force is currently and probably fatally underfunded. Regardless, to some critics, the BUR force structure cannot carry out now the objectives of the two major regional conflict scenarios and therefore is flawed for operational reasons. To other observers, the BUR force exceeds the nation's genuine needs. No matter whether either of these or even another view is correct, the criticism remains that an imbalance of one sort or another exists among funding realities, force capabilities, and planning objectives. While this criticism suggests that little may have changed from the days of the "2-1/2 war" and the "1-1/2 war" scenarios regarding a "force-budget mismatch," what is different today is that the harm done by the structural erosion of military might has become far worse. Without the real threat, with growing demands on the defense share of the budget by non-defense priorities, with growing "cost creep," and, finally, with an unhealthy disparity between "teeth" and "tail," the new mismatch will prove far more challenging to military power than perhaps any time in the nation's history.

After Les Aspin's resignation as secretary of defense, President Clinton has held firmly to supporting the rationale for and the conclusions of the BUR. Aspin's replacement, William Perry, was a key member of the team that conducted the BUR. Thus, it is unlikely that complete abandonment of the BUR will occur in this administration even though a "BUR II" reappraisal seems likely and may alter or revise some of the orginial construct.

Second, only one of the four dangers that provided the foundation for the BUR is fully relevant to defense as a principal mission. The need to wage war in line with the MRCs is clearly the principal and legitimate responsibility of the DOD. However, what seems as the equal status of the other three dangers to national security should be questioned as the continuing basis for DOD planning. There is no doubt that the failure of democratization in the FSU is a real danger. There is more than doubt over the question of whether this should be a principal foundation for DOD planning or should rest, instead, elsewhere in the government.

Economic security and the danger of its failure are vital matters in framing national objectives. This danger is not, however, a principal objective for DOD. The Congress, NEC, Treasury, Federal Reserve, and other financial institutions are more centrally concerned with economic security than is DOD. To be sure, defense conversion is important, as is maximizing the military value gained for the defense dollar spent. But on the grounds of the size of the economic impact of defense (i.e., less than 4 percent of GDP) and relevance, economic security should not be principally a DOD concern or function.

Finally, the dangers of proliferation of advanced weapons and weapons of mass destruction are, of course, real. However, the implications of these dangers for the DOD should be more properly viewed as subsets of the MRCs and not as principal or stand-alone responsibilities for setting overarching DOD policy. For example, eliminating an adversary's air force or armor may be first-order wartime priorities, but neither is the overriding objective in establishing DOD priorities. Surely, as with arms control and foreign military assistance, DOD has a substantive but secondary role to play. The same should be true of proliferation.

This discussion leads to several important conclusions for DOD and its principal responsibilities. First, from a management and resource perspective, DOD must be primarily concerned with organizing, equipping, and training the forces to fight and win across a range of wars and conflicts. The MRCs provide the criteria and the operational requirements that rightly should guide and determine DOD programming and budget decisions.

Second, the planning assumption of two MRCs must be reexamined in terms of how many MRCs are enough and what is needed to win an MRC. As currently envisaged, the requirements posed by the MRCs will exceed the planned force capabilities if the budget shortfalls are not closed and if full simultaneity (i.e., meeting both MRCs at the same time) is not achieved. On the other hand, U.S. capabilities may have increased since 1991 as many more of the systems that helped win Desert Storm have entered service. Indeed, the demands of the MRCs may well have been set in excess of what could prove to be operational reality as a safeguard to ensure that enough U.S. military capability was available to win decisively.

Third, requirements for forces outside those generated by the MRCs to carry out missions of presence, forward basing, and overseas deployments must be carefully assessed as to whether they are additive (or additional) or should be met by the force levels and capabilities established only by the MRCs.

Fourth, to obtain broad understanding, consensus, and support for U.S. military power not only at home but also overseas, a basic and understandable framework for articulating the strategy for and use of these forces must be developed beyond responding to only MRCs. This articulation becomes more important if the four dangers posited by the administration and underpinning the DOD rationale are revised and more vital as domestic priorities dominate strategic and operational considerations giving rise to worries about American retrenchment.

In the past and during periods of danger and turmoil, the United States was able to make do with relatively small standing armies, relying on other policy tools for protecting U.S. security. From the onset of the Cold War, the general and more recent strategy was to deter and contain the USSR from aggressive or hostile actions, and the use of force was always vital yet symbolic and political in that sense. In practice, only against other states or actors did the U.S. actually apply force in anger. In the post-Cold War world, the concept seems to be to extend the role of deterrence and containment to a regional basis. Yet, deterring or containing regional instability, the new rationale for U.S. strategy, lacks the specificity for defining future military capability and perhaps the plausibility for generating domestic consensus on that strategy.

* * *

Before moving to solutions, the actions of three previous presidencies are relevant, perhaps surprisingly so, to the challenges facing us. These examples are drawn from three presidents not normally associated or grouped together—George Washington, Harry Truman, and Richard Nixon—regarding foreign and strategic matters of their day.[62] Spanning nearly the full life, thus far, of the nation, the sweep, scope, and reasoning for their actions offer an interesting perspective from which to address the issues of today and tomorrow.

America, during the last quarter of the 18th century and well into the 19th century, was in a most precarious form of isolation. The fate of the republic literally rested in the hands of England and France and was modulated by other European states, principally Spain and Holland. American diplomacy of that period, conducted by Thomas Jefferson, John Adams, Benjamin Franklin, John Jay, James Madison, and others, was both sophisticated and finely balanced. During the War of Independence, cajoling and keeping France as an ally was vital. After the Treaty of Paris ceded independence to the colonies, one of George Washington's major tasks was to protect and nurture a small and weak United States as a separate, independent country by maintaining this delicate perch between Britain and France.

---

[62] The lessons of George Washington as well as arguments supporting a complementary approach to foreign policy based on objectives similar to my own are found in the exceptionally useful book *A Breakfast for Bonaparte* written by Dr. Eugene Rostow and published by The National Defense University in 1993.

That George Washington is invariably misquoted in his famous farewell address delivered at Frauncis Tavern in New York in March of 1797 is suggestive of the failure to understand the nature of these policies. Washington is alleged to have counseled to "steer clear of foreign entanglements." What he said, in fact, was to avoid "permanent alliances." What he meant was the need for the United States to remain agile and flexible in its security, balancing the appetites and interests of larger more powerful states against each other. The result was a highly sophisticated diplomacy that simultaneously protected the United States from possible foreign domination[63] and would facilitate its extraordinary growth largely through future purchases and acquisition of the bulk of the continent that would lead to and assure prosperity and greatness.

The skill and flexibility of security policy under presidents Truman and Nixon were described earlier. From Truman comes the lesson of relying on non-military instruments of policy and less on raw military power during times of momentous and unsettling change. From Nixon comes the value of strategic vision using the rapprochement with China and the Nixon Doctrine as the basis for the transition from planning for "2-1/2 wars" to planning for "1-1/2" wars. While slogans and shorthand expressions are no substitute for sound strategic thought and plans, the lessons and applications are obvious and instructive in using flexibility, agility, common sense, and strategic vision. The implications hold for future U.S. security.

Constructive U.S. leadership and engagement in international matters remain vital. The United States provides stability, continuity, and reassurance in an otherwise turbulent world with perhaps greater emphasis on regional rather than global events. However, a greater degree of dexterity and agility is required in these unfolding times of turbulence. The lesson from George Washington underscores the value in balancing the interests of others against the interests of the United States. This is more than a simple balance-of-power model or a condition trivialized by the view that my neighbor's neighbor is my ally and is my neighbor's foe. The geostrategic era

---

[63] During the first, infant decades of the United States, the nation fought Britain after the Revolution in the War of 1812 and fought an undeclared war with France in 1801–1803.

with emphasis on military force and great power interaction has receded, perhaps indefinitely. Skill and subtlety in advancing security and geoeconomic interests are the orders of the new day in which regional tensions and conflict may be assuming more relevance.

The Truman legacy is one of grace under fire and the realization that rationality and common sense are essential, particularly when events are transpiring against U.S. interests. But the obverse is also true when events are conspiring to advance U.S. interests. Imagination and pragmatism can reinforce or multiply these advantages and opportunities, especially when applied across the many instruments of policy.

The Nixon legacy is a mixture of the actions of the first and the thirty-third presidents. Dexterity and flexibility combined with strategic imagination and common sense can yield new frameworks for security. These became the Nixon Doctrine. By adapting relevant aspects of each of the legacies, a framework of new and rejuvenated strategic alliances, based not on the quantitative or numerical level of U.S. involvement measured in military force but instead on qualitative criteria that combine strategy, diplomacy, imagination and common sense, can better and more effectively respond to the fundamental challenges posed by strategic uncertainty.

* * *

In developing any policy or strategy, there first needs to be a basic formulation of objectives. National security objectives can be translated into foreign policy goals, and the two sets of criteria can serve as the framework for defense policy, defense strategy, and the operational requirements that define force structure and employment. In November of 1993, Secretary of State Warren Christopher outlined the major priorities for U.S. foreign policy before the Senate Foreign Relations Committee. These priorities specified economic security; support for political and economic reforms in Russia and the newly independent states (NIS); Europe and NATO; Asia and the Pacific; the Middle East; non-proliferation; and other global issues.[64]

---

[64] The best formal statement of U.S. national security and foreign policy views is contained in the President's *Budget of the United States for Fiscal Year 1995*. See Chapter Six.

In general, the Clinton administration has pursued these goals through highly specific and visible single issues such as assistance for the FSU, NAFTA, GATT, and the American-Pacific Economic Cooperation Conference. However, unlike George Washington, Harry Truman, and Richard Nixon and their presidencies, there is no broad framework or design for integrating and implementing these priorities as part of a grander national security strategy and policy. Instead, the Clinton administration has chosen to react serially to events attempting to allow solutions to each to form the texture of broader policy.

Creating such a framework is not inherently difficult. For example, the United States is vitally committed to peace and security and to the rule of law and order in international politics and diplomacy. The demise of the USSR has consigned to the United States the role of single superpower and the opportunity as global superpower of applying its good offices to ensuring peace and security and the rule of law where and how that may be appropriate. This responsibility is real, readily understood, and generally supported by most Americans.[65]

In this role, the U.S. simply does not have (and probably never did have) the resources in treasure, blood, and national interest to envisage itself as the global cop. Arrogance aside, certain physical limitations cannot be dismissed. Hence, the commitment to peace, stability, and the rule of law cannot and should not be matched with a policeman's uniform or with a strong declaratory preference for morality and human rights that may prove unachievable or unenforceable.

While human rights are noble and important objectives, in many cases unfettered pursuit of this goal is simply counterproductive. Not every state has the same view of human rights as we do. Indeed, had China the oil capacity of the Gulf states, perhaps U.S. actions on human rights in both regions would be vastly different. The U.S. record at home is not without blemish. As long as careful

---

[65] Note that this responsibility is not to become the world's policeman nor to enshrine human rights or a related moral preference as the key or major criterion for basing U.S. policy. Certainly this point on the place of human rights is not without controversy, but the discussion on both points is short and, beyond this discussion, outside the boundaries of this book.

choice must be made as to where and when the U.S. should intervene on behalf of human rights and as long as the U.S. is unable to show a pure or perfect record itself, the use of human rights as an enforceable policy must be tempered. Indeed, there are cases where national interests far outweigh considerations of human rights. The World War II alliances against Hitler are most relevant in which autocratic and repressive Russia and China were staunch partners with the democratic West.[66]

Consequences for foreign and defense policy must flow from this general policy framework of commitment to peace, stability, and the rule of law. Here, the legacies of the three presidents are relevant. The U.S. must be engaged internationally in a manner that combines elements of flexibility and reassurance and, in many cases, as a facilitator in pursuing peace and security. Commitment to this new regime for policy, as in the Nixon Doctrine, must place more responsibility on regional states and partners buttressed by the "qualitative" support of the United States. That qualitative support includes but is not limited to the United States' good offices, its strategic "sinews," and military strength, including interlocking communications and intelligence networks, logistics and lift capacity, and, of course, trade and economic relationships.

All this suggests that the United States should be fashioning a worldwide network of positive interactions, building in some cases on its vital alliances such as NATO and through new regional security mechanisms created for discussion, debate, and, as appropriate, action in pursuit of peace, security, and the rule of law.

In parallel, there must be a series of major domestic actions at least equivalent to this reformulated foreign policy framework. These actions must deal with the consequences of introspection and preoccupation with domestic policy as they affect the broader security and correcting the extraordinary cost and expense of governance.

To make this work, there needs to be a considerable expenditure of courage, endurance, and political capital. Opponents, critics, and skeptics will abound on the need and ability for making substantial

---

[66] On the other hand, the strategic use of human rights as employed against the FSU had an important objective. The distinction, however, was between strategic and moral purposes, a distinction not to be ignored.

changes in national security and defense. Many will raise powerful objections and reasons why this cannot be done. Uncertainty about the future of reform in Russia and the occasional presence of autocrats and neo-fascists will be alleged as hard evidence to mitigate major defense policy shifts. Economic fears over the loss of military and military-related employment and the diminishment of the industrial and technical base are only likely to grow and to be used as counters to downsizing. Predictions occasioned by defense reductions will flow about the irreversible damage likely to be done to the perception of a strong and actively engaged United States by allies and adversaries alike. Last, some may argue that President Clinton's record on the Vietnam War and his lack of military service will become greater political liabilities if defense is reduced much further. But, on balance, these and related arguments will prove largely off the mark.

U.S. military power is certainly going to be reduced, and perhaps substantially, by the very nature of the political process that will cut spending while possibly imposing additional operational tasks or assignments and by the corrosive factors long in place that attack efficiency and effectiveness in using resources wisely. Something must be done. If corrective actions are taken to avoid the syndrome of "in irons," then, even at a certain fraction of its current power, the U.S. military will still be the most formidable and the most capable force in the world. Concurrently, with this passage of strategic eras, there is the unique but temporary opportunity to reexamine and adjust many of the assumptions on which our security has been based. These assessments can lead to defining more concise and relevant strategic and infrastructure objectives and, ultimately, to the smaller, right-sized force to serve our needs.

To complete the arguments for implementation of actions made possible and desirable by strategic change is the issue of the future role of force and how much will be enough. Regional instability and civil and ethnic strife are endemic and, for better or for worse, are part of global politics. It is very difficult to see, however, how force can be directly and effectively applied to ending all these civil instabilities except at levels of loss and cost that are unacceptable certainly to the U.S. public.

Suppose, for example, reform fails in Russia and an autocratic or despotic regime seizes power. Whether the U.S. has one million or five million people under arms is not immediately relevant to preventing the failure of democracy in Russia unless direct U.S. or Western intervention was contemplated. Should that same regime look outwardly to expand or to lean on its neighbors at a future point, appropriate counteractions would have to be taken. But, it is hard to imagine at this hypothetical time in a future that may never transpire, that the situation would be more perilous than it was in 1946, 1947, or 1948, when the U.S. had demobilized its forces and NATO and other alliances still remained largely gleams in various strategic eyes.

Admiral Arleigh Burke, who served as U.S. Chief of Naval Operations from 1955 to 1961, provided the appropriate and prophetic metaphor for describing how we should proceed in this new era. Confronted then by debate and intent to build thousands and thousands of nuclear systems, in his view beyond our needs and beyond what could be strategically useful, Burke remarked of his childhood in Colorado. As a boy, he was alive at a time when there were still lots of cowboys alive and well in the West. They all wore "six-guns." But, observed Burke, "you never saw a cowboy with three guns. Two were usually enough." Indeed, in this new era, the equivalent of two six-guns is certainly enough.

Chapter Ten: New Strategic Alliances

The challenges of strategic uncertainty for national security rest in the inability to predict the future and the unknowable long-term consequences of the end of a single massive and unifying threat around which a suitable strategy and sustainable accompanying level of military force could be built, maintained, and justified. Regardless of which of the broader choices may be taken, one means of strengthening U.S. security and defense is through rejuvenating old strategic alliances and creating new frameworks. This approach is independent of force levels and is applicable in virtually every case. What is required, however, is commitment to putting in place a more rigorously defined and articulated policy framework to draw together the many distinct and often loose threads that characterize the current condition of U.S. national security.

Assume for the moment that the United States accepts and articulates as its major security objectives the commitment to safeguard or advance security, peace, and the rule of law in conjunction with its interests and those of its friends, allies, and partners. In other words, the United States is expressing the need for cooperative or collective security in which it is prepared to play a significant and even dominant role *provided* a sense of partnership can be sustained. That "partnership" can be defined in different ways across different regions and different strategic needs dependent upon the different circumstances.

For example, the NATO alliance would be regarded in this view as the closest form of partnership bound by treaty, history, and nearly fifty years of unparalleled success. Partnership with Central Europe and the FSU would be defined in different terms but with the ultimate objective of bringing those states into NATO or a NATO-like security arrangement. In Asia, partnership through bilateral treaty arrangements with Japan and Korea could be complemented by new frameworks that could include even North Korea. Nor should Africa be exempt.

The thrust of these actions would be to construct the equivalent of a "new Nixon Doctrine" or at least a modified version of one. Responsibility for regional security would rest largely with regional states. In some cases, the U.S. role would be vital and central, such as in NATO. In other cases, the U.S. role need not always be so essential or visible as leader. The United States would provide the strategic framework and, perhaps more importantly, the "strategic sinews" in the form of its vast communications and logistics and its economic capacity. In other words, the U.S. would be the facilitator and provider of capabilities not available in the region. The majority of military forces would come from within the region. The combination of these contributions would serve as reassurance for security, peace, and the rule of law. Regional states would assume specific responsibility perhaps for peacekeeping and other initiatives that may be required.

Peace and security would be defined and measured in broad strategic, economic, social, and military terms, but not necessarily with a universal or absolute bias. In other words, any U.S. ideology or conviction about what defines peace and security would be muted and would not be automatically applicable in each case or region. And, the role of the United Nations would be appropriately integrated or modulated. How would this work?

The most vital alliance for the United States and for global stability among industrial states remains NATO. NATO is the linchpin for assuring security and stability throughout Europe and, with skill, perhaps could assume a broader role throughout Eurasia. While fundamentally and overwhelmingly an alliance based on mutual defense of its membership, NATO has the flexibility to adapt to a changing future, as it demonstrated at the 1991 Rome Summit. The future condition, health, and construct of NATO, however, have yet to be defined, certainly in irreversible terms. Specific realities, challenges, and issues will inescapably bound that definition and direction.

NATO is, above all, a threat-based military alliance. This simple proposition was a great strength during the Cold War. In the future, the issue around which NATO's relevance will rest is how well or how badly NATO makes the transition from what was a single threat-based military alliance to "something else." The first steps were begun at Rome in 1991 and continued at the Brussels Summit in January 1994. This "something else" will be a function of many overlapping, sometimes competing, and occasionally contradictory factors.

There are four concentric groupings of states and regions with interests and security concerns of direct relevance to NATO. The first grouping is the alliance itself and includes the competing interests and differences, as well as the common interests, of member states on both sides of the Atlantic. The second is the former Soviet Union.

The third comprises the Eastern and Central European states outside the FSU. Fourth are the so-called "out of area" regions, principally the Middle East and Persian Gulf, which are of immediate interest to NATO as an alliance and to its membership. Each of these four groupings will and must be affected by and will affect whatever course of action NATO follows. Unlike during the Cold War, there are no East-West constraints or bipolar forces that mitigate the impact of oblique, colliding, or diverging interests from complicating future action by NATO.

Within NATO, certain powerful centrifugal forces are at work. These forces tend to be exacerbated by normal economic competition, particularly at times when economies are retrenching or receding. There continues to be erosion in the strength of the transatlantic link. The end of the Warsaw Pact has been the obvious contributing factor. However, differences over policies and responsibilities to resolve the conflict in Bosnia have been serious. Unless and until there is more clarity in defining NATO's needs and responses regarding alliance expansion eastward, this erosion will not be reversed.

Concurrently, national political and domestic economic concerns of NATO member states cast darker shadows over the broader interests of the alliance. The growing trend towards regionalization of and preoccupation with subregional and proximate security concerns is not abating. Declines in defense expenditures continue in all of NATO's members and certainly in the non-Russian states of the former Warsaw Pact. Current estimates suggest that, during the remainder of this decade, European NATO states will reduce their military forces by half or more from the levels that existed during the waning days of the Cold War.

In light of these perspectives, it is not surprising that intuitive understanding and support of NATO by its publics vary considerably on both sides of the Atlantic. In Europe, there is inherent appreciation of the continuing need for NATO and for active American leadership and participation. Two world wars and one cold war this century are ample reasons for these beliefs. The alliance, with strong U.S. engagement, offers reassurance and insurance. Furthermore, only the United States can act as a restraint or ultimate arbiter should tensions among European NATO partners escalate to dangerous levels. Serious and even seemingly irreconcilable differences over particular policy issues such as whether and how to intervene in Bosnia and how or how quickly to extend membership eastward may come and go. However, from a European perspective, these divergences can be balanced by the realization that there is no alternative to strong U.S. leadership and involvement in a NATO that is at least relatively vibrant.

The U.S. public, on the whole, does not appear to share this level of intuitive understanding, interest, and support for NATO. The end of the USSR, in the view of many Americans, has ended the rationale and need for NATO. The prospect of expanding U.S. commitments eastward to include possible defense of former Soviet republics as distant as Kazakhistan is not credible. The threat of an expansionist or remilitarized Russia is not sufficiently daunting to much of the U.S. public as justification for continuing the size and expense of current commitments to NATO. Perhaps emergence of a serious and dangerous neo-fascist leader could change these views.

The current U.S. proposal for NATO that was unanimously approved by the membership in January 1994 is the Partnership for Peace (PFP). The purpose of the PFP is "to deepen NATO's engagement with the East and draw the new democracies to the West."[67] The partnership is open to all European countries, including the states of the former Warsaw Pact and Soviet Union. The PFP is an "evolutionary...and step by step" process that, with NATO approval, could lead, over time, to expanded membership. Active partners will have representation at NATO headquarters in Brussels, and military cooperative efforts will ensue. In crisis or imminent threat to the "territorial integrity, political independence, or security of any partner state, it will have the right to consult and engage in intense political dialogue with alliance members."[68]

There is a purposeful vagueness about the PFP that offers the promise of security to the East while not forcing or rushing any timetable. The details will evolve and will have to be worked out over time. By deferring specific action now, events in Russia and Central Europe will have the opportunity to run their course and perhaps be sorted out. All in all, the PFP could be successful once

---

[67] See Warren Christopher, "NATO Plus," the *Washington Post*, January 9, 1994, p. C7. In June 1994, Russia accepted membership in the PFP.

[68] *Ibid.* The article by the U.S. secretary of state is perhaps the most concise discussion of the PFP available.

a set of long-term conditions and criteria for NATO expansion can be defined and approved.

There are, however, inherent problems likely to arise from any set of long-term objectives for the alliance and the PFP. The dilemma posed by the transition from a threat-based alliance to something else is the most obvious. Because nurturing "reform and democracy" are purposes of the PFP, the vision or outcome of all this would seem to be a more stable, more economically viable, and presumably peaceful western, central, and eastern Europes, including the FSU. But that outcome directly contradicts the purpose and core mission of NATO, which is defense of the alliance. In this happy case of future success, what is to be defended against? The logic of success appears to be Marxist: a withering away of the alliance as the grounds for its existence evaporate.

Should the PFP lead to expansion of NATO membership, the question of extending commitments and security guarantees eastward is non-trivial. Ultimately, the incorporation of all former members of the Warsaw Pact into NATO, however remote the prospects are, could obviously transform the character of the alliance into a mini-UN or some other large and perhaps unwieldy organization more appropriate to the Conference on Security and Cooperation in Europe (CSCE) and the Western European Union (WEU). Incorporation of some but not other or all European states into NATO could establish political boundaries and divisions that foment and do not alleviate tension. Thus, the future of the PFP is not without certain difficulties and cannot be assumed, as yet, as an automatic cure. Indeed, in 1994, the impact of the PFP on future Pentagon plans is still an embryo.

For the moment, NATO has deferred taking decisions on resolving and defining the specifics of the PFP and what could become the irreconcilable issue of expanded membership. On the U.S. side, there will be grave reservations about expanding U.S. commitments eastward that would have to be met by some level or promise of U.S. military capability. In a bizarre situation where perhaps Belarus, Georgia, and Ukraine applied for and were granted NATO membership, if any of those states were threatened or attacked by Russia, conceivably, U.S. forces could be sent as part of a NATO response. Or, indeed, the threat of nuclear escalation could reemerge perhaps with ten or more instead of the original four nuclear states. On the other hand, without dealing seriously with changed conditions in European security, NATO could be signing it own death warrant.

NATO has had long and successful experience in dealing with and resolving seemingly intractable or irreconcilable dilemmas. Greece and Turkey have been at each other's throats for centuries, and Cyprus has been an island of contention and spilled blood between these erstwhile allies. In October 1956, the alliance was nearly fractured by the Suez Crisis and an Arab-Israeli war. British, French, and Israeli troops seized the canal and occupied a substantial part of Egypt. They were forced to withdraw by the United States, verbally supported by the Soviet Union then in the midst of a bloody suppression of the Hungarian revolution. Despite the most bitter feelings among the most important allies, the NATO alliance survived.

The most difficult strategic dilemma for the alliance, however, was probably over the tension between nuclear weapons and conventional forward defense in Europe. European members of NATO favored a strong dose of U.S. nuclear deterrence in which the battlefields were likely to be the superpower homelands at the receiving end of a nuclear exchange. Hence, this threat of strategic nuclear war would be sufficient to deter the USSR and, ultimately, to lead to less rather than more spending on conventional forces—a variant of Eisenhower's "new look" and, for the Europeans, defense on the cheap.

In the mid to late 1960s, as "massive retaliation" capabilities were being matched by the Soviet Union, the United States began to favor enhanced forward conventional defense in Europe that would blunt any Soviet conventional attack at the border—or so the theory went. In many ways, U.S. and NATO Europe views on this issue were seemingly irreconcilable. The solution was "flexible response," not only a military concept but, indeed, a brilliant political solution to an otherwise intractable problem.[69]

---

[69] Flexible response was fully described in Chapters One and Two. To review for the reader, the idea was to have a full spectrum of capabilities from strategic nuclear to conventional. Under this umbrella, the European allies could focus on strategic nuclear deterrence with their publics; the U.S. on forward defense.

Whether the PFP will have the same positive political effect that "flexible response" had is a good question. There is always the risk that PFP could become merely a slogan with no real basis for implementation.[70] The most important means for assuring success is to establish basic objectives and visions of where a future Europe ought to be headed. Then, the PFP and other policy instruments can be brought to bear to achieve those aims.

At a minimum, U.S. and NATO Europe objectives should entail a stable and secure Europe. NATO remains the best insurance policy to that end. At the same time, the fact that the preponderant military might in the world remains vested in NATO and the NACC suggests that there should be ongoing military ties and arrangements that could facilitate the deployment of some of these forces through this system and network of integrated and cooperative military structures. This means that NATO, acting as an expanded alliance or as individual members acting in their own interests as in Desert Storm, can call on these cooperative arrangements and associated facilities, experiences, and integrated command and logistic military structures to deploy forces when or as needed.

Thus, in the case for a "minimalist" NATO in which stability and security in European and the former Warsaw Pact states approach the level that exists in NATO today, a formal alliance structure would remain in place as insurance, and the military relationships would continue so that the capacity to deploy force in crisis was always present. To repeat, these are the minimum criteria on which NATO would have to operate while remaining an enduring and effective alliance. This still leaves unresolved the broader centrifugal pressures affecting NATO.

Addressing and containing the centrifugal forces can draw on the wisdom and lessons of Washington, Truman, and Nixon and apply a "qualitative" rather than "quantitative" approach. Qualitative simply means that ideas, concepts, and alternative policy actions rather than reliance on raw numbers of military forces and other exact measurements of power have greater relevance to the viability of the alliance. As a starter, the alliance can minimize hand-wringing and complaining about declining defense budgets

---

70 The cynic is reminded of the "search and destroy" policy in Vietnam— a slogan that really failed in every respect.

and requirements to keep specific levels of forces in hand. By moving towards cooperative task forces and increasing military-to-military relations, the most important sinews for training and employing forces will be protected.

Large numbers of standing forces, to a point, are not vital to training and preparing for contingencies. For example, in the 1930s when the Wehrmacht was very small and ill-equipped, its training and maneuvers were nonetheless predicated on corps and army levels of deployments. Thinking large while perhaps being relatively small in numbers must become the order of the day. This also means that innovation will be at a premium, and NATO should tailor its military capabilities against what is affordable at national levels rather than exacerbate alliance tensions by setting unnecessary and unreachable spending goals across its membership.

To deal with the issue of restoring transatlantic cohesion and averting potential crises within the alliance, the first step should be to take the numbers of U.S. forces permanently stationed in Europe out of play as a political issue. In other words, a future boundary or floor ought to be set at around the 50,000–100,000 troop level so that the question of cost is below the political threshold of pain in the U.S. Indeed, NATO should set what looks like its likely aggregate of national capability as the five-year projection for NATO needs. Although that U.S. number will lead to a militarily significant force of a few brigades or a division, and will be well under the stated military objective of maintaining a deployable three-division corps, those military consequences can be addressed through other means such as mobilization and reliance on allies. Most importantly, the pressure to withdraw or reduce U.S. engagement in NATO for domestic political and cost issues will be largely neutralized.[71]

---

[71] These reductions will also serve to deal with the dilemmas attached to extending memberships east. To the degree Russia has genuine concerns over NATO's military might, the reduction of U.S. forces in Europe is symbolic of NATO's defensive character. Of course those forces could be replaced or returned in crisis, but surely Russia understands that a severe crisis would be necessary for a redeployment of that magnitude. Hence, U.S. force reductions in Europe would respond strategically both to U.S. and Russian political realities.

To deal with the most important military and operational issues and the regionalization of security concerns within NATO, there should be greater emphasis on regional command structures. The Combined Joint Task Force (CJTF), just approved by NATO, will enable European NATO members to act on their own in crises outside NATO with military force through a NATO structure. At the risk of seeming to introduce undue complexity, this CJTF concept should be expanded so that the "flanks" (NATO North and NATO South) and perhaps the Standing Naval Force Atlantic would have CJTF staffs focusing on matters of both regional and broader NATO concerns. These staffs could be extensions of current staffs with new responsibilities for contingency planning, coordination, and training for potential new or different uses of NATO forces.

Instead of using these responsibilities to increase the size of NATO's bureaucracy, however, the reverse is important. There must be cuts, and perhaps a five-year goal of reducing NATO staff and bureaucracy by about 50 percent should be established. The reason, as with the U.S. case, is national domestic unhappiness with retaining large military staffs when the threat has changed. In other words, preemptive cuts might make for the best political outcome.

Employing the parallel of "flexible response" to reconcile other difficult and major divergences leads to some interesting solutions to the question of expanded membership. Assuming criteria and timetables for new NATO membership can be fashioned and accepted, one operational and political problem will be the effect of seeming to draw new "lines" in Europe as some states enter NATO and others do not or must wait to join. Using the military-to-military links that will be constructed through the PFP for both member and non-member states, it may be expedient to establish certain security "baskets" or categories by region and then address their absorption into NATO through these "baskets" and regions rather than on a state-by-state basis. To be sure, this may be viewed as a guise to obscure the drawing of "lines." However, these "lines" are transparent, porous, and temporary and no less visible than the current lines distinguishing NATO members from their neighbors.

One further step could be through the introduction of security zones or *de facto* local alliances. In this approach, for example, the four Visegrad states could be loosely formed into a security basket. NATO would extend military cooperation and training to provide the basis for a defensive capability. Then, this "bloc" could engage in agreements with NATO for friendship and, ultimately, security in concert with the PFP. An external attack on this bloc, rather than an attack on a single state, would form the basis for further responses. And, this organization would remove the confusion and complications of ethnic conflict among the members as a *casus belli* for NATO. In other words, ethnic factions in Slovakia attacking Hungary would not be tantamount to an attack by Poland, Russia, or some other power.

This arrangement would be simultaneously extended east. Russia could be either an independent state or part of the CIS. Bloc-to-bloc relations and military agreements would complement the PFP, would still permit the establishment of military-to-military relationships, and would remove the bizarre consequences of aggression against a former and distant Soviet republic becoming the unlikely trigger for unleashing a crisis over Article 4 and 5 commitments in the NATO treaty over defending member states.

In conjunction with this security arrangement, and as part of an inducement to overcome Russian recalcitrance and sensitivity to seeing itself surrounded by an expanded alliance or a new system of security blocs, a more substantial aid and assistance package should be put in place. The problems, so far, with Western efforts at aid have been too little, too slowly. Unlike Germany and Japan forty-five years ago, market reform in Russia will occur or fail without foreign occupation. The U.S. tendency to replicate its own systems elsewhere (i.e., the "Vietnamization" of Russia) is also unlikely to work. Yet, something needs to be done both to ensure some stability in Russia and to build a potentially huge, new market economy.

On the Russian side, centuries of autocratic rule, a bloated bureaucracy, corruption, and the absence of a civil code, banking system, and currency convertibility, among other impediments, have resisted the reform effort. Thus, only a very large program with tens and hundreds of billions of dollars in the offing is likely to provide the actual means for ensuring reform and the incentives to make reform work. A double security track is therefore essential if NATO is to remain the centerpiece in Europe and the thorny issues of European security and stability are to be resolved successfully.

* * *

The implications of these actions on U.S. defense planning are clear. Through formal resolutions, declarations, or other means, the U.S. would restate its commitment to NATO and Europe. The long-term goal would be a safe, secure, and stable Eurasia (i.e., NATO plus NACC), and the minimum structure and role for NATO would be as a military insurance policy and a military alliance capable of deploying the forces of the collective or smaller units as the situation dictates.

In terms of U.S. force planning, the number of U.S. service personnel permanently stationed in Europe would be flexible and probably much lower. Because it is unlikely that the U.S. public will continue indefinitely to pay for 100,000 of its troops in Europe, that level can be reduced to eliminate many of these legitimate criticisms.[72] What is more interesting is the effect of the PFP on MRCs.

If, through the PFP, NATO is to become the *de facto* means of deploying military force in many or most circumstances, whether collectively or unilaterally, then the perspective of the MRCs alters substantially. For example, if war were to break out in Iraq or Korea, very much as was the case in Desert Storm, the U.S. could deploy forces both directly and through the NATO network. This reality reinforces the need for focusing on "qualitative" solutions and instruments to facilitate future possible uses of force. Rather than restricting U.S. options, the NATO instrument can be very useful in expanding those options. However, there will have to be great care, sophistication, and balance in implementing the actions to make this work. Washington and Truman would be proud and Nixon approving.

* * *

Where a new mechanism or regional framework can and must be fashioned is in the northeast Pacific. U.S. bilateral treaties with Japan and Korea must be maintained. However, for the moment,

---

72 The cost of keeping U.S. troops in Europe has already been estimated by members of Congress as more than what the U.S. will spend on beefing up local police forces. Politically, the assertion that the U.S. is spending more on forces stationed in Germany than on protecting its citizens from crime by enlarging police forces could be devastating.

there is no serious mechanism for incorporating the major regional powers into some effective forum. The Conference on Security and Cooperation in Europe (CSCE), nearly twenty years old, provides a useful model. A Pacific Conference organized along the lines of CSCE and initially including the U.S., China, Japan, Russia, and South Korea, should be formed. The principal areas of common interest for this "CSCP" are regional stability and economic development. Specific issues for more immediate discussion could include discussions to resolve the Japanese-Russian territorial dispute over the northern territories occupied by the USSR after World War II and means to secure arms reductions in the Korean peninsula.

A third regional framework needs to be developed for the Middle East and Persian Gulf. The agreement between the PLO and Israel offers an opportunity for expanding this breakthrough. A CSC-like mechanism is a relevant and appropriate model in this region. Along with the U.S., the Gulf states, Syria, Lebanon, Jordan, Egypt, and Israel would be initial members. As with the CSCP, discussion would be the principal mechanism for beginning the relationship.

Finally, the U.S. ought to look towards establishing a similar type of security framework for Africa. This perhaps could be administered through the UN with the U.S. providing strategic sinews. The Organization of African Unity (OAU), perhaps in collaboration with the UN, would provide peacekeeping for tragedies like Rwanda and Sudan. The U.S. would contribute the sinews.

In parallel with these structures and engagement to promote security, peace, stability, and the rule of law, there needs to be a strategic concept for reward, penalty, and enforcement beyond the standard run of commitments and treaty obligations and the ultimate sanction of applying military force. Deterrence, as argued, was unique to the thermonuclear, bipolar age when both superpowers had the power to destroy each other and, thus, the strongest disincentive to war. That condition no longer obtains politically, but the punitive basis for deterrence may have future relevance.

If regional states with interests inimical to ours become the potential sources of conflict, would the threat of societal incapacitation or destruction be limiting or deterring? To make good any such threat, it is clear that thermonuclear weapons possess the necessary destructive characteristics. It is less certain but arguable that advanced conventional munitions offer an alternative through destroying the infrastructure and networks on which the functioning of society rests while killing relatively few civilians. Whether this threat, manifested in either form, is credible and whether the United States would actually impose this type of punishment are vital questions. A further question is whether it is the vulnerability of any society to obliteration as a functioning entity or the vulnerability of the population to annihilation that is the point of applying successful leverage in any construct of deterrence.

Return to the example of North Korea. Without direct outside military intervention, and with enough of its own determination and competence, North Korea cannot effectively be denied a nuclear weapon. Assuming the case that current U.S. antiproliferation policy does not work and North Korea builds one or more nuclear weapons, what are the likely policy options for the U.S.? They would include a range of sanctions and steps aimed at isolating North Korea politically and economically. The military option, if nonproliferation fails, is not very likely because of the cost and risk of another Korean War.

Suppose, however, the U.S. applies a doctrine of selective deterrence to North Korea. Should North Korea either threaten or use weapons of mass destruction, the U.S. would be prepared to respond by destroying that society's ability to function as well as attempt to eliminate the nuclear capacity. That threat could entail targeting the networks and infrastructure of Korean society, the population, or both. This threat of retaliation is specific in that it relates only to being triggered by the use of weapons of mass destruction, yet ambiguous in that it leaves open which strategic objectives would be used, which targets would be hit, and with what type of weapons. But there would be no gradualism or escalating ladder of response. As far as the potential target is concerned, the response would be total, massive, and devastating.

Under these circumstances of selective intent, the reaction of major powers such as Russia, China, and Japan is likely to be muted. The prospect of North Korea reacting as the Soviet Union did by developing a large nuclear deterrent force of its own is difficult to imagine and is beyond Korea's capability for a very long time if not forever. And, with positive steps such as the CSCP, this selective deterrence doctrine need be only a fall-back position. The application of selective deterrence, of course, could extend beyond North Korea to other potential problem states.

* * *

One implicit assumption underwriting the use of new strategic structures to address the consequences of strategic uncertainty is that fewer U.S. military forces will be needed and that their employment and deployment can be carried out in different forms. A long-standing assertion has been that numbers count and substantial U.S. military contraction or withdrawal will create adverse political and strategic perceptions and conditions for us among allies and adversaries alike. In many ways, this prediction has meant to be self-fulfilling as the best prevention to U.S. disengagement. However, as the role and utility of military force have less strategic importance to our major allies and adversaries, this forecast of automatic adversity needs to be reexamined.

At some point, there surely is a level of military strength below which the United States can no longer remain or be seen as a military superpower. It is hard to imagine that at a level of a million or so active-duty personnel and with an arsenal of the world's most capable weapons, this condition of non-superpower status would apply. The devil is in the detail, but common sense surely suggests that innovative ways to demonstrate and symbolize commitment, leadership, and engagement exist. Thus, by shifting more to qualitative rather than quantitative actions, this new framework can effectively deal with the rigors of strategic uncertainty.

CHAPTER ELEVEN: ASSURING THE BEST MILITARY IN THE WORLD

Whether we admit it or not, as with solutions to most issues of national importance, ultimately, the size, shape, rationale, and condition of U.S. military might has been and will be determined by the complex and often orthogonal interaction of politics and judgment occasionally tempered or influenced by analysis. Judgment, shaped or informed by politics, and politics, shaped or informed by judgment, have set the basic assumptions on which U.S. strategy and military capability have broadly rested. On this sometimes clear, sometimes ambiguous foundation, analysis was supposed to provide specific direction as well as justification for underwriting the military forces. To repeat, this analysis never had a universal formula or law that inspired absolute solutions. To advance on solutions to these issues, however inexact, three questions were posed earlier as vital to this process of determining what should and should not constitute responsible levels for future U.S. military might:

- What forces are needed strategically and operationally?

- What level of capability and what types of force structure are politically and economically sustainable and justifiable for the long term?

- How do we safely, sensibly, and affordably get from today's forces to those of tomorrow and properly balance the threat, strategy, force structure, budget, and infrastructure relationships?

These questions, in turn, lead to a three-part answer.

The first part of the answer rests in the examination and debate of, and ultimate agreement on, the objectives, criteria, strategy, and policy that must define U.S. military might. These answers form the assumptions, valid or otherwise, that set the qualitative and quantitative measures for deriving the entire threat, strategy, force structure, budget, and supporting infrastructure equation. From these assumptions and measures for that equation, the mix of combat systems and capability can be assessed against expectations of what can be achieved operationally, what cannot be achieved, and where there is uncertainty.

The second part of the answer rests in those actions for reforming this process and generating more effective and efficient use of our resources. It would be the height of folly if, in seeking to retain a highly capable force, we purposely chose to impose reductions in the hopes of balancing smaller budgets with reduced operational needs and, instead of sustaining a future military of highest quality and capability, ended up with a smaller but more hollow residual version of what is in place today. In other words, without dealing with the root causes of the growing costs and expense of the process of governance as they affect U.S. military might, the spiral towards fewer, less ready, and less capable forces becomes inevitable.

The third part of the answer rests in assuring we get safely from today's force to tomorrow's. This means properly balancing the interplay among threat, strategy, force structure, budget, and infrastructure. To implement the necessary remedial actions, there needs to be sufficiently compelling incentives to generate public and political support and then to permit navigating the dangerous rocks and shoals that endanger any safe passage of policy.

The three parts of this or any answer are indivisible and are necessary and sufficient conditions to assuring the best military in the world.

* * *

No matter the declaratory style, U.S. national security has been and will be articulated on the partial basis of contributing to global peace and stability as we Americans perceive these measures. Some level of force will be required to assure that end. This means the U.S. must have the ability to bring to bear, or to threaten credibly, the necessary force to resolve the issue at hand to our satisfaction.

In this regard, the use of the MRC in the Bottom-Up Review must be correct. The obvious and most demanding sizing scenario in this era of strategic uncertainty continues to be the major regional conflict. This is the most (or only) plausible and logical scenario in which the United States would bring substantial military force to bear. From this point, specific determinants for future force structure can be introduced.

In dealing with the planning consequences of a generic MRC, three specific considerations must matter most: the demands of the MRC—specifically, strategic and operational threat assessments based on enemy capabilities and intentions; the number of MRCs to be dealt with by the forces or other policy instruments; and the degree of simultaneity or seriality to be pursued in dealing with more than one MRC, as well as the other policy tools that might be brought to bear in the case of a second contingency. These other instruments include allies, mobilization, and perhaps even threatening or using nuclear weapons to compensate for any conventional military weakenesses. The Bottom-Up Review also defined presence as a basis for setting the level of military forces beyond what was needed for the MRCs.

Strategic and Operational Demands

Prudence suggests and history shows that occasions of a second crisis igniting during a first international crisis are surprisingly more frequent than might be expected.[73] There would be little popular dissent with the proposition that the U.S., at a minimum, must be able to cope with one MRC. Given the dangers and risks posed by an overlapping second MRC, the United States cannot entirely dismiss or ignore retaining some countervailing or contingency capability, if only to serve as a potential deterrent to a second conflict. Three MRCs occurring simultaneously have no recent historical precedent and would seem simply not plausible short of world war. Whether or not the BUR requirements for two MRCs are sustained, few would argue with the proposition that the U.S. must plan for at least one MRC.[74]

---

[73] For an excellent discussion of the record of second crises during much of the Cold War, see Jonathan T. Howe, *Multicrises: Seapower and Global Politics in the Missile Age* (MIT Press: Cambridge, MA, 1971), 412 p.

[74] The BUR calls for dealing with two MRCs "nearly simultaneously." During World War II, there were, in essence, two MRCs—the war in Europe against Hitler and the war in the Pacific against Japan. U.S. strategy was clear: win in Europe first and hold in the Pacific. As in that war, either consecutive or simultaneous operations may unfold regardless of the declaratory policy issued in advance of the conflict. And, allies and mobilization may provide the ultimate means for bringing sufficient force to bear.

The second MRC and forces required for presence will form central topics for debate and for determining how much is enough.

Regarding a single MRC, the Bottom-Up Review concluded that about 500,000 U.S. personnel would be required to fight and win. These forces would be divided among 4 to 5 Army divisions, 4 to 5 Navy carrier battle groups, 1 to 2 Marine Expeditionary Forces, 10 Air Force tactical fighter wings, 100 bombers, and sufficient logistics and supply support. They would be deployed to the MRC in three to six months. This force was designed to fight an Iraqi or North Korean type of enemy with military strength comparable to each of those countries. However, using the predictive outcome of any hypothetical military action as the basis for planning is bound to have inherent failings. Indeed, the case can be made that U.S. capabilities, for the time being, are both relatively and absolutely greater than they were during the Gulf War, meaning fewer forces might be sufficient to win an MRC. This argument, however, poses a certain contradiction.

How is it that U.S. military power can be evaluated as both more capable now than during the Gulf War and at the point of approaching a future state of "in irons" or worse? The answer is vital to understanding the fragility of our current condition and the dangers of complacency.

As of 1994, the U.S. maintains both enormous relative and absolute advantages in its military capabilities and in its ability to employ them decisively against any would-be adversary. However, as resources and defense budgets are cut, the actual operational capabilities of these otherwise superior weapon systems will erode as maintenance, overhaul, and repair parts needed to keep those systems up and ready diminish. At the same time, the personnel to operate and maintain these systems will suffer from these same budget cuts. Training and morale will plummet. Retention will decline. Overall capability then will fall off precipitously. This vicious circle becomes more vicious, and a hollow force or worse must result as it did in the 1970s. We have entered the first steps of decline.

Despite this impending decline and before its effects are fully felt, there is substantial evidence that shows or suggests the extent of U.S. military superiority today. Regarding air warfare, the United States has the best and most capable combat aircraft in the world with the best command-and-control systems. AWACS, the airborne warning and control system, is a premier example. U.S. electronic warfare capabilities include the most advanced active jamming, decoys, homing, antiradiation missiles, and standoff weapons. The U.S. has stealthy and virtually undetectable aircraft and cruise missiles in large numbers. B-52 and B-1 bombers have the capacity for conducting saturation bombing. U.S. fighters will dominate air space. And, these assets have been improved since the Gulf War, in some cases from the lessons learned during that conflict.

In the "air-land" battle, the U.S. continues to improve its impressive ground and maneuver warfare advantages. During Desert Storm, not a single M1A1 tank was lost to enemy fire. With thermal imaging sights, the M1 has killed the formidable (former Soviet) T-72 tank at ranges of 3,500 meters. U.S. attack helicopters, Bradley fighting vehicles, and the most advanced artillery, including the Multiple-Launched Rocket System (MLRS) with smart and scatterable submunitions are further examples of this superiority. The Advanced Tactical Missile System (ATACMS) will increase this advantage as will Hellfire II anti-tank weapons and better integrated C^{4}I.

At sea, no other state is capable of even the most limited contest over command of the oceans. These ocean-going combat capabilities are in the hands of highly professional, enormously well-trained U.S. forces. Since the Gulf War, the U.S. has more rather than fewer capabilities in place as more systems have continued through the production pipeline. These include nearly 500 F/A-18 aircraft now equipped with laser guidance systems.

This is a brief summary not a quantitative analysis of why current U.S. military advantage may be greater than we think. If this assessment is correct, then perhaps fewer than 500,000 U.S. forces may be required for a single MRC. The number could be as low as 350,000–400,000, provided these operational advantages are maintained. This means keeping the force fully funded or at least a sizable "core" portion sustained with sufficient resources to maintain high states of readiness to win an MRC.

It may be assumed that for the United States to respond (nearly) simultaneously to a second MRC, regardless of forces on hand, the full support, commitment, and concurrent deployment of forces by at least a few allies will be forthcoming, and whatever mobilization is needed by the U.S. will be carried out at home. This assumption is vital because it means that for the U.S. to engage fully in a second MRC, real stakes and real interests are involved and are seen to be involved. By definition, if neither allies nor domestic support is available, the grounds for categorizing the crisis as an MRC evaporate. For an aggressor who bets on a combined failure of allied and U.S. domestic support before embarking on what could be a second MRC, there is no absolute guarantee he will be proven right. On the other hand, the threat of a response, given the extraordinary military capability of the U.S., must be taken very seriously. In fact, without domestic support, U.S. response to a first MRC is highly questionable.

It follows that in order to meet the operational demands of either one or two MRCs that are likely to occur with minimal warning, a substantial portion of the active-duty force must be ready for service in all respects. While assumptions about warning and preparation time in responding to any MRC are as vital in planning for future contingencies as they were during the Cold War, it would be a most unlikely stroke of good fortune if another Desert Storm conflict were refought. In Desert Shield and Desert Storm, months of uncontested buildup and preparation time took place in a region with among the world's best logistic bases. Replaying these formidable advantages should not be seen as axiomatic. Also, given the political visibility and volatility in the U.S. of applying even small amounts of military force, that force must be seen to operate competently, decisively, and with minimum losses. This reality, in turn, reinforces the assumption of high readiness.

How Many MRCs?

If the United States follows a course of "Steady as you go," two MRCs will remain the objective. Given the degradation in military power likely to occur, except in worst-case conditions, from an operational perspective, the U.S. should still be able to deal with one MRC. This means a second MRC would be consigned to some sort of sequential operation, presumably with heavy reliance on allies and mobilization. Perhaps nuclear deterrence or a variant might find application in this case as well.

If the United States chooses to "Fully fund the BUR force," it should be able to deal with two nearly simultaneous MRCs. Whether that capability is worth the cost remains a vital but separate question.

If the United States chooses to "Readjust or change," several prospects are possible. If the advantage in military superiority is as large as suggested earlier and is sustained, perhaps a force of 350,000 to

400,000 would be enough to deal with a single MRC. Working backwards, that means that an overall military force of about 1 million, as opposed to the planned 1.4 million, might be enough.

On the other hand, the United States could opt for a single-MRC requirement or a "one plus" MRC planning basis. The notion here would be to deal with a second MRC much as we dealt with World War II. The "plus" capability could be defined as the ability to deploy, simultaneously to a second MRC, a corps of about 100,000 elsewhere. Working backwards, these requirements for a "one" and "one plus" MRC also lead to a force of a million or less.

Using largely arbitrary criteria based on the projected erosion of capability, evaluation of each of the three policy choices leads to this assessment regarding possible outcomes in dealing with the MRCs:

Predicted outcomes

Choice	Conflict scenarios			Likely annual budgets
	1 MRC	1 MRC "plus"	2 MRCs (BUR)	
"Steady as you go"	Sufficient	Marginal	Not sufficient	$250 billion
"Fully fund"	Sufficient (with excess)	Sufficient	Sufficient	$270 billion
"Readjust"	Sufficient	Sufficient	Marginal (or possibly sufficient)	$200 billion

To allow a comparison of this MRC analysis with the basic force options discussed in Chapter Six, table 20 is repeated here as table 35.

The $150 billion option is omitted from further discussion on the grounds that it and the 600,000 personnel force are simply not large enough for the American public. The reconstitution choice, while conceptually feasible and possibly valid, is deferred on the grounds that a substantially sized and highly ready force must be on hand whether or not large-scale combat contingencies occur. The global leadership position of the United States and the international

Table 35. The universe of future U.S. military might

I. BUR force fully funded at $270–280 billion per year (current dollars)

1.4 million active-duty force (approximate numbers)

• Army	450,000	15 divisions
• Navy	420,000	12 carriers, 340–350 ships
• Marine Corps	179,000	3 expeditionary forces
• Air Force	400,000	20 tactical fighter wings and up to 184 bombers

II. Alternative Choices and Budgets

Annual budget:	$150 billion		$200 billion		$250 billion	
Active forces:	0.75 million		1 million		1.2 million	
BUR force extended	• Army	225,000	• Army	310,000	• Army	370,000
(assumes	• Navy	220,000	• Navy	290,000	• Navy	350,000
maximum	• Marines	90,000	• Marines	130,000	• Marines	140,000
readiness)	• Air Force	215,000	• Air Force	270,000	• Air Force	340,000
Garrison force	• Army	280,000	• Army	400,000	• Army	450,000
(assumes	• Navy	180,000	• Navy	220,000	• Navy	250,000
maximum	• Marines	50,000	• Marines	80,000	• Marines	100,000
readiness)	• Air Force	240,000	• Air Force	300,000	• Air Force	400,000
Maritime force	• Army	180,000	• Army	220,000	• Army	290,000
(assumes	• Navy	280,000	• Navy	400,000	• Navy	450,000
maximum	• Marines	120,000	• Marines	150,000	• Marines	180,000
readiness)	• Air Force	170,000	• Air Force	230,000	• Air Force	280,000

- **Staggered readiness** For each of the spending levels, forces would be placed in one of three categories: fully ready; partial; and reserve. For example,

  Fully ready: 50% of the force

  Partial readiness: 25% of the force
  (i.e., 3–6 months to bring to full readiness)

  Reserve readiness: 25% of the force
  (i.e., more than 6 months to bring to full readiness)

  or some combination of the above

- **Reconstitution** Since the bulk of the force structure would be dependent upon reconstitution, no attempt is made to show a quantitative assignment of forces to any categories either by service or degree of readiness.

responsibilities it must accept mandate that U.S. military power be constituted in usable and deployable ways, certainly over the short term. U.S. domestic realities mandate that whenever U.S. force is used, it must be as ready, effective, and capable as we can make it. Of course, if these assumptions about readiness are rejected, reconstitution as well as other options can be justified.

Geography suggests that the garrison force is likely to prove too inflexible.[75] The U.S. must be able to project power, often at great distance and often with alacrity. The future strategy preference should stress agility, in keeping with needs of an uncertain world. Agility would also be reinforced by the network of new and rejuvenated alliances that should be created and the need to respond perhaps quickly to a range of unpredictable events abroad. Garrison forces inherently lack this agility. This does not mean the U.S. will not and should not selectively rely on garrison army and air forces stationed in Europe, Korea, or the United States, but those land-based forces would be counted as part of the total allocation for each service and not be used as "force-builders" in driving the overall force structure design.

This means force design will follow either the "BUR force extended" or the "maritime force" construct. The BUR extended has the advantage of being the least bureaucratically difficult to implement since each of the services must equitably share and support the reductions. The disadvantage would reside in whatever loss in strategic and operational agility occurs from maintaining a large land-based component of the force structure.

The maritime force has the advantage of strategic agility. Indeed, to the degree that additional land-based air power assets could be incorporated into this force design, it is perhaps a more attractive alternative than the BUR extended. In this case, the function of air power could be to blunt initial attacks in an MRC and to support ground operations as well as to conduct a strategic campaign

---

[75] Moving large numbers of land-based forces to regions that lack basing facilities is a time-consuming and expensive proposition. That said, it also should be noted that the largest amphibious invasions during World War II, like Normandy, were conducted by the Army. In the future, however, we simply may not have the time to mount such an operation.

from the air. The lessons of the Gulf War are relevant. The disadvantage is that, bureaucratically, it would be more difficult to implement because ground forces would absorb a disproportionately large share of the cuts. Depending upon the assumptions that underwrite the strategy and objectives, U.S. presence and commitments could be redefined, physically reduced, and augmented through an expanded framework of regional alliances and security arrangements and through emphasis on qualitative rather than quantitative means to underwrite U.S. commitments. This approach would reduce demand on the numbers of forces needed in service and to carry out obligations of presence and commitments.

In other words, the Cold War characteristic of automatically associating commitments with some (generally high) level of military force could be replaced with a more flexible regime that restructures, reconfigures, and, in some cases, reduces the need for U.S. military presence and overseas deployments. The new objective for this regime would be based on preserving access. Access, in turn, requires more than only presence and offers flexibility and relief in maintaining constant deployments. Regional familiarity, logistical support, overflight and basing rights, and other characteristics of preserving access follow.

MISSIONS OTHER THAN WAR—NEW WAYS OF DOING BUSINESS

The term "missions other than war" is becoming more prevalent in defense discourse. Presence and peacekeeping-related tasks are two of the most widely discussed missions. However, these new tasks should be more closely examined before they are adopted into new and expanded formal U.S. military roles and missions.

The BUR has specified "presence" as a sizing factor for forces beyond the MRC requirements. But presence as defined in this sense still carries a Cold War connotation and currently imposes operational demands on the forces that, for the longer term, will hurt morale and probably are not sustainable for other reasons relating to funding cuts. Reductions in the size of the force, combined with unrelenting demands for maintaining U.S. forces on deployed status, have led to high levels of operational tempo equivalent to the most intense days of the Cold War. Without compelling reason, it will prove difficult to convince the forces that this stress is in the country's best interest. At this point, traditionally, morale and retention begin to suffer.

The hard-nosed assessment must be that the military demands of the MRCs should be the basic sizing factors for U.S. forces. Forces for presence will be drawn from this aggregate and cannot be regarded as additive because higher numbers of forces will prove neither strategically necessary nor politically and economically affordable. To reduce the operating tempo and the operational demands that, ironically, put as great or greater requirements for deployments on our forces now as existed during the Cold War, readjustment must be made to current commitments, deployments, and presence objectives.

If presence is removed as a criterion for rationalizing and establishing force levels, other "new missions" may be contenders for this force-building function. Among the most visible and perhaps most tempting of publicly discussed "new missions" for U.S. forces is the family of so-called peacekeeping tasks. Peacekeeping is used in a broader sense as shorthand for using military forces not only in specific missions embodied by the symbol of the UN's "blue hats and helmets" but also in more expansive, related nation-building assignments. Peacemaking, peace-imposing, and nation-building are inexact phrases that suggest the boundaries for a range of these possible new missions. For example, should a peace settlement be reached in Bosnia, the U.S. has pledged a peacekeeping force of 25,000 to 35,000. That size force requires a pool of about 75,000 to 100,000 to support such a deployment on the standard planning rule of "two back for every one forward." This peacekeeping requirement would require nearly 20 percent of the current U.S. Army if it were dedicated to this single task. If these roles were assumed, the implications for force planning could easily reach the numerical equivalent of a single MRC.

Although there is an obvious and understandable need for organizations or nations to carry out these broader tasks, it does not follow necessarily that peacekeeping-related missions should be a principal U.S. responsibility or a U.S. Department of Defense assignment. Peacekeeping requires absolute neutrality, great endurance and patience, and an ability to bring ambient political temperature to as low a point as possible. Culturally, politically, and emotionally, this would prove to be an extremely arduous task for America and Americans. Largely but not exclusively for domestic reasons, the U.S. is not well-disposed to take up a posture of absolute neutrality. In Bosnia, for example, while atrocities have been committed by all three factions—Serbs, Bosnians, and Muslims—Bosnian Serb radicals have been by far the guiltiest parties. It would be extremely testing, given America's sense of fair play, not to see U.S. peacekeepers lose the required sense of neutrality and favor, even subjectively, the most aggrieved party.

Americans are also results oriented. Endurance and staying power, especially when human lives and substantial costs are involved, are not our long suits. To be sure, the U.S. stayed and remains in Europe, Korea, and Japan. But this forward basing is not peacekeeping, and the important reasons for continuing U.S. presence are well understood.

Americans also make among the best political targets for radical or terrorist groups. Given American visceral disapproval of taking casualties, this understandable and commendable trait is the final reason why broader peacekeeping missions should not be our cup of tea. This does not mean there are no new missions or areas where the U.S. should intensify its efforts to identify relevant tasks for military forces. Two bear scrutiny.

The first relates to support of peacekeeping. The United States does maintain the most formidable training; logistics; command, control, communications, and intelligence; and lift capabilities in the world. These are strategic "sinews." Where the U.S. and the U.S. military should be prepared to play a role is in providing these strategic sinews to support the peacekeeping family of missions carried out by other states. As the Swiss were known for centuries as the most reliable guards in Europe, the U.S. could become the principal support component to these peacekeeping-related tasks through its strategic sinews.[76]

---

[76] Alternatively, if the United States determines it must play a major role in peacekeeping and station large numbers of peacekeepers abroad, consideration can be given to establishing a separate "peacekeeping" organization, perhaps under the State Department and outside DOD. DOD might provide the military protection. However, this alternative would relieve some of the problems of associating peacekeeping with combat forces and deserves further review.

Second, to cope with the tasks of preventing both potential proliferation and MRCs from starting in the first place, the U.S. should examine the new mission of extending selective deterrence through purely countervalue means against would-be Third World adversaries. The ability to defeat an opponent's armed forces is part of the MRC responsibility. However, the ability to threaten that society, either with nuclear or conventional weapons, may be one method of appropriately limiting proliferation in general and the use of weapons of mass destruction specifically against us or our friends.

NEW ORGANIZATION

If caution is suggested in the rush to embrace certain missions other than war, quite the opposite approach is advocated in exploring new ways to employ forces through organizational change. There are two types of organizational change to be investigated. The first is through "jointness," that is, drawing on the capabilities of each of the services to complement, multiply, or create higher levels of military effectiveness. The second is to structure traditional units differently.

Regarding "jointness," given the resource constraints and the need to operate the forces in the demanding new environment, there is no reason traditional service responsibilities and capabilities cannot be more broadly shared. For example, why could there not be an automatic, standing, operational, organizational structure in which the ground commander assumed control of naval forces that, in turn, had Air Force units flying off its ships or perhaps even Army ATACMS loaded in the vertical launch tubes of surface combatants or some equally innovative variant? Another term for this type of highly flexible organization is "adaptive."

The first commander in chief of the new U.S. Atlantic Command, Admiral Paul D. Miller, and the Vice Chairman of the JCS, Admiral William A. Owens, have been proponents of "adaptive joint force packages." The concept embellishes General Powell's metaphor of designing a "tool box" of forces for field commanders by repackaging sea, air, and land forces into appropriate operational units tailored for specific missions. The innovative configuration of the U.S. aircraft carriers in the Haitian intervention, replacing air wings with soldiers, is a relevant example.

Although this seems an obvious and uncomplicated idea with great merit, the coordination and effort needed to continue along these lines are considerable. There is resistance, which is understandable. Operational commanders may think they need force packages different from the ones being provided. Hence, the traditional approach is seen as satisfactory. But, exploring these operational changes in organization is essential and offers great potential in maximizing the way in which force can be effectively deployed and used, especially when budgets make the old, tried-and-true system unaffordable or less affordable.

The second approach is to reexamine the organization and equipment of the basic unit building blocks for the force—the carrier air wing, the Army battalion, and the Air Force squadron or wing. The argument here is that, given U.S. absolute military superiority, the amount of equipment—specifically aircraft, tanks, artillery, and other large systems—might be reduced in each unit. The reduction of the carrier air wing from about 90 to 60 aircraft is the example that could become the rule. Whether this applies to other units in the Army and Air Force needs to be closely examined.

To summarize, future U.S. force structure should be constructed on the operational requirements posed by the MRC. In "Steady as you go" and "Fully fund," two MRCs would be the driving requirement. In the first case, the requirements would be objectives (partially) unmet by the capabilities. In the second, the forces would meet the mark.

Should the "Readjust and change" choice emerge as policy, overall reductions in force levels from the planned 1.4 million to about 1 million in active-duty strength would be made over a period of three to five years. These or any reductions will be hotly contested by many, including those who argue that there is a certain critical mass in the size of the force below which it will be fractured or broken. The current Army Chief of Staff, General Gordon Sullivan, argues vehemently that the U.S. Army, for example, cannot descend below a level of about 495,000. If it does, General Sullivan believes and warns the Army will be "broken" and will become incapable of carrying out its current roles.

The notion of force fragility and the attendant concern that size is crucial beyond or above a certain point cannot be lightly or easily dismissed. This issue is one of military judgment, and, aside from parochial service preferences that are understandable and legitimate, the nation can ill-afford to make significant cutbacks that ultimately will lead to shattering the surviving force.

On the other side of the coin, there is no hard evidence that forces cannot be substantially reduced. It is obvious that if forces are reduced in a callous or unplanned manner, if operational demands and deployments are not accordingly reduced, and if readiness and maintenance are degraded, the morale and fighting fiber of the soldiers, airmen, and sailors and marines will suffer grievously. Indeed, although there is a large degree of unfairness in the following comparison because of significant overhead, infrastructure, organizational, and operational differences, some would argue there is already a land force in the United States a third the size of the U.S. Army. It is the Marine Corps. Although the Marine Corps lacks the armored punch of the Army and the associated heavy capabilities for waging long-term high-intensity conflict, it numbers about 175,000, showing that a smaller ground force can be both sustained and kept at high levels of readiness.

The arguments that total numbers as large as 500,000 are needed so as not to shatter the Army rest on several assumptions. The rule of thumb is that for every forward-deployed division three are needed for rotational purposes. With over 100,000 soldiers deployed, this requirement quickly builds the numbers. In the Army, the argument arises that there are two forces: one that is trained and one that is in training. Thus, in this view, large numbers are seen as vital to sustain a given endstrength if the force is to be effective.

The Navy, however, would seem to be less affected by this notion of shattering. Because the bulk of naval striking power rests in a relatively small number of ships (the carrier, Aegis-class destroyers and cruisers, and nuclear submarines), a 250-ship Navy need not be much less capable than a 500-ship Navy provided the right ships were kept and the operational needs and deployments sized accordingly. Twelve carriers with enough Aegis escorts are maintainable at both the 250- and 500-ship level. The difference is that with the end of a major threat at sea, the Navy can and has slimmed down in total numbers. At the same time, reductions in amphibious capability could be mitigated by retaining the big-deck LHAs and other large ships that carry substantial numbers of Marines.

The response to those who see the risks of a shattered force as real will never be entirely convincing. However, given the trends, the U.S. military seems irreversibly headed in the direction of a much smaller and weaker force if a 1.4-million active-duty strength cannot be fiscally sustained. Hence, if reforms are not made to deal with the efficiency and cost issues, it is a matter of time until a shattered force or, certainly, a desiccated one occurs. Reforms also must be highly innovative in promoting new or alternative organizations for enhancing fighting power. For better or worse, the Army attempted major strategic and organizational change in the 1950s when no less a military general than Eisenhower presided over the strategic "new look" and the pentomic Army.

If the change is, in fact, made, under either the BUR extended or maritime force choice, how might commitments and presence requirements be tailored? Tables 27, 28, and 29 showing that tailoring are reproduced here as tables 36, 37, and 38.

Table 36. Central Europe and the former USSR (objectives, commitments, deployments, and presence)

Objectives	Commitments	Deployments	Presence
Current			
Support democratization and open market reform	SALT, ABM, CFE START, INF treaties	N/A	N/A
Support aid and assistance	Funding	—	—
Reduce nuclear and conventional armaments	Advisory personnel	—	—
Defense conversion	"Partnership"	—	—
Alternatives and additions			
Extend NATO "partnership"	Defense of FSU, Central Europe	U.S. forces	Part-time (?) Low-level
Extend NATO membership	Defense of FSU	U.S. forces	Full-time
Extend economic partnership	Treaties, agreements, funding	—	Low to medium level
Peacekeeping in Bosnia	Impose peace	U.S./NATO forces	Up to 25,000

Table 37. Northwest Pacific (objectives, commitments, deployments, and presence)

Objectives	Commitments	Deployments	Presence
	Current		
Assure U.S. engagement	Treaties (U.S.-Japan; Korea)	Seventh Fleet	All U.S. military forces
Promote stability	Peace	U.S. in Korea	
Promote trade, economic development	Security and stability	U.S. in Okinawa	Full-time Robust
Reduce grounds for conflict	Troop presence	Exercises	
	Restraining N. Korean nuclear proliferation		
	Alternatives and additions		
Broaden security framework through CSCE-type mechanism	As above	Greater military cooperation and exercises	Probably larger
Seek arms control agreements	Treaties	?	?
Seek alliance, nonaggression treaties	Treaties	?	?

Table 38. Non-regional/"global" issues (objectives, commitments, deployments, and presence)

Objectives	Commitments	Deployments	Presence
	Current		
Promote democratization and open market reforms	GATT, IMF, international agreements	In concert with other objectives	In concert Selective
Free/fair trade		Selective, i.e., Kurdish, Somalia relief	
Antiproliferation	UN		
Antiterrorist	MTCR; non-proliferation treaty	?	
Promote human rights			
Promote humanitarian actions	Maintain access "enablers"		
	Alternatives and additions		
Provide a UN force/make the UN the ultimate arbiter of international disputes	To subsume national authority and autonomy to UN decision	?	?

In general, the key assumption for this particular type of tailoring is that the U.S. would structure its deployments on the basis of maintaining access to a particular region. The degree of access would be in keeping with commitments and with the needs for responding to contingencies or special circumstances relating to that region. In Europe, the 100,000 U.S. troop level most likely would be reduced to about 50,000 to 75,000 as a means of preventing or preempting politically driven pressures in the U.S. from making that number even lower. In the Mediterranean, the U.S. would keep a full-time presence, but one that was flexible and need not always include an aircraft carrier. Instead of a carrier on station about 75 percent of the time, that figure could be reduced to a third or half time on station. Flexible deployments and alternatives, such as sending a mix of air and ground units on short deployments to a region, would complement maritime presence.

The same regime of operational flexibility and tailored deployment patterns would be expanded globally to other regions where presence is to be maintained and access assured. Development of these types of innovations, as well as the concurrent and specific practical actions, must be left to the JCS, the CINCs, and the military staffs who have the expertise necessary for implementation. Under this arrangement, the tempo of operations would be reduced in large part to prevent wearing out people and machines. To the degree that allies could join in these deployments, as well as through cooperative training and exercising, for example, as envisaged in the PFP, powerful complementary mechanisms for demonstrating U.S. engagement and commitment will be put in place or reinforced.

STRATEGIC NUCLEAR FORCES

Regarding strategic nuclear offensive forces, with the demise of the USSR, the longstanding strategy, doctrine, targeting, and, indeed, purposes of these forces have been immutably changed. As long as nuclear and thermonuclear weapons exist and guarantees for their permanent elimination are less than absolute, the United States must retain some of these forces for the reason of prudence. Beyond this single reason, establishing consensus or policy on what nuclear strategy and forces are required must rely on intuitive factors and judgment. There are, however, a few indicators of possible future direction.

At the same time that the U.S. and Russia move towards reducing total strategic nuclear warhead inventories to 3,500 or less, it is imperative to understand what the new basis should be for rationalizing and maintaining these weapons. Default in fully addressing this case is possible and risks implementing actual or formal policies before they have been well thought out. But we know the following. At a minimum, France, Britain, and China will possess substantial nuclear arsenals numbering in the hundreds of warheads. Pakistan, India, Israel, and North Korea, if all those states are or go "nuclear," will possess handfuls of nuclear weapons. These systems will be nuclear and not thermonuclear. Furthermore, the residual FSU republics are likely to reduce or eliminate their nuclear arsenals and, for planning, can be considered added together with Russia. And the distinction in destructive capacity between nuclear and thermonuclear weapons should not be dismissed.

What is the purpose of nuclear and thermonuclear weapons? Strategic nuclear deterrence could be seen as nothing more than a relic of the Cold War. And enough U.S. and Russian nuclear weapons will remain as insurance against a future confrontational situation that could be no worse than the Cold War standoff if Russia were to become a threat again. Beyond that, there are other purposes for these nuclear systems.

First, it would be a good idea for the United States to be able to prevent potential adversaries or proliferators from threatening the U.S. with weapons of mass destruction (in addition to a very distant future when super-conventional weapons conceivably could cripple a society by destroying its infrastructure). Until such time as those nuclear threats are eliminated, the U.S. must maintain a thermonuclear and nuclear arsenal that is perceived as one of overwhelming superiority. In other words, the ability to obliterate potential adversaries should not be dismissed or assumed away. Such an arsenal would require perhaps hundreds or even a thousand or so warheads and weapons. This also means that targeting has to expand to include a range of potential adversaries, and retargeting options and capabilities as well must be enhanced or put in place.

To ensure cooperation and mutual understanding among the major nuclear states regarding the role of these weapons, perhaps a Nuclear Planning Group (NPG) type of arrangement, as exists in

NATO, ought to be set up, with nuclear states as members. The principal purpose would be to demonstrate that the old Western and Eastern blocs are not targeting each other as has already been agreed by Russia and the U.S. The assignment, say, of U.S. and Russian officers to the strategic nuclear forces of the other is a wise step. Because one state's potential target may be someone else's ally (i.e., North Korea), this NPG could focus on how to prevent or respond to proliferation and the use of or threats of use of weapons of mass destruction.

In this future arrangement, the U.S. would move almost certainly to a largely sea-based deterrent force. The remaining bombers—the B-1, B-2, and older B-52s—would be assigned principally to non-strategic non-nuclear roles. Intercontinental ballistic missiles (ICBMs), consistent with strategic arms agreements, should be reduced. A minimum of ICBMs, perhaps numbering well under 100, should be retained. The vast bulk of capability should reside in the submarine force, with ships that can patrol while staying in American homewaters or in port, as the reach and accuracy of the D-5 missile is sufficient for most target coverage.

The area where the U.S. should persist, although at responsible and appropriate levels, is in improving ballistic missile defense. Because these implications for U.S. force structure are modest in affecting design, size, or the level of defense spending, missile defense is noted as a significant area but beyond this particular study effort.

Once agreements with the FSU can be reached on descending below the 3,500-warhead limit, movement towards the sea-based, more flexible force supported by NPG-type arrangements will form the future capabilities. The purpose remains to provide an overwhelming counter to any state that uses or threatens to use mass-destruction weapons. The implications for the nuclear defense industrial base are more significant and follow.

* * *

To summarize, the United States faces three basic choices regarding future military might. "Steady as you go" will result in a military that retains as its objectives the requirements set by two MRCs. For reasons noted, over time, without full funding, the force will lose perhaps a third or more of its aggregate capability. It will become largely "hollow."

If this choice is made, whether by default or design, the underlying reasons are clear. The lack of threat, the amount of warning time likely to be available if a dangerous threat were to arise, and the primacy of domestic issues provide the rationale for maintaining course, speed, and the inevitability of decline. For those who disagree with this judgment and potentially abhor the consequences, perhaps the more open and public manner in which this choice was deliberated and debated would mitigate some of these concerns.

If, however, a hollow force resulted because Congress and the president chose either not to recognize or to defer the consequences of this case, that would be irresponsible. But, it could happen.

"Fully funding the force" will produce a balance between the requirements of two MRCs and military capability sufficient to meet those needs. It is arguable whether more money will be spent on defense or whether reform will free up the necessary resources to fund this force fully. However, this choice is reasonable and responsible if it can be carried out. If not, the flaws and inherent shortcomings of the first choice apply.

"Readjust and change," by far the most ambitious choice, requires change both in structure and in process. The ability to impose reforms in both of these areas could be impractical or impossible. The siren song of avoiding a "hollow force" is unlikely to be powerful enough to overcome the enormous political inertia and opposition. Incentives will be vital. The specific design and composition of the readjust and change choice would best be reflected by either the BUR force extended or the maritime force. However, as noted, savings and efficiencies and creation of incentives to that end must be implemented.

The United States could maintain the current active force planned at 1.4 million. Either more money would be spent every year or reforms would be imposed to overcome the consequences of the excessive inefficiencies and insatiably growing costs. With reforms, steady-state defense spending and capability could be maintained, but, given the choice between an active force of 1.4 million that is "hollow" and one of 1.0 million that is ready, it is obvious that military leaders strongly support the latter.

The argument has been presented that, as Arleigh Burke noted, "two guns are enough," and a highly capable force of about a million should prove sufficient. The provisos are that this force must be kept ready and capable; a new strategic framework must be put in place to facilitate the engagement of the United States internationally on a qualitative basis; and reforms must be made on the excessive costs imposed by the process and, specifically, by the defense infrastructure.

To answer Mr. McNamara's question, in my view, the recommended definition of "enough" is an active-duty force of about one million and an annual budget of about $200 billion. Designed around a "one-plus" MRC requirement, a full second MRC could conceivably be handled with the remaining forces on hand. Should more capability be required, a mix of allies, mobilization, sequential operations, and perhaps a selective nuclear deterrent strategy would follow. However, no matter which of the three choices is made, both a rejuvenated network of international alliances and structures and repair and reform of the process are necessary and attainable steps to be taken.

Chapter Twelve: Reform and Consolidation

The defense infrastructure poses among the most inordinately complex, incestuously interrelated, and inherently political set of challenges, obstacles, and problems for assuring the common defense. As with Siamese twins, it is unambiguously clear that U.S. military might is irrevocably attached to and dependent on this infrastructure for its life's blood. However, in this case, the infrastructure twin is consuming an ever greater share of increasingly scarcer nourishment at the expense of military might. The trends and graphs presented earlier show how much the "tail" of infrastructure is exacting greater and greater percentages of the DOD budget at the expense of "teeth." The divergences are increasing. The consequences are predictable: less and less military capability.

The defense infrastructure correlates largely with the political and constituent or civilian side of the DOD budget. In crass terms, this translates into jobs and bases. Hence, the practical impact of the politics of infrastructure is to make inseparable its link with the larger question of how much is enough. Strategic and operational logic is a vital ingredient in any defense considerations, but it is not enough. Politics will and must intrude—a measure not of cynicism but of the legitimate and reasonable representation of constituent interests by members of Congress. The result, however, will always skew this interaction, often at the expense of combat power and in favor of the other side of this equation—the infrastructure.

The natural ascendancy of infrastructure over military power is further distorted and exaggerated by the actual structure of the budget, the annual budget process, and the phenomenon of escalating cost growth. Because defense represents the majority of all discretionary federal spending, it is likely to receive the largest and even disproportionately greatest share of future budget cuts. Because these cuts must ultimately be realized in outlays or current spending, it is the manpower, training, operations, and readiness accounts that are most greatly affected. These characteristics and realities of the budget and the process bias against fighting power and towards preserving infrastructure. The cumulative effects of these bureaucratic and process-driven costs and inefficiencies across government were spelled out in the remarkable *Report of the National Performance Review*, chaired by Vice President Al Gore in 1993.[77]

The phenomena of escalating (unit) costs and cost growth have been well documented. President Coolidge is credited for remarking on the perils of cost growth some 70 years ago. At some stage, the United States would end up with one ship, one aircraft, and one tank. The generals and admirals, according to Coolidge, would take it in turn to drive or fly the single unit in service. With the current costs of the major weapon systems as high as they are today, Coolidge's complaint may come true. The price of a nuclear-powered aircraft carrier and air wing is about $8 billion. The B-2 bomber, originally programmed for a purchase of 100 aircraft and later cut to 20, will cost over $2 billion a copy as the costs of R&D and other expenses are prorated against only one-fifth of the intended buy. The experience with the new F-22 fighter, for which the order was reduced from about 650 to 450, showed both that the program total costs grew due to "stretching out" the buy, and that unit costs increased to over $100 million.

In parallel to these trends, the costs of the acquisition process have continued to increase. The instability of an annually approved budget process virtually guarantees continuing changes to the number of weapon systems to be procured. Almost any program change outside cancellation or major reduction, whether adding or cutting, increases the total costs of that program. The contracting, pricing, and accounting systems are so extensive, different, and filled with cost anomalies that inefficiency is the general rule.

Last but not least, the failure of trust and confidence in government has imposed a most extraordinary regulatory, oversight, audit, and micromanagement regime. The combination of all of these factors probably consumes 20 or 25 percent of the total defense budget. If this 20 or 25 percent, or perhaps some $50 billion to

---

[77] See "Creating a Government That Works Better and Costs Less," *Report of the National Performance Review*, (Washington, DC; GPO: September 7, 1993) 168 p.

$75 billion a year, can be seen as the price of defeating "waste, fraud, and abuse," that price is unaffordable.[78]

The first conclusion must be that reforms, if they are to work, have to be made on the process and structure rather than on individual programs, because, unless and until these structural and inherent inefficiencies and cost-drivers are redressed, broad reform won't work. The 1994 legislation on procurement reform, while containing some useful and unexceptional provisions, was only a step in this direction. It is not enough. Sadly, however, this legislation may be the best that can be expected.

At the same time, antitrust and competition regulations must be carefully reviewed in light of consolidation of defense industries. The government has formidable means to demand and achieve fair value for dollar spent even through sole sources of supply. However, public education and information on how DOD will deal with a "monopsonic-monopolistic" business environment is vital if trust and confidence are to be maintained.

Bases and Supporting Infrastructure

Both the executive branch and Congress recognized the necessity for closing or realigning military bases. The BRAC was empowered by law to that end. The last round of this current BRAC will take place in 1995. But, since this process started, there has been an ominous, significant, and understandable reaction in Congress.

The "up or down" single vote in Congress was meant to take the politics out of base closings. This format provided political cover for members of Congress to use when local bases were shut. As a result, much but not all of the politics of base closings had been removed. Because of the two-year window between these closings, the uncertainty of what bases would go or stay in the next round

---

[78] It is, of course, very difficult to calculate with precision the costs of governance and inefficiency. The Packard Commission and the CSIS Defense Acquisition Study in 1987 estimated that, depending upon which reforms were taken, $25–50 billion a year could be saved. The most extensive study on cost reductions was done by Honeywell. That analysis showed that without major reform DOD could take safe actions and reduce the costs of buying virtually all systems by about 17 to 20 percent.

has practically and inadvertently placed more pressure on Congress by constituents rightfully anxious to know their future status.

What happened is that Congress has not always appropriated the full amount of money required to carry out the base closings as previously approved. If this trend continues, the BRAC process will be delayed, rendered less ineffective and perhaps impotent. Furthermore, a constitutional challenge to the BRAC 1990 Law was made by Senator Arlen Specter of Pennsylvania. Specter's argument was clear. The Navy, he asserted, withheld information regarding the value of the Philadelphia Naval yard. Therefore, in his view, the yard was put on the closure list illegally. Under these circumstances, because DOD offered no relief, the law must be subject to judicial review; otherwise, it is unconstitutional.

Even though the Supreme Court agreed with the government and sustained the lower court decision rejecting the suit, this precedent is not likely to remain unique. If these types of suits increase, any rational form of downsizing the nation's defenses will be made increasingly more difficult. On the other hand, Specter's suit and argument over the constitutionality of forgoing judicial review are strong and with merit. Thus, the original departure point of legislating around roadblocks and impasses of the political system is called into question. The tragedy is that there may be no alternative.

On the other hand, there is no serious alternative to a rigorous, comprehensive, and enduring base realignment and closure program. With 1995 the year of the last round of BRAC, this may be a final opportunity to downsize the supporting bases in line with operational needs. Three actions are required and are proposed.

First, the DOD should specify as its highest priority the maintenance of an effective, ready combat force. Against that directive, the services should be ordered to propose, in a coordinated, combined, and consolidated plan, a bare-bones minimum of bases to be kept in service, closing or realigning the remaining facilities accordingly. However draconian the nature of this process, if military power is to be preserved, the BRAC recommendations must be carried out without exception.

Second, the BRAC recommendations must be part of a broader and more comprehensive national defense plan that encompasses the entire range of DOD responsibilities from strategy and force structure to budgets and infrastructure. These broader findings will focus the BRAC, and, once recommendations are made by the commission, the broader defense plan can be adjusted to meet these findings. The comprehensive plan and the BRAC recommendations, once approved by the president, would be sent to Congress as part of one package. The point is to coordinate a comprehensive defense plan in advance to reduce the impact of another, Specter-like constitutional challenge.

Third, Congress must agree, preferably by law or other binding measure, to fund fully the recommendations of BRAC that it approves.

It is also very desirable, if not essential, that the DOD present to Congress its assessment of what failure to address the base closing issue effectively and comprehensively will mean for the readiness and fighting power of the forces. In essence, Congress must be presented with the military consequences of two base closing conditions—taking effective action and taking insufficient or ineffective action. Congress cannot be allowed to ignore or defer these future prospects.

THE RATE OF TECHNOLOGICAL INNOVATION

One of the greatest pressure points concerning research, development, testing, and evaluation programs is the rate at which technology and technological innovation are pursued. In a sense, the word "rate" is misleading. It suggests that there can be a quantifiable expression against which to measure technology and to establish the priority for allocating resources.

In a hypothetical case, for example, an innovation rate of A might equate with X dollars. A rate of $2A$ might equate with a multiple of X. Because an explicit and high-priority objective of DOD has been to exploit technology, the emphasis has generally been on the urgent side. Thus, we have chosen to spend more rather than less to support this emphasis. However, because it may take 15 to 20 years or more to move from system conceptualization to full-scale production, it can be argued either that urgency is of the essence to keep this period as short as possible, or that urgency is not relevant, also because of time—namely, over two decades it may be more cost-efficient to spend at a lower rate.

During a competition or conflict with a known adversary, there may be no substitute for urgency. America's determination to field nuclear weapons before Nazi Germany did is a virtually incontrovertible example of where urgency was and is a necessity. Now that the Cold War is over, the insistence on maintaining such a rapid and expensive pace to assure technological superiority is subject to review. For the moment, any linkages between various rates of pursuing technology and spending shares of the budget to achieve that objective are deferred. Also and from the outset, the issue is not whether to pursue technology but rather how and how quickly.

The first stage of assessing the degree of dependence on and the rate at which to pursue technology must rest in understanding the relative strengths, weaknesses, advantages, and potential vulnerabilities of the U.S. and its technologies *vis a vis* potential adversaries. Such an assessment would require volumes to ensure complete and specific coverage of myriad systems and technologies and is beyond the intent of this book. However, a less comprehensive but satisfactory alternative for assessment exists. Indeed, the larger and mandatory effort is presumably under way on a continuing basis by the relevant offices of government, especially the intelligence community.

This broader evaluation is expedited by placing technology in one of two categories—it is either "known" or it comes as a "surprise." "Known" covers the obvious universe; "surprise" has two subsets: a known technology used in an innovative or unexpected way to achieve operational surprise, or a new or different technology that presents itself for the first time. Precision-guided munitions and mines are examples of known technologies that can be used unexpectedly and can achieve tactical surprise. Vulnerabilities of current weapon systems to countermeasures, whether electronic or mechanical, are part of this subset. German V-2 rockets and the atomic bomb constituted technologies of surprise. These categories should form the methodological bases for ongoing assessments.

From this methodology, the area of principal concern should focus on potential vulnerabilities of U.S. systems, doctrine, and tactics rather than on the emergence of new and surprise technologies.

Because no other state assigns as large a share of resources to military R&D as the United States, and because the more likely threats and adversaries possess far less technological capability than the United States, the major military risks are likely to lie in countering U.S. systems with operational means as opposed to "wonder weapons."

Finally, because the relative and absolute military advantages possessed by the United States are so great, it is difficult to see how even relatively short-term, step-function improvements in these capabilities will add much more utility or effectiveness. Hence, although the U.S. must still be vigilant regarding "breakthrough" technologies, it should be able to draw on its huge superiority and consider alternative means to exploit technology.

There is, at present, discussion and anticipation of the "revolution in military affairs" (RMA) or "military technical revolution" (MTR). The hypothesis is that the operations and organization of military forces have been or will be profoundly affected by advancing or new technology. Precision, in the form of information and target location data, combined with great weapon accuracies and instant or near-instant communications, is asserted as the mechanism that will dispel much or most of the "fog of war." These technological revolutions, so the argument goes, will enable the side possessing these capabilities to have as close to perfect knowledge of the enemy as possible. The conduct and organization of forces and operations will be redesigned accordingly. If this argument proves correct, Desert Storm and the intensity, lethality, and decisiveness of the air and land campaigns were precursors of things to come. By focusing on this MTR, the U.S. would simply build on its already superior operational advantages.

There are, of course, many sides and facets to this debate. The objectives of this new "military revolution," if it exists, are far from new. The means, of course, are relatively new, with further systems and technologies presumably to be invented and fielded. However, to those who have fought in war or who understand the "fog of war," prudence and common sense suggest caution for several reasons. What happens if and when both sides attained a similar or equivalent capability, as was the case in the Cold War standoff? Alternatively, if the United States is assumed (with its allies) as the sole possessor of these types of military-technical advantages, what would keep a "have-not" adversary from neutralizing that advantage through a different strategy or tactic as happened in Vietnam?

A lesson driven home in Vietnam is that technological superiority is never the only guarantor of victory. More to the point, cultural arrogance is a recurring fragility. As Stanley Hoffmann pointed out three decades ago, the problem with Americans is often that we expect adversaries to reason as we do or to be in need of education to bring them up to our standards. This cultural arrogance may prove to be a more formidable problem than technological surprise.

The conclusions are mixed. On the one hand, experience shows that many more revolutions in military affairs have been predicted than have occurred. On the other hand, technology can provide powerful and invincible countervailing force—whether French knights in armor being slaughtered under the fire of English longbows at Crecy or, centuries later, Iraq's tanks being pulverized by enormously superior U.S. weapons in the 1991 "100-hour war." The issue becomes one of balance, which suggests an intellectual or conceptual rather than a resource-driven approach simply because there are too many technological avenues through which to spend money.

In this case, the "roll-over" model suggested for acquisition may prove useful in assessing rates of innovation. The "roll-over" model would conduct the R&D and produce a working prototype ready to enter full-scale production. There would be no need for the latter unless or until crisis or changed conditions intervened. In essence, the prototype would be kept funded at a minimum sustainment level pending further and future use, which might never be required.

What the United States should do in this regard becomes clear. In the past, a common practice of government and industry has been to form "red teams" to take part, any way they could, in critiquing a particular plan or system. In some cases, these "red teams" or red cells would pose alternative choices or designs. But the notion was akin to providing "a devil's advocate" and a contrarian view to test and challenge the program or plan under review as rigorously as possible. This process should be expanded and institutionalized. Indeed, at a time when most staffs and programs in DOD are shrinking, analytically enshrining a permanent "red team" within the bureaucracy runs counter to this trend.

Across both the operational command and OSD/service organizational structures, two trends have emerged. The notion of "jointness," that is, using the strengths of a particular military capability regardless of service ownership, has become both mantra and modus operandi. The role of doctrine, largely to reinforce the benefits of jointness and largely to respond to the changed strategic and operational environments, has been thrust on the unified commanders.[79] These matters are being taken very seriously and have the full support of the chain of command. The test is that new doctrine and jointness requirements are setting budget and program priorities.

Against this background, a technology "red cell" program should be institutionalized and given the highest priority. The aims of this program are uncomplicated. First, U.S. doctrine and operational concepts must be examined with a rigorous, ruthless, and uncompromising perspective to adduce weaknesses and potential vulnerabilities. Second, the steps that could be taken to defeat, neutralize, offset, or counter U.S. military capabilities and employments by possible adversaries should be posited. Finally, other steps (some technological, others strategic, still others tactical) that, while not operational, to the best knowledge under consideration could pose similar obstacles to using U.S. force successfully should be created or identified.

These "cells" would appear, nominally, on unified and specified command staffs, on the Joint and OSD staffs, and on service staffs. The results of their assessments would often highlight specific technologies and operational characteristics that require special evaluation. In some cases, the "roll-over" model might be appropriate. In others, design and plans rather than actual hardware or software would suffice. And, in still other cases, it might be sufficient to draft only the blueprint for designing the means to apply and test the particular technology.

The meaning and rationale for this approach are unambiguous. Too often the United States has tended to spend its way clear of danger. Now, stringent budgets must place a premium on other resources, in this case ones of intellect. The message for this era of

---

[79] In or near Norfolk, Virginia, for example, the Army's Training and Doctrine Command and the Navy's new Joint Doctrine School both report to the Commander in Chief, U.S. Atlantic Command.

strategic uncertainty is the necessity to think rather than spend our way clear of many dangers.

Quantitative analysts and technicians are unhappy with this type of solution. However, given the way the budget for technology is structured, there is no alternative. In FY 1994 and 1995, the DOD budget for research, development, and testing and evaluation (RDT&E) is as shown in table 39.

Table 39. DOD research, development, testing, and evaluation (budget authority in billions of dollars)[a]

	1994	1995
Technology		
Basic research	1.2	1.2
Applied research	2.7	3.0
Advanced technology development		
Ballistic missile defense	2.6	1.2
Other technology development	3.6	3.9
Total science and technology	10.1	9.3
System development		
New systems	10.1	12.7
Modifications for existing systems	11.4	10.9
Total	21.5	23.6
R&D management support	3.2	3.3
Total RDT&E	34.8	36.2

[a] *The Budget of the United States for FY 1995*, p. 228.

Although $34.8 and $36.2 billion are substantial sums, the six program areas shown consist of hundreds of thousands or more of specific items and contracts that make up the whole. Determining the actual number of programs is perhaps impossible. The point is that the bulk of these items are relatively small in funding. Because they *are* relatively small and are in the million, hundred thousand, and tens of thousands of dollars categories, even a small reduction could effectively terminate the contract. Hence, across-the-board reductions, given how those cuts would be carried out, are likely to prove extremely inefficient and wasteful.

There are, however, two means for improving the efficiency of allocating R&D resources. First, the overhead costs of administering, managing, auditing, and providing oversight can be reduced through changes to the overall process. These will be discussed shortly. Second, using the "red cell" approach, the total number of individual projects, programs, and contracts can be reduced. This means elimination of some or many rather than arbitrary reductions imposed across the entire account. Only through these actions can efficiencies, economies, and actual cost savings be achieved.

The Defense Industrial Base

As discussed in Chapter Eight, there are three basic paths for dealing with the defense industrial base. *Laissez-faire* will let the market determine survivors and victims. "Nationalization" will shift the ownership of the base to government. "Industrial policy" will navigate between the two with a hybrid type of future industrial base.

The constraints and realities that largely will determine how this industrial base issue unfolds are also straightforward. The unyielding discourse over competition and monopoly and how much competition is enough is powerful politically and ideologically. The survival instincts of the industries and facilities that compose the base are strong and not suicidal. And the question of autarky and the argument that national security justifies maintaining certain sectors and capacity regardless of economic costs will not be dismissed.

Because these constraints and realities are as old as the republic and run to the core of the nation, there may not be any solution that appears rational, economic, or efficient. To the degree that defense becomes a surrogate for jobfare or welfare, the nation may be faced with a permanent and costly infrastructure that exceeds all likely needs, imposes a great drain on the budget, and consumes resources at the direct expense of military might. Conversely, from a strategic, operational, and economic perspective, the defense industrial base must be rationalized, compressed, and consolidated.

Reforms to the acquisition system are an essential part of this process. Relief from competition and antitrust laws and regulations must be granted on a case-by-case basis. Finally, redundant capacity in the industrial base and in certain areas, such as between private and public overhaul or production facilities, must be eliminated or reduced. All these actions will require the most powerful incentive; otherwise, there is virtually no chance that any of them will be implemented.

The starting point is a comprehensive and relatively stable overarching defense plan that will be made reliable and credible through the long-term manner in which it is enacted into law. Downsizing defense, combined with the turbulence guaranteed by yearly approval and debate and changes to the budget, makes assurance of any semblance of an orderly transition for planning virtually impossible.

Attaining stability in planning will require collaboration between government and industry that heretofore has been missing. Government must be able to specify what it proposes to spend and to buy for a period of at least three and perhaps five years and stick to it. Industry, armed with this information that is reliable and relieved of some of the antitrust and competition requirements, can respond through mergers, acquisitions, and other suitable business transactions to reshape and downsize itself. For those facilities and organizations, government and civilian, that will be closed and for those jobs eliminated, there must be some better incentive than only unemployment insurance or welfare. Chapter Thirteen details such a plan.

As the "red team" approach was applied to the area of technology and technology investment, the BRAC process should be expanded for determining the future industrial base. Specific companies cannot and would not be targeted, but sectors like defense electronics, aerospace, shipbuilding, weapons, armored vehicles, and artillery would be assigned aggregate levels of industrial capacity that stem from projected budgets. It would be up to the private sector to respond. Government would facilitate, adjudicate where necessary, and provide certain incentives to ease this transition. Without this type of approach, there is no likely alternative. The result will be a continuously bloated infrastructure and a military placed "in irons."

THE ACQUISITION PROCESS

Despite all the studies, commissions, and attempts at reform, the process of acquiring the goods and services for defense remains excessively costly, wasteful, and inefficient. It simply takes too long and costs too much to acquire weapons of war. Remarkably, the process of super-regulation, micromanagement, and extraordinary oversight withstanding, the United States still turns out the best systems of the world. At this stage, however, the costs are becoming unaffordable.

Responsibility and blame for past and current excesses in the broader sense no longer apply. The executive branch, Congress, and the private sector, willingly or inadvertently, have all contributed to the present situation. From an American perspective, the issue is not who is at fault; the issue is correcting this condition.

Thus, reforms must be taken by the executive branch, Congress, and the private sector. Thus far and to be fair, although the executive branch and private sector have been the exclusive targets of reform, reform has not worked. Congress must be part of the solution. If not, no solution or reform will work.

Table 40 illustrates the growth of government. By extension, this growth and intrusion of government have created a series of bureaucracies, rules, laws, oversight, and procedures that are strangling any hope of achieving economies or efficiencies. The *National Performance Review*, noted earlier, records that nearly 10 percent of GDP, or more than $600 billion a year, is required to meet the regulatory and oversight demands of all levels of government.

Table 40. Growth in Federal Government

		Executive branch				Legislative branch	Judicial branch
Year	President	Cabinet positions	Executive agencies	Independent and emergency agencies	Civilian employment	Civilian employment	Civilian employment
1789	George Washington	5	0	0	>4,000	>200	—
1850	Zachary Taylor	7	0	0	26,000	386	177
1900	William McKinley	8	0	0	232,000	5,690	2,730
1940	Franklin Roosevelt	10	4	59	1,023,000	17,019	2,468
1950	Harry Truman	9	6	60	1,934,000	22,896	3,772
1960	Dwight Eisenhower	10	7	65	2,371,000	22,886	4,992
1970	Richard Nixon	12	11	69	2,944,000	30,869	6,887
1980	Jimmy Carter	13	10	108	2,821,000	40,000	17,000
1990	George Bush	14	14	101	3,067,000	38,000	22,000

The executive and legislative branches, therefore, must undertake a series of reforms to correct as many of these excesses as possible. These reforms, specified below, must concentrate on rationalizing the excesses of the process; the bureaucracies; the rules, regulations, and oversight; and the inherent political tensions between Congress and the presidency.

- First, the current budget process should be streamlined and compressed. The annual and redundant budget, authorization, and appropriation bills should be turned into a single bill and a single review process. This will mean reducing committees and subcommittees with jurisdiction over defense.[80]

- Second, a two-year appropriation bill should be adopted. Congress would pass the bill in year one and provide a review and oversight function in year two.

- Third, acquisition rules, regulations, and laws must be streamlined and codified by statute.

- Fourth, wrongdoing and misdeeds must be dealt with using the appropriate legal code so that the tendency to criminalize all or most offenses is limited to criminal and not civil offenses.

To ensure these functions are effectively carried out, Congress should establish a Joint Committee on National Security and Defense. The long-term purposes of this committee would be to replace the current system of overlapping committees and to induce the executive branch to develop a basic outline for the revised defense plan.[81] If the president were reluctant to act or chose to defer taking action, this Congressional committee could, in the last instance, serve as a surrogate and produce its own plan. Given some of the bad results that have taken place when Congress has acted to redress problems, such as the S&Ls, this approach is neither recommended nor desired. But, there must be some backup and even threat if the president is unwilling to fulfill the responsibilities as commander in chief. These items would include for vote into law matters pertaining to U.S. alliances, strategy, force structure, defense spending,

---

[80] The current annual budget cycle has three phases. The budgeting phase, overseen by the respective budget committees, sets overall spending limits now defined by the 1993 Omnibus Law. The armed services committees oversee authorizations, that is, the intent to fund programs. Finally, the appropriations committees approve what will be spent each year in the form of 13 separate appropriations bills to be voted on by both houses.

[81] A simple majority vote would be required to approve any plan. Hence, unless the two-party system no longer obtained, no matter which parties controlled the White House and each house in Congress, a majority vote would always be forthcoming if voted along party lines.

commitments, deployments and presence objectives, rationalizing the infrastructure (including acquisition reform), and other appropriate topics. Congress would approve or reject this plan without amendment and by a one-time vote in each house. Each year, or every two years with the budget, this plan could be resubmitted.

RESERVE AND GUARD FORCES

Reserve and guard forces would be part of any comprehensive plan. Under the arguments and strategic plans advanced in this book, reserve and guard forces would be restructured and reduced to conform with the new requirements for the MRCs that specified the presence of allied forces and mobilization. This would mean moving from about 900,000 reservists to about 650,000 to 700,000 or even less over a three- to five-year period.[82]

FINAL THOUGHTS ON INFRASTRUCTURE REVISITED

The infrastructure is not inherently the villain or albatross draped around the neck of America's fighting forces. Without an appropriate infrastructure, there could be no fighting power. The issue is downsizing the infrastructure to a level that fully supports the fighting forces with minimum demand on the available resources.

The broadest issue facing the nation regarding defense rests in governance and the ability of the process to withstand and to respond to the extraordinary demands of a complex, fractionated, 21st-century, post-industrial society. The defense infrastructure is a direct outgrowth and subset of this larger issue. The solution, if there is one, is inherently political and not entirely strategic or operational.

Many metaphors and analogies can describe the role of the infrastructure. The Siamese twin analogy is accurate only in that this irrevocable joining means that separation of the two would prove to be fatal, at least to the weaker twin. In this case and in the worst of worlds, or if trends continue, unless action is taken, we will be left with a large and insatiable twin in the form of infrastructure and a frail, undernourished, and, in a sense, dying twin of military might. This specter or the logic of the case will not magically change this forecast. Incentives will.

---

82 Obviously, if a reconstitution strategy were chosen, reserve and guard forces could be increased. The point is that the reserve and the guard must be part of a comprehensive approach.

Chapter Thirteen: Incentives for Action

Change is generally motivated by responses to some combination of factors that can be characterized in terms of incentives and disincentives. The latter obviously will arise from crisis or failure and derive their motivating power in those cases largely for fear-induced reasons. That fear can be as basic as the threat of losing one's life, livelihood, or liberty, or more complicated as less clear-cut values are at stake.

Regarding the common defense, although the issue is anything but trivial, defense just does not register as a concern or even as a topic of interest to the vast majority of Americans. The disincentive raised by the alarm that U.S. military power is headed towards a future state of "in irons" not only will fail to penetrate the body politic; the alarm will simply not be heard, and left to future generations to heed. Hence, if the future of defense is to be put on a track other than one of deferral, sufficiently strong incentives are vital both to forcing attention and to motivating different behavior—that is, assuming a war or real crisis does not intervene first.

Given the political conditions and priorities in the United States in the 1990s, are there any feasible incentives that might be applied to the business of defense? Or, are those incentives likely to be ones of only rhetorical, intrinsic, or spiritual value, such as those based on honor, duty, and patriotism, and therefore without tangible reward and benefit? In blunt terms, it is perhaps only economic and monetary rewards that, in the first instance, can provide an incentive powerful enough to induce the political system to deal with defense in a different light. Of course, as one moves down the political hierarchy of authority from the chief executive and Congress to the military forces that must be prepared to fight and win, other incentives no doubt must be created to motivate any change.

How might incentives be created or assigned to each of the three policy choices facing the nation and its government? This assumes, of course, that the disincentive of stumbling into a future crisis or catastrophe remains uncompelling as an inducement for change and not really relevant to the defense debate.

Steady as You Go

If a process of default or neglect occurs and the White House and Congress choose to defer, dismiss, or ignore the trends towards a hollow force, the incentive is the politics of following the path of least resistance. By deferring this defense issue, other more important priorities and problems can be addressed without the dilution or division caused by another controversy or political fight. In fact, this incentive is really in the form of not provoking other disincentives that could complicate or impede progress on what are seen as more significant non-defense matters.

Alternatively, if the White House were to recognize the impending defense condition and voluntarily elect to allow that state to unfold on the grounds that the international environment has created a breathing space such that a substantial decline in military power will not be harmful to the nation, the incentive is much different. Truth and candor would be seen as rallying political support for the current agenda. Of course, many would argue that increasingly permitting military power to decline significantly was irresponsible.

FUND THE FORCE

If the White House and Congress agree to fund the force fully, the incentive would be derived from the political and geostrategic benefits arise from maintaining the objective and the ability to fight two MRCs. The actual merits and demerits would be subjective and extremely difficult to measure regarding what that level of military power does for U.S. security. Although the hundreds of billions of dollars needed for this funding would be marginal when compared against the nation's GDP over those years, the social, political, and economic opportunity costs of non-defense programs forgone would be argued by some as enormous. This, however, would also be done on a subjective basis.

If some of the resources for funding the force came down from reform of the process, that would be a substantial incentive in itself. Making government perform more effectively and efficiently, without changing the nature of that government, inherently must be of value. Of course, the political costs of imposing reform create very strong disincentives.

READJUST AND CHANGE

If the White House and Congress agree to readjust and change the nation's military posture, the largest potential incentive rests in reducing the resources that go to defense *provided* national security is appropriately and adequately protected. If less defense is appropriate (for example, the "one plus" MRC strategy), it is imperative that reforms are also implemented to ensure that a steady-state level of capability can be maintained, or provisions made to fund that level as may be necessary. Assuming the "one plus" MRC could be maintained at $200 billion per year, over the next five-year defense plan of $1.2 or 1.3 trillion, several hundreds of billions of dollars could be available for other national purposes.

The disincentives of this approach rest in the political costs of making this significant change, and in dealing with the many service personnel and civilian constituents whose employment depends upon defense and who would become redundant. Within the military, further downsizing could easily harm morale and the esprit necessary to maintain any effective fighting force. Thus, incentives to mitigate or revise these disincentives must be created and must provide satisfactory and sufficient transition and employment options as well.

ONE INCENTIVE

How might this incentive work assuming the nation avoided the path of political default?

First, the president must take a strong stand on defense in his capacity as commander in chief. There is no alternative to this, no matter how strong the magnetism of the domestic agenda may be. He can either direct his national security team to produce major and comprehensive alternatives, reflecting the choices that lie ahead, or he can establish a Presidential Commission on National Security and Defense to achieve the same purpose. These results—perhaps done best with liaison with Congress, or, more precisely, its leaders during the process—would then be presented to Congress along with the defense budget for that year. As with the BRAC, perhaps a legislative exception can be made, and Congress would approve or disapprove the entire package through an up or down vote in both houses. Amendments or resolutions would not be permitted on the basic bill.

The results of this NSC or Commission effort would be a range of alternatives representing the three policy choices, or ones like them, and possibly a recommended course of action. Specifically, the general content of each alternative would include:

- *Threat*: the nature of general and specific threats to the security of the U.S. over the next ten years or so, and a statement of the instruments to deal with these threats that include old and new alliances; the role of international organizations; diplomatic and aid initiatives; the role of military force, including a statement of U.S. commitments, deployments, and presence requirements; and arms control, arms transfers, and other related matters.

- *Strategy*: the definition of U.S. strategy that specifies objectives, relates policy issues to objectives, specifies the MRC and other military objectives that set military requirements, and shows how the strategy will be argued to both domestic and international audiences.

- *Force structure*: the definition of the size, shape, and composition of U.S. active and reserve forces to meet the strategy, its objectives, and the ensuing requirements. Also specified will be the criteria for setting standards of readiness, training, maintenance, operational tempo, and other related criteria.

- *Budget*: the statement of the actual costs of maintaining the force at a steady-state level of capability and readiness.

- *Infrastructure*: the definition of what size and shape infrastructure is needed to support the forces.

- *Plan of action for change and reform*: the definition of how to move from the current structure to the proposed choice over the next three to five years, including a cost-benefit analysis of the risks and rewards.

- *Incentives*: the definition of what is required to make any change or reform work.

The president would make his choice and send the complete package to Congress for approval.

Let us assume the first NSC Review or Commission on National Security and Defense convenes in FY 1996. It is fairly clear how such a review would respond to the first two choices. The most interesting case is that of readjust and change. The recommendations made by the NSC or the Commission on the choice of "Readjust and change" could be summarized as follows.

THE READJUST AND CHANGE CHOICE: A SUMMARY OF THE REVIEW BY THE NATIONAL SECURITY COUNCIL ON NATIONAL SECURITY AND DEFENSE

- ***Threat:*** Direct dangers and military threats to the 50 U.S. states will be isolated and limited almost exclusively to terrorism or to limited use of weapons of mass destruction. Absent mass destruction weapons, the direct threat to the physical security of the 50 states is minuscule and will be so for some time to come.

  Abroad, regional conflicts remain the basis for major contingencies and therefore the only basis for organizing, planning, and justifying the bulk of U.S. military power. A "one plus" MRC is deemed the appropriate planning basis for these forces.

  Threats can and must also be dealt with using allies; old and new security frameworks; international organizations; diplomacy and traditional quasi-military instruments; economic and trade incentives; and common sense.

- ***Strategy:*** U.S. military might will be postured to meet the requirements of the "one plus" MRC scenario. Approximately 500,000 troops, dispatched and deployed over three to six months, set the upper limits for the single MRC; 100,000 troops constitute the "plus." The support of allies and mobilization at home will be assumed as occurring or available in any crisis. The ultimate U.S. objectives in the MRC would be to "win" through defeating the adversary as decisively and quickly as feasible.

  U.S. commitments, deployments, and presence would be readjusted accordingly in line with such other instruments as new or rejuvenated alliances. Flexibility in substituting different types of deployed forces for presence would occur.

- *Force structure:* An active-duty force of about 1 million and a reserve component of about 700,000 would be required. The composition would be either the BUR force extended or the maritime force. High levels of operational readiness would be maintained across virtually all of the forces in a deployed or deployable (i.e., ready) status.

- *Budgets:* About $200 billion per year is required. If reform is imposed, that figure could be lower. If reform is not imposed, annual real increases of about 3 percent will be needed to keep a steady-state level of capability.

- *Infrastructure:* Infrastructure must be consolidated and streamlined by a total of about 50 to 60 percent. Realignment and reduction, rather than outright closing, are probably the preferred alternatives. Another BRAC-like process will be part of these recommendations and result in these changes. The specifics would follow in the report.

The specific plan of action for making this transition is best left to DOD. The details obviously are crucial and require expert input. In addition to the obvious incentive of reducing defense expenditures, incentives to facilitate this transition are vital.

Balance among threat, strategy, force structure, budget, and infrastructure was set to carry out a "one plus" MRC requirement. This leads to an active-duty force of about 1 million and an annual defense expenditure of $200 billion. This transition will take three to five years if it is to be done without destroying the fiber of the forces. But, to make this transition politically acceptable, incentives for military and civilians and local communities must be created. These incentives would include programs like "GI education bills," retraining and re-education, financial support, and continuation of health insurance. Funds for these new expenses would be derived by starting with the current plan to spend about $1.3 trillion on defense over the next five-year period. The differential between that level and the actual monies expended on the smaller force would make up the account from which these incentives would be funded.

At the end of the five-year period, presumably with the defense spending level at $200 billion, whatever resources were left from this $1.3 trillion account would be available for other public uses. To achieve this endpoint, the annual procedures would be roughly as follows:

- Congress, with a biannual appropriation would approve $200 billion a year for two years for defense—a total of $400 billion.

- For FY 1996, Congress would establish an off-budget "defense escrow account" in which it would appropriate $100 billion. These funds would be used only for defense transition.

- For FY 1997, perhaps an additional $50 billion would be appropriated to this fund.

- For FY 1998, 1999, and, if necessary, 2000, more funds would be added if required, up to $50 billion.

If the process went smoothly, funds remaining in the "defense escrow account" would be returned to the treasury. In any event, the total expenditure would be $1.2 trillion at most. And annual defense spending would be steady at the $200 billion. Obviously, the rates of supplying and using this escrow account would require detailed analysis. There would also be scrupulous control of this account through a joint DOD-Congressional oversight committee.

To give this incentive teeth, these appropriations and spending levels would be binding and relaxed only in the event of national emergency or by a 2/3 (or super—i.e., 60 percent) majority vote in both houses of Congress to grant relief. The defense plan would be approved concurrently, which would provide an unprecedented level of stability for planning.

For the White House, this plan would lead to retaining the finest military in the world at the right level and the right expenditure. If all went well, substantial savings could be realized as well.

For the DOD, there would be longer-term certainty and agreement on strategy, force structure, funding, and planning, and the knowledge that the future force, although smaller, would be the best in the world.

For Congress, there would be these same rewards plus the credit for legislating a defense downsizing plan that worked efficiently and fairly. This would also free up resources for other programs.

For individuals and communities that were transitioned out of the defense work force, there would be sufficient financial and psychic incentives to make that change with minimum pain.

There are, of course, counter-arguments to a plan like this at least as truculent as the arguments against making further reductions to defense. The chance of Congress moving to a two-year defense budget is remote. The reasons why Congress or DOD would stick to these spending levels are disingenuous. The incentive would be to do otherwise. The experience with the Gramm-Rudman-Hollings Deficit Reduction Act proves the rule. Incentives for the transition could require a new bureaucracy. Administration of benefits would be ripe for fraud. And so on!

On the other hand, given, in essence, a clean slate, government has the opportunity to make major and vital changes to defense and national security. If there is no consensus or movement to change, the U.S. military force will evolve by default. This is the nature and result of the democratic process as it exists today. But that is not the best excuse for failing to impose the vital reforms to defense without which no steady-state level of a ready military capability can be sustained.

In addition to the military incentive of maintaining a high and steady-state level of capability, further incentives will be required to sustain esprit and fighting power while drawing down. Fewer rather than more deployments and reduced operating tempo will be needed. One incentive applies to innovation.

Despite the advance of technology and the embrace and institutionalization of the highest standards of military professionalism and competence, as forces are downsized, the understandable tendency will be to preserve "core" capabilities. "Core" capabilities could relate both to systems and to specific military formations and units. It is unlikely that the services will renounce their equivalent of the capital ship or the current basic design of military formations. Although these preferences and conclusions may be absolutely justified, true innovation may be stifled.

Two initiatives bear scrutiny and comparison with the current organization and design. The first is to rely far more heavily on "jointness," especially through new organizational structures. Jointness means, in part, exploiting the fungibility of service capabilities. The uses of adaptive joint force packages and far more integrated and cross-service oriented task forces were cited as examples of this approach.

Pursuit of jointness and the advantages that may accrue can be accomplished through detailing the very best officers to the appropriate command tasked with this responsibility. For the time being, this responsibility is assigned to the (new) Atlantic Command. The capacity and spirit to look innovatively at new ways to carry out both old and new tasks must be reinforced and nurtured by the most senior leadership in DOD.

The second initiative deals with how we will fight, and the alternative is derived from what the British called the military style of fighting practiced by "Easterners." Easterners served in places like the Gulf, Malaysia, and Burma, where conditions such as topography or remoteness demanded different means of fighting. Generally configured as light or special forces, Easterners used stealth, cunning, and mobility in lieu of heavy, mechanized systems. Lawrence of Arabia and Field Marshal Slim of Burma come to mind.[83]

The opposite style of war, called by the British after the so-called "Westerners," was based on traditional, heavy, armored forces supported by heavy firepower. Montgomery and the "Desert Rats," who defeated Rommel's Afrika Corps, are representative of this school. "Westerners" reflect the more traditional, long-standing approach to war—and the 1991 Desert Storm campaign is the most current example.

The Easterners initiative would place the focus of warfare through this less conventional lens. The obvious consequences of this form of warfare would dramatically change the style, systems, and designs for military formations, especially if stealth, cunning, and high degrees of mobility were adopted as chief criteria supported by firepower from advanced weapon systems. These changes would reflect the type of future adversaries and conflicts the U.S. would likely fight. Of course, the tried, true, and traditional approach of the Westerners may prove more relevant and convincing.

---

[83] I am indebted to John Barry of *Newsweek* magazine for calling attention to this most useful distinction.

A further variant of both styles of waging war involves heavier reliance on signature management. Signature management is the ability to control or regulate those visible signals or signs seen, heard, or detected by an adversary. This goes well beyond stealthy aircraft invisible to radar or infrared detection.[84]

Suppose, for example, an Army platoon could alter its "signature" to look like a division, or even a carrier battle group or amphibious group if close to the sea. Or suppose a division could disguise itself as a platoon or even smaller unit. The ability to adapt or readapt to a tactical situation and apply force accordingly could have decisive impact. Because the technologies and procedures for those approaches are presumably closely held, signature management is not discussed in greater detail. However, the concept offers some interesting possibilities.

Taken together, emphasis on innovation and actively seeking out new ways to deal more effectively with both traditional and nontraditional tasks are exciting. This excitement and challenge can form a stimulating incentive within the military.

* * *

The choice is ours. If, in this rather small but vital sector that is about 4 percent of GDP, government can be made to work more effectively and efficiently, the prospects for applying that success to the larger issues are brighter. If, at the bleaker end of the scale, no reform or progress is made, the consequences are almost certain. We can change the direction of the Ship of State and sail with ample winds and calm seas. Or, we can merely trim the sails and hazard the risk of finding ourselves placed "in irons."

---

84 I am indebted to former senior DOD official Dr. James P. Wade, Jr., for the basic idea for this approach.

EPILOGUE: THE COSTS OF FAILURE

For well into its second century of existence, the United States narrowly interpreted the constitutional directives "to maintain a navy" and "to raise an army." As a result, the nation kept only a small standing military force. The Civil War years of 1861–1865 were exceptions. Indeed, after World War I ended in 1918, the United States demobilized and returned to the traditional posture of a relatively small standing armed force. World War II, the Cold War, and, now, the era of strategic uncertainty have reversed that traditional posture. For the foreseeable future, the United States will maintain a large standing military force and an annual defense budget probably in excess of what the rest of the world collectively spends on armed might.

Two ironies underscore the difficulties ahead as well as the important consequences for the condition of the future U.S. military establishment. The relative and absolute advantages in military capabilities possessed by the United States were arguably never greater. Yet, exploiting or using these advantages to national benefit is easier said than done. The powerful influence of geoeconomics and regional concerns further complicates exploiting the utility of American military force.

Although most Americans continue to prefer having the best or most capable military force in the world, those preferences cannot be isolated from the absence of genuine military threats to the nation's security and the preoccupation with problems at home that impose increasing demands on limited national resources.

The second irony stems from success. Public expectations of cost-free and decisive, quick success in applying American force on every occasion have been intensified by political and social conditioning of the past decade. It is quite possible this cultural pattern could become disabling to future policy needs by setting military requirements that could not be met or fully guaranteed even though the use of force was justified.

It is therefore not inconceivable that in a decade or two, because of these factors, the United States could return to the more traditional posture of maintaining only a relatively small standing force.

This condition could occur naturally, by default, or through a dramatic change in policy. Today, although history has shown it would be exceedingly unwise for America to disarm either structurally or premeditatively, there can be no absolute conclusion about what such a condition would mean for America's future well-being.

In the mid 1990s, the prospect of a militarily weakened America is not registering very high on any list of national concerns. However, simply because the symptoms are not visible does not mean the pathology is automatically benign or, in certain ways, not highly destructive and dangerous to the body politic. To specialists in national security, quite the opposite diagnosis of damage is likely.

Today, the common defense is threatened not by clear and apparent dangers abroad, but by conditions, events, and politics largely within these shores. The absence of a worthy and credible enemy replete with awesome and frightening weapons of war poses a fundamental challenge to any chief executive of the nation. How can the defense of the nation be based on a threat that is quite small and, over time, becomes less and less clear or apparent?

At the same time, the extraordinary expense of governance, manifested in diseconomies and inefficiencies long imbedded in the political process and the soaring costs of administering society's overhead in which there is little value added and probably a lot forgone for the resources expended, will and must erode whatever level of military power the nation retains unless change and reform occur.

Finally, it is clear that the Cold War structure of international politics has been irreversibly and fundamentally changed. The view or sense of what kind of a replacement structure, if any, will fill this vacuum is not only unclear, it is opaque.

That the arguments and forecasts presented in this book may turn out to be absolutely accurate is preempted by the issue of relevance. Why should a president of either party when confronted with issues of burning domestic importance such as health care and welfare reform, public safety, and economic recovery expend precious time and even more precious political capital in responding to a diaphanous, dynamic, and, at this point, unpredictable regime for national security? One answer is that without the incentive or fear posed by a major crisis or new threat, any president would not.

On the grounds of logic, politics, and the demands of the Constitution, it has been and will be exceedingly difficult to argue, except in crisis, that providing for the common defense is a more important priority than safeguarding the general welfare and the domestic tranquility of the nation. For those who correctly may argue that defense is of a different texture because the fate of the entire nation is concerned and defenders may be called upon to shed their own blood in answering the call to arms, there is the response that reflects a grimmer reality. Increasingly, the domestic community and society at home are placing Americans in harm's way. Hence, the patriotism and service often associated with defending one's country are arrested by the cynical changes in American society at large.

There are, however, two islands of refuge for a president wishing to put national defense on a better and more solid footing. The first is the political judgment and historical experience that the United States has no alternative except to be well defended by a powerful and capable military able, when necessary, to destroy or neutralize the will and capacity of potential enemies to oppose us. The second is the courage to recognize that a combination of factors—exacerbated by political expectations that exceed economic means, a political process not easily disciplined to make tough decisions, and understandable complacency—has become a dagger inadvertently pointed at many vital national organs, including the heart of military capability. By returning that dagger to a protective scabbard, the president can preserve this military structure. By imposing reforms and remedial actions to this relatively limited sector of national interest, the president can do more than only reduce the demand on crucial resources. These initiatives make a much larger and important point.

Many observers believe the United States has reached a crucial juncture in its history. The pessimists see decline as inevitable, a result of the end of America's greatness. The absence of any recent major successes by government in redressing major American problems contributes to this pessimism. Perhaps the military establishment represents one small sector where decline and disarray can be prevented. If that is the case, this example of success may have broader benefit and relevance. But, only time will tell whether U.S. military might in the new century is the best and most formidable in the world or whether it is consigned to a fate of "in irons."

INDEX

W

Y

Z

*U.S. G.P.O.:1995-387-330:20003